THE
WORLD WATCH
READER
on
Global
Environmental
Issues

OTHER NORTON/WORLDWATCH BOOKS
Lester R. Brown et al.

State of the World 1984   *State of the World 1995*
State of the World 1985   *State of the World 1996*
State of the World 1986   *State of the World 1997*
State of the World 1987   *State of the World 1998*
State of the World 1988   *Vital Signs 1992*
State of the World 1989   *Vital Signs 1993*
State of the World 1990   *Vital Signs 1994*
State of the World 1991   *Vital Signs 1995*
State of the World 1992   *Vital Signs 1996*
State of the World 1993   *Vital Signs 1997*
State of the World 1994

ENVIRONMENTAL ALERT SERIES

Lester R. Brown et al.
Saving the Planet

Alan Thein Durning
How Much is Enough?

Sandra Postel
Last Oasis

Lester R. Brown
Hal Kane
Full House

Christopher Flavin
Nicholas Lenssen
Power Surge

Lester R. Brown
Who Will Feed China?

Lester R. Brown
Tough Choices

Michael Renner
Fighting for Survival

MAGAZINE STAFF

THE
WORLD WATCH
READER
on
Global
Environmental
Issues

W · W · NORTON & COMPANY
New York · London

The text of this book is composed in Galliard, with the display set in
Goudy. Composition by Worldwatch Institute; manufacturing by the
Haddon Craftsmen, Inc.

First Edition

Library of Congress Cataloging-in-Publication Data

The World Watch Reader on global environmental issues / magazine staff: editor,
Ed Ayres; senior editor, Chris Bright; associate editor, Curtis Runyan, editorial
committee, Lester R. Brown .. [et al.]

ISBN 0-393-31753-6

W. W. Norton & Company, Inc., 500 Fifth Avenue, New York, N.Y. 10110
http://www.wwnorton.com

W. W. Norton & Company Ltd., 10 Coptic Street, London WC1A IPU

1 2 3 4 5 6 7 8 9 0

This book is printed on recycled paper.

WORLDWATCH INSTITUTE

CONTENTS

3 Biological Instabilities

4 Bread and Water

5 Better Use of Materials

6 Social Instabilities

FOREWORD

When the first edition of the *World Watch Reader* was published in 1991, we wrote in our foreword that "the global economy is literally destroying the natural systems that support it." And yet, we noted, no major government or international institution—not the White House, not the World Bank, not the United Nations—had developed a coherent vision of what a sustainable society would really look like.

Since then, world leaders have begun to awaken to the urgency of this need for a new kind of economy—one that allows us to thrive without continuing our deforestation of the planet, destruction of species, or disruptions of climate. A series of landmark global summits have taken place—the Rio Earth Summit in 1992, the Cairo Population Summit in 1995, and the Kyoto Climate Conference in 1997, among others.

Despite this awakening, however, most institutions have been distressingly slow to change. The World Bank still puts the bulk of its funding support into fossil fuel projects that emit dangerous quantities of greenhouse-warming gases; the U.N. is still mired in emergency efforts that leave it with little capacity to focus on the more pervasive threats to human security that arise from disrupted environments. The world's most powerful nation, the United States, now officially recognizes the need to reduce carbon emissions, but played a heel-dragging role in the formulation of the Kyoto Climate Treaty—agreeing only to reduce emissions by 2010 to slightly below the level they had reached in 1990—the year the first *World Watch Reader* was written. In that 20 years, however, the world's population will have increased by another 1.6 billion; tens of thousands more species will have gone extinct, and another fifth of the world's forests will have been cut or burned.

One reason progress has been slow is that in this age of exploding information, experts are becoming increasingly specialized—and find it more and more difficult to view the "big picture" of how their disciplines can contribute to the broad restructuring of the global economy that will be need to stabilize the planet's life systems. An agricultural business manager, for example, may believe that it is important to use every possible acre of land to maximize farm productivity. Yet, an expert in plant pollination may explain that wild pollinators thrive in the strips of meadow or woodland left around traditional farms fields, and that wild pollinators are essential to a large percentage of the world's crops—so if their habitat is plowed up, the fields may actually produce less. A key role of *World Watch* has been to integrate the findings of numerous specialities in a way that lets us see that missing "big picture."

In doing so, we have come to an important general conclusion: that the greatest dangers confronting humanity are often self-inflicted; they result from unanticipated side-effects or misuse of powerful technologies—whether mechanized equipment for clearing forest, or nuclear power once billed as "too cheap to meter"—for which we once had only the brightest hopes. Yet, the solution is not to become hostile to what we have invented or created. Rather, it is to use the same powers of invention and creativity to learn how to live in ways that allow the natural systems underpinning our economy to regenerate and thrive, rather than to continue their dangerous decline.

The seven chapters of this book show how we can do that. First, to provide an unflinching look at the challenge we face, they show how human activities over a range of basic industries—energy, food, water, timber, paper—are continuing to undermine natural systems at a dizzying rate. Second, they show how alternatives could be put in place to stabilize these systems. In most cases, readers will find that the task of developing appropriate technology is not the main impediment; it is the resistance of vested interests or fearful politicians that stands in the way.

In the opening chapter on *Energy and Climate*, for example, we address one of the most important single issues to face humanity since the beginning of the industrial revolution: how to supply energy for a rapidly developing human economy in ways that won't catastrophically destabilize climate. While resistant industries have argued about the economic risks of phasing out coal and oil, the section by Molly O'Meara examines the much larger risks of *not* phasing those fuels out. Christopher Flavin's section on the Second Energy Revolution shows that new clean-energy technologies are already available, and that they can provide immediate help for the tens of millions of people in the developing world who do not have access to centralized electricity grids—and for whom these large coal- or oil-powered systems could not be built without adding dangerously to the world's carbon emissions.

The second chapter, *Oceans in Distress*, shows that the interdependence of human and environmental well-being is far closer than may be apparent to many of us who live in cities or suburbs. Examine a map of human settlement patterns, and we find that the majority of the world's people live near coasts, yet it is precisely these coastal areas that are ecologically most vulnerable. As Peter Weber shows in his section on Failing Coasts, the biological wealth of the world is greatest in those areas of land and water nearest to where land and water meet—yet this is just where people have dumped the most pollutants, destroyed the most wetlands and forests, and done the most dredging, paving, and building. Anne Platt McGinn's section, Failing Seas, observes that it is the coasts surrounding the world's great seas, particularly, that have been the cradles of civilization. Her analysis makes it clear that for human activity to become sustainable, communities on every continent will need to renew their appreciation—and protection—of the ecosystems that allowed them to first arise.

Chapter 3, *Biological Instabilities*, shows why increasing human dominance at the expense of the rest of the planet's life would be self-defeating in the long run. The most obvious measure of our dominance is our increasing occupation of available land—and our destruction of the habitat of other species. When their habitat disappears, the species begin to die off. In a section on the Decline of Primates, John Tuxill reports on how this global land-grab, combined with increasing use of firearms, is decimating the populations of our closest relatives outside the human family. And even when habitat isn't completely destroyed, it can be severely weakened or degraded. The section on Bio-invasions, by Chris Bright, shows how today's voluminous travel, tourism, and trade have allowed non-native species of pests and weeds to spread and do increasing damage. The section on Nature's Secret Economy, by Janet Abramovitz, while acknowledging that economic productivity is an important measure of human wellbeing, powerfully refutes the often-heard argument that economic and environmental priorities are in conflict. Her analysis shows that the products and services provided "free" by nature actually have as much economic value as, if not more than, the ones we provide with our own industry—and that if we don't begin to value them more highly, we could lose them.

In the chapter on *Bread and Water*, Lester R. Brown and

Sandra Postel show that there are real limits to the Earth's capacity to satisfy our growing demands for food and fresh-water. Postel's section notes that rivers once thought to be inexhaustible sources of water are now subjected to such heavy demands—for agriculture and industry, as well as for municipal use—that in many cases they are drying up before they can reach their natural destinations. Lester Brown's two sections, when originally published in *World Watch*, had extraordinary effects on the food policies of the world's most populous country, China—and may eventually affect our management of food production worldwide. Brown shows that global food production capacity is no longer keeping up with population growth, and that the time has come to make major changes in how we use our land.

The chapter on *Better Use of Materials* introduces a fast-emerging issue in global environmental economics: the unsustainable rate at which we are both depleting resources that are hard to replace, and generating pollutants that are hard to dispose of safely. Alan Thein Durning's section on the New World View briefly reviews the history of our "extrac-tive" industries—those that thrive by consuming the planet's once-abundant natural capital—and then argues that we need to find ways of achieving more with less—providing services and products that allow us to enjoy life to the fullest without diminishing the quality of life over the longer term. One strategy is to recycle materials so that we don't have to cut so much forest or dig up so much of the planet's surface. John Young's section on recycling shows how that strategy became a part of our mainstream economic thinking in the early 1990s, and suggests that large-scale recycling could eventual-ly replace traditional timber or mining operations as the world's primary source of raw materials.

The chapter on *Social Instabilities* makes it clear that ulti-mately, if the ecological underpinnings of the human econo-my are too disrupted, society itself begins to come unglued. The section on the Chiapas rebellion in Mexico, by Michael

Renner, offers a case study of what can happen when people are economically marginalized—cut off both from their traditional livelihoods and from participation in the fruits of the new globalizing economy. And Anne Platt McGinn's report on the New Epidemics shows that social destabilization does not stop at anger, rebellion, or refugee flight. Overcrowded and uprooted populations become more vulnerable to illness; one symptom of a disrupted world has been a pattern of increasing outbreaks of new and resurgent diseases.

The last chapter, *Paying for Change*, focuses on the hard question of financing reform. Hilary French's report on Private Investment looks at the historic shift of development financing from public to private sources. Christopher Flavin's section on the World Bank examines a fundamental challenge of reform: how can we best employ the financial muscle of the developed countries to help the less-developed ones catch up? Flavin observes that the World Bank has been the world's largest financier of giant development projects (hydroelectric dams, coal-powered electric plants, highways, etc.) that were built with good intentions but that have turned out to be environmentally and sometimes socially disastrous—yet because of that same financial muscle, he sees the Bank as having enormous potential to help the world get back on a sustainable course.

In each of these chapters, the *World Watch* strategy is to link the specific problem area—whether it be declining fisheries, rising greenhouse gas emissions, or impending food scarcity—with the larger challenge of achieving a sustainable global economy. In each case, the problem is analyzed in terms of the full range of costs, benefits, and risks that are entailed in various courses of action. The analysis is not limited to the kind of financial assessments cited by industries, which often don't count hidden or deferred costs that are not included in conventional accounting (such as the eventual costs of diseases caused by industrial pollution, which are not currently included in the prices of those industries' products or in the liabilities disclosed to shareholders). Instead, the *World Watch* authors consider the long-term effects of alternative strategies not just for the immediate producers and consumers, but for other communities, generations, and species. From this analysis, the authors recommend policy changes or actions that we have reason to believe are economically and politically feasible, as well as scientifically and technically sound.

These issues are not just of concern to environmentalists, but to every living person—and to everyone yet to be born. While there may have been times and places in the past where small elites could isolate themselves from environmental degradation, that is no longer true. Pollutants carry on the winds and waters, across all borders; pests and diseases spread faster as the global economy grows faster; and resource scarcities in a few places can drive up prices and social instabilities virtually everywhere else. We hope many readers of this book will join the growing legions of far-sighted people who now recognize that it is now in the best interests of everyone, from the most affluent entrepreneurs or investors to the poorest peasant farmers, to make the transition to a more resilient, livable, and sustainable kind of world.

Lester R. Brown
President, Worldwatch Institute

Ed Ayres
Editor, *World Watch*

ACKNOWLEDGMENTS

The modest size of this book belies the number of people it took to produce—and the extraordinary commitment their work represents. Not only the authors whose work we compiled, but the whole staff of the Worldwatch Institute, contributed to this effort. The Institute's research, library, and editorial staffs, as well as its indefatigable administrative staff (all listed on page 7) made this project possible by providing the unsung support services that go into producing *World Watch* magazine and the Institute's other publications.

The *Reader* editors are particularly grateful for the expertise and energy of our designer, Liz Doherty, who did not have the luxury of being able to take time out from the unrelenting schedule of producing a magazine virtually single-handedly, in order to produce this book along with our annual *State of the World* and a number of other projects. She managed to do all this while still keeping both her good cheer and her sanity. Human civilization, in its search for sustainability, could learn from her example!

No useful enterprise can be undertaken without a cost, and at Worldwatch we have always been concerned about who *pays* the cost. Although most prominent magazines are heavily dependent on revenue from advertisers, we have always wanted Worldwatch Institute publications to be free of any obligations that could compromise the objectivity and forthrightness of the recommendations they offer to decisionmakers. As a result, only a fraction of the cost of a book like this is covered by the price it brings in a bookstore.

Much of the cost was borne by three groups of contributors who have recognized the need for human societies to move toward more sustainable economies with clear-sightedness and speed. These groups, to whom we are deeply thankful, are as follows:

First, there are the foundations that have provided specific funding in the startup phase of *World Watch* magazine or as continuing support during its ten years of publication. They include the George Gund Foundation, the John D. and Catherine T. MacArthur Foundation, the Curtis and Edith Munson Foundation, and the Rockefeller Brothers Fund.

In addition, we want to thank the many foundations that have supported the Institute's research program, and have thus contributed indirectly—but importantly—to the preparation of the *World Watch Reader*. Those foundations include: The Carolyn Foundation, the Nathan Cummings Foundation, the Geraldine R. Dodge Foundation, the Energy Foundation, the Ford Foundation, the Foundation for Ecology and Development, the William and Flora Hewlett Foundation, the W. Alton Jones Foundation, the Andrew W. Mellon Foundation, the Mertz-Gilmore Foundation, the Charles Stewart Mott Foundation, the John Edward Noble Foundation, the David and Lucille Packard Foundation, The Pew Charitable Trusts, the Lynn R. and Karl E. Prickett Fund, the Public Welfare Foundation, the Rasmussen Foundation, the Rockefeller Foundation, the Winthrop Rockefeller Charitable Trust, the Summit Foundation, the Surdna Foundation, the Turner Foundation, the U.N. Population Fund, the Wallace Genetic Fund, the Wallace Global Foundation, the Weeden Foundation, and the Winslow Foundation. In addition to these foundations, the newly established Council of Sponsors contributed to the overall support of the Institute in 1997—and thus of the magazine. Council members are Toshishige Kurosawa, Kazuhiko Nishi, Roger and Vicki Sant, Robert Wallace, and Eckart Wintzen.

Finally, a number of individual readers have felt so convinced of the importance of the Institute's work that they have made substantial contributions. Their names are too numerous to list here, but we have listed them in the magazine itself—on pages 36–38 of the March/April 1998 issue.

We should also note that outside the United States, there are numerous organizations and people who have found the Institute's research to be of such value that they have been willing to put their own resources into distributing one ore more of our publications in their own language. To them, too, we are deeply appreciative. Thanks to their commitment, our research has now been published in over 30 languages and *World Watch* magazine itself has been published in Chinese, German, Italian, Japanese, Spanish, and Russian, in addition to English.

1

Energy and Climate

THE RISKS OF
DISRUPTING CLIMATE

By Molly O'Meara

L as Vegas and Monte Carlo, with their myriad roulette wheels and blackjack tables, are famed gambling meccas. Kyoto, Japan is not. Glitzy casinos cannot be found in Kyoto, center of Japanese culture since the late eighth century. The streets are lined instead with manicured gardens, ancient Buddhist temples, and Shinto shrines. But for 10 tension-filled days at the end of 1997, Kyoto became the site of a huge, high-stakes gamble. In December, the city hosted a critical meeting of the parties to the 1992 United Nations Framework Convention on Climate Change. Delegates from more than 160 countries convened to address some of the largest risks the world has ever faced: the potentially catastrophic consequences of global climate change.

The Earth is experiencing a twentieth century warming trend. As economies around the world have industrialized, they have been powered by fossil fuels. Ever greater burning of these fuels and ever faster rates of deforestation have released precipitous increases in carbon dioxide. Along with other "greenhouse" gases, carbon dioxide traps heat, enhancing the natural greenhouse effect of the Earth's atmosphere. Continued, unrestrained emission of these gases, most scientists agree, will invite large-scale climate disruption (see figure, page 28).

Already, phenomena consistent with an enhanced greenhouse effect abound. Polar ice shelves are cracking and splintering, and mountaintop glaciers around the world, from the Alps to the Andes, are in retreat. Temperature-sensitive coral reefs are bleaching under stress, the timing of seasons has changed, and the geographic range of optimal temperature for various plants, animals, and disease vectors has shifted. In theory, there is a small chance that this warming falls within the climate's natural variability. But it would be dangerous to bet on that chance by allowing nations to maintain or accelerate their emissions of greenhouse gases. The resiliency of nature, availability of food and water, health of human populations, and vibrancy of economies all hinge on climate. As Stanford University climate scientist Stephen Schneider puts it in his new book, *Laboratory Earth*, continuing to alter the climate at the current rate is akin to taking a "planetary gamble we can't afford to lose."

As gamblers, human societies have become ever more adept at working the odds. In fact, it was casino-style gam-

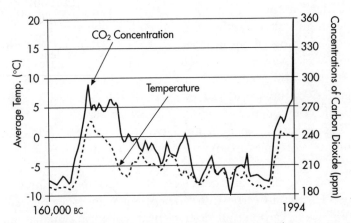

Source: Worldwatch Institute, *Vital Signs 1995*; IPCC, *Climate Change 1995: The Science of Climate Change.*

Correlation of Temperature with Carbon Dioxide Levels, Vostok, Antarctica, 160,000 BC–1994 AD

bling that led us to the tools we now use to assess many risks. During the mid-seventeenth century, mathematician Blaise Pascal and lawyer-turned-math enthusiast Pierre de Fermat—actual Renaissance men—teamed up to calculate the odds in a game of chance. In doing so, they developed an important mathematical idea, one that is the basis for our modern concept of risk: the theory of probability. Peter Bernstein, author of *Against the Gods: The Remarkable Story of Risk*, describes risk as "the revolutionary idea that defines the boundary between modern times and the past... the notion that the future is more than a whim of the gods." Although many early peoples, such as the ancient Greeks, had mathematical skills, they did not apply them to predicting the future; for them, the future was the sole province of the oracles.

Today, however, a mathematical appraisal of the odds often informs our plans for the future. Assessment of risks helps patients to decide on surgery, investors to buy stocks, and military advisors to devise defense strategies. Modern patients seek explanations of medical conditions that are couched in probabilities: what could the worst outcome be? Is it more risky to have surgery or to forego it? When faced with a range of potential outcomes—in health care, engineering, finance, defense, or any other field—we have learned to weigh risks, in order to ignore the small dangers and hedge against catastrophe. To underscore this point, a managing director at the large investment bank Morgan Stanley reportedly likes to quote J.R.R. Tolkien: "It doesn't do to leave a live dragon out of your calculations if you live near him."

Potentially severe climate disruption is a lurking "dragon" that we must now include in our future planning. For instance, we must realign the energy industry if we are to see a reduction in the burning of fossil fuels. The envoys sent to Kyoto in December 1997 began to improve the odds of the current climate "gamble" by agreeing to a legally binding climate treaty protocol. If negotiators are able to strengthen the protocol, it may eventually prove tto be the mt important risk management strategy of the next century. In fact, dealing with the uncertainties of climate change in the twenty-first century may assume the same overiding importance as has military planning in the twentieth. Governments are spurred to build defense capacity not by the knowledge of certain conflict, but by the *risk* of war. It's the same kind of thinking that we use on a personal level, when we purchase car insurance. We know we might never have a car accident, or have only a small accident with minor costs. But, recognizing that we could total the car, or be found liable for a catastrophic injury, we buy the insurance to avoid financial ruin. Diplomats in the ongoing cimate negotiations have the chance to agree on some form of "insurance" too—but in their case the entire planet stands to lose from a "crash." These envoys are crafting insurance not just for the citizens of their home countries, but for those without a seat at the bargaining table, including future generations.

As the Kyoto treaty process continues, some skeptics continue to focus on a single question: "Is climate change real?" In doing so, they purposefully misguide public debate. The majority of scientists have agreed that climate change is real, but they also agree that the local effects of climate change are highly uncertain. Therefore, among the questions we should be asking are: "What do we know about the risks?"; "What level of risk is acceptable?"; and "How can we avoid unacceptable risks?" Even British Petroleum, a corporation that mines the fuels that stoke greenhouse warming, has recognized the importance of asking such questions. In explaining BP's decision to move into climate-friendly solar technologies, chief executive John Browne conceded in May 1997 that the grave risks of climate change "cannot be discounted."

LEARNING TO ASSESS CLIMATE RISKS

If we approach climate change as we do other risky situations, then our first step is to systematically identify the range and probability of possible outcomes. For instance, companies that sell car insurance classify the riskiest clients—say, male teenagers who drive sportscars—by studying historical data on car crashes. Large investors, trying to ascertain the risks of investing abroad, consult *Institutional Investor*'s country credit ratings, based on the economic, financial, and political risks in a given country. The closest analogue for climate change is the rapidly growing body of relevant scientific research, which is continually reviewed by a global network of climate experts. This group, the Intergovernmental Panel on Climate Change (IPCC), was created in 1988 by the World Meteorological Organisation and the United Nations Environment Programme to help decisionmakers around the world understand the scope of the climate change problem.

The IPCC has been as methodical as any actuary or financial analyst in its step-by-step approach to studying climate change. The scientists first examined the range of projections for future population growth, economic development and technological innovation—the key trends that will influence our emissions of greenhouse gases in the future. Then, translating these scenarios into possible levels for carbon dioxide concentrations, the scientists determined that we can expect to see at least a doubling of preindustrial levels of carbon dioxide by the middle of the next century. Consensus is that this doubling will raise the average global surface temperature 1 to 3.5°C by 2100. This change far exceeds any recent natural fluctuation and will occur at a rate faster than any since the last Ice Age more than 10,000 years ago.

Climate is weather averaged over the long term: decades, centuries, and millennia. It is a tremendously complex system that comprises not only the atmosphere, but also the oceans, ice, the land and its features, as well as rivers, lakes, and subsurface water. The Sun's output, the Earth's rotation, and the chemical composition of the atmosphere and ocean all affect this system. Changes in any of these internal or external factors are responsible for the climate's variability. While the climate has undergone some wild shifts over the course of geological history, it has been relatively stable during the period in which modern human society has evolved.

With the warming that is projected from the gases that humans are adding to the atmosphere, this stability may come to a man-made end. Sea level is expected to rise between 15 and 95 centimeters over the next century as oceans expand and ice melts. The largest rises in temperature will occur at higher latitudes. Higher temperatures will enhance evaporation and precipitation, altering the global cycling of water. Some areas will become wetter while others become drier. And dramatic events such as floods and storms could become more variable.

These changes may occur faster than we will be able to respond. And because both nature and climate are so complex, we may be startled by some unwelcome "surprises." For instance, climate change could magnify *other* global problems that stem from a larger human population. Even as average temperatures are rising, we expect to see human population rocketing from 6 billion today to 9 billion within the first half of the next century; ever greater numbers of rural dwellers migrating to urban areas, especially coastal cities; and the use of land rapidly changing—as, for example, in the conversion of forests to farmland. In concert with soil erosion, water and air pollution, and a host of other ills, climate change could push ecosystems past tolerable thresholds. These unhealthy combinations, or "synergisms," may already be spurring events such as the worldwide decline of various animals, the large-scale growth of toxic algae, and the death of coral reefs. Moreover, the warming we cause may trigger more warming, spinning the climate into an inhospitable state. Climate operates over such a long time scale that adverse consequences may take centuries or millennia to reverse. Other changes, such as the decimation of species, are likely to be irreversible. Such surprises may be our greatest risk, the equivalent of the financial catastrophe we try to avoid by buying insurance.

THE STAKES

Surprises, by their nature, are difficult to foresee, but many simpler, "linear" responses to climate change are the subject of intense study. Looking to clues from history, current observations, and lab and field studies, scientists have begun to suggest how projected changes (i.e. temperature increases, sea-level rise, and variation in the global cycling of water) might affect nature, food production, water availability, human health, coastal areas, and other systems vulnerable to the vagaries of climate.

For instance, the icy Antarctic ecosystem is particularly sensitive to warming, as the story of the South Pole's Adélie penguins suggests. Midwinter temperatures have risen 4 to 5°C on the western Antarctic Peninsula over the past five decades. University of Montana ecologist William Fraser has studied the Adélie penguins for 22 years, has seen their population drop 40 percent, and thinks that warmth could be causing changes that make it hard for penguins to find food and breed. The Adélie normally feast on a shrimp-like creature called krill, found in plankton-rich areas near sea ice. But increases in Antarctic temperatures have melted sea ice, apparently causing krill populations to plummet. In addition, increased spring snowfall, as a result of warmer, moisture-laden air, may be thwarting the penguins' attempts to breed. Their eggs may be getting buried under snowbanks. Scientists agree that the penguins' home is likely to be one of the first spots on Earth to feel a temperature hike. Thus, the plight of the penguins could be a small, early example of changes we may begin to see on a much larger scale.

Consider the fate of the world's plants, which are all adapted to certain ranges of temperature and moisture. Entire ecosystems could unravel if changes in climate force plants out of their current ranges. Over time, the population of a plant species can move, as seeds, dispersed by winds and animals, take root in a more hospitable habitat. While past changes in climate forced plants into different geographic ranges, those prehistoric plants did not have to contend with urbanized landscapes. Today, temperature shifts, combined with fragmented habitat, could strand many plants in regional pockets and consign others to extinction. A Dutch study suggests that major vegetation changes will take place by 2050 in 24 percent of the world's parks and protected areas. In some cases, park boundaries may eventually undermine the protection of some species, as roads, farms, and urban areas prevent species from moving.

If warming trends persist in mountain ecosystems, for instance, plants that are adapted to warm conditions may gradually move toward summits, and colder-weather varieties could be caught in shrinking ranges. Already, ecologists at the University of Vienna have found that plants have been "climbing" the Alps as fast as 3.7 meters per decade over the past 90 years. In the U. S. Yellowstone National Park, University of Oregon researchers concluded that warming projected by the IPCC could cause the range of high-elevation trees, including several species of pine, to decrease to such an extent that the trees will not be able to survive. The rate at which we continue to emit greenhouse gases will influence the speed of climate change—and a fast pace could prove disastrous for the Yellowstone pines and countless other plant species.

Animals, too, are vulnerable to changes in climate. For instance, if plants are squeezed out of their ranges or into extinction, the animals that depend on them for food or shelter will be threatened. This could be the case with the Adélie penguins going hungry as their krill stocks dwindle (the marine plankton that the krill eat seem to be diminishing as sea ice melts). A University of California ecologist, Camille Parmesan, published an article last year in the journal *Nature* that is thought to be the first climate-related study to cover not just a local population, but the full range of a species. She found that warmer temperatures could be responsible for the

160-kilometer shift northward of a North American butterfly, the Edith's checkerspot.

Nature not only is affected by changes in climate; it also influences climate. The carbon dioxide that warms the atmosphere enhances photosynthesis, promoting plant growth. Plants take up carbon dioxide, so one might expect their heightened growth to curb global warming. This could be an example of a "negative feedback," in which one change sparks a counteractive response. Indeed, initial laboratory tests of increased carbon levels led scientists to foresee greener forests and more verdant fields. However, labs cannot replicate nature's complexity. Outside of the lab, warming contributes not only to plant growth but also to pest outbreaks that can kill the plants. When plants die, they can no longer take up carbon dioxide; instead they release it. While the future response of nature to ever greater levels of carbon dioxide cannot be predicted, the fact that concentrations of this gas are now at their highest in at least 160,000 years suggests that human carbon dioxide production has already exceeded nature's storage capacity.

Further complicating the picture are other large changes made to the planet by humans, such as the global excess of nitrogen from fossil fuels and industrial fertilizer. With the amount of industrial fertilizer used on crops during the 1980s alone exceeding all industrial fertilizer applied previously in human history, the amount of biologically active nitrogen on land has doubled from preindustrial levels. The double stress of too much carbon dioxide and too much nitrogen was observed in a 12-year field study of grasslands. In the short term, nitrogen spurred plant growth, and the plants took up more carbon dioxide. But in the long term, the added nitrogen caused a change in the species mix, favoring plants that are less adept at taking up carbon. One of the lead authors, David Wedin of the University of Toronto, concluded: "The ecosystems that do a good job of storing carbon are the very same ones we're losing because of the added nitrogen." The same sort of shift could also occur in forests, which play an even bigger role in carbon storage.

One-third of the world's forested area could undergo major changes with a doubling of carbon dioxide. Climate change could be a further stress on forests already under siege from acid rain and fragmented habitat. In the North, boreal forests are particularly vulnerable. Forest fires, a normal part of forest ecology, are likely to increase in frequency and severity, substantially decreasing forest cover and releasing additional carbon dioxide. Several studies predict a dramatic surge in Canadian forest fires that could increase by 40 to 50 percent the area burned each year. In Russia, an additional 7 to 12 million hectares are projected to burn annually within the next 50 years, affecting 30 to 50 percent of the land area. Scientists cited by the IPCC expect that during the next century, boreal forests will be diminished to such an extent that the supply of industrial roundwood will cease to meet demand.

The effects of climate change on nature promise to cascade into the global economy. A shifting climate threatens not only the goods that nature provides us, such as timber, food and genetic resources, but also such vital services as the cleaning of air and water and the pollinating of crops by insects. (See Janet Abramovitz, "Nature's Hidden Economy" in Chapter 3.) Robert Costanza, a University of Maryland economist, and colleagues recently estimated the cumulative value of these services to be in the neighborhood of $33 trillion per year, which compares to the Gross World Product of $28 trillion.

By continuing to load the atmosphere with greenhouse gases, we are putting many of these valuable services at risk. Canada's MacKenzie River Basin, for instance, depends heavily on water transport. Climate change is projected to lower the minimum water levels in the region's waterways, which would hinder navigation—an important natural service. Coastal wetlands also provide us with myriad services: habitat for lucrative fisheries, protection against storms, and improved water quality through sediment, nutrient, and pollution removal. While coastal development is already encroaching on wetlands, climate change brings the added risk of sea-level rise and the potential for more intense storms. Along with many other industries, tourism stands to lose in the face of such changes. Without coastal protection, attractive beaches will erode—a particularly dire prospect for many small island states, where tourism often accounts for more than a third of GDP.

RISKING OUR FOOD AND WATER

As farmers are well aware, the availability of fresh, salt-free water is a crucial service we obtain from nature. Farmers in the midwestern United States are not likely to forget the summer of 1988. Below normal rainfall and record-breaking temperatures combined to create a crop-withering drought. Grain yields dropped by 30 percent, causing production to fall below demand for the first time in U.S. history.

By itself, this single drought is not evidence of climate change. It is, however, a scenario that we may see more frequently in a warmer world—and it highlights the risks that climate change poses to our food and water supplies. On average, the interiors of large continents are expected to warm up and dry out, prompting increased demands for water. One study cited by the IPCC suggests that many midlatitude locations, like the United States, would experience more droughts: the frequency of severe droughts that currently occur only 5 percent of the time could rise to 50 percent by 2050.

Water is already scarce in many areas. Humans now use more than half of the world's fresh water. Even without climate change, countries with high population growth rates are likely to suffer water shortages. Nations that are already water-limited, such as Kuwait, Jordan, Israel, Rwanda, and Somalia, are likely to face substantial costs. In the United

States, the Environmental Protection Agency (EPA) predicts that the warming from a doubling of carbon dioxide would reduce by 7 to 16 percent the annual water supplies in California's Central Valley basin, where water demand is expected to rise by more than 50 percent as early as 2010.

The possibility of more droughts is a risk to food production, but in the absence of droughts, warmer temperatures may actually be a boon in some places. Decreased frequency of severe frosts may help to boost crop productivity. While some crops may benefit, climate change is likely to sharpen agricultural inequities between the rich and poor. Wealthier countries may employ "technological fixes" to evade some climate hazards, but the developing world is far more vulnerable. A study commissioned by the US EPA found that climate change was expected to decrease global production of wheat, rice, and other grains 1.2 to 7.6 percent by 2060. Poor countries, the study estimated, would take the brunt of this shortfall. Industrial countries would see production decrease slightly, or perhaps even increase by as much as 11.3 percent. Developing countries, on the other hand, would see losses of 9.2 to 11 percent.

Even assuming reduced levels of population growth and full trade liberalization, climate change would likely increase the number of people in developing nations at risk of hunger. Depending on the assumptions, the population at risk would increase by 18 million to 412 million. At greatest risk for famine are those who rely on isolated agricultural systems in sub-Saharan Africa, South and Southeast Asia, tropical areas of Latin America, and some Pacific Island nations. But if climate change causes famine in one part of the world, then other countries will feel the pain too, as environmental refugees course across their borders. Nobel laureate and MIT physicist Henry Kendall believes industrial nations in particular ought to see this as a national security risk, warning U.S. President Bill Clinton: "it is not the case that one end of the boat can sink."

The productivity of lakes and oceans is also at risk. Fish thrive in nutrient-rich waters. Warming is expected to reduce the vertical mixing of lake water, impeding nutrient distribution. This would harm freshwater fisheries in lakes such as Africa's Lake Malawi, habitat of 500–1,000 fish species that are an important source of food to local people, and prey to local birds.

Oceanic fisheries, too, are temperature sensitive. Paleo-climate studies indicate that earlier warmer eras were marked by a decrease in global oceanic productivity. Worldwide, about 90 percent of commercial fish are caught within 200 nautical miles of the coast, many in coastal upwellings of cold water. Warmer temperatures could weaken the mechanisms that produce these upwellings. Off the coast of California, a warming of the sea surface by as much as 1.5°C since 1951 has led to an 80 percent decline in zooplankton, which are vital to the oceanic food chain.

Warmer sea water, however, speeds up the metabolism of the more toxic species of algae. Algal blooms, often in the form of red or brown tides, can kill fish and sicken people who eat contaminated seafood. A recent surge in toxic algal blooms worldwide may be the result of new synergisms. Algal blooms thrive in warmth, as well as in nitrogen-rich waters, which are increasing thanks to human activities. As industrial fertilizer production and fossil fuel burning release more nitrogen, coastal wetlands and mangroves, which normally filter out nitrogen, are being lost to coastal development and aquaculture.

Coastal wetlands and other shoreline habitats, at tremendous risk from sea-level rise, sustain valuable fisheries: about 70 percent of the ocean's fish depend on near-shore areas at some point in their life cycle. As sea level rises, fish production could initially increase as marshes fragment, flood, die, and decompose, and nutrients become available from leaching of soils and flooded peat. But ultimately, the loss of nesting sites and refuge would likely damage fisheries.

Coral reefs, dubbed the "tropical rainforests of the sea"

for their rich biological diversity, are another marine habitat at risk. Reefs are already suffering from overfishing, pollution, and enhanced sedimentation—stresses that may increase the corals' vulnerability to a blip in temperature. An increase of 1 to 2°C can cause corals to "bleach," as they expel the algae that provide them with food and lend them their vibrant colors. Sustained increases of 3 to 4°C can cause significant coral death. Warmer than normal sea water has contributed to extensive coral bleaching near the Galapagos Islands off the coast of Ecuador and elsewhere in the eastern Pacific, Caribbean, and adjacent Atlantic.

THREATS TO HEALTH

When corals bleach, they offer a particularly vivid sign of a species under stress. Humans can provide another striking example. In July 1995, for instance, a heat wave paralyzed the city of Chicago for nearly a week. Sustained high temperatures directly contributed to the death of 500 people.

As we continue to add gases to the greenhouse stew, we may be increasing the risk of heat-related deaths. Even a small hike in average temperature can increase the risk of heat waves. The U.S. National Climatic Data Center has shown that a 3°C increase in Chicago's average July temperature would increase the probability of the heat index (a measure of temperature and humidity) exceeding 49°C during the month from one in 20 to one in 4. More very hot days translates into more deaths; studies analyzing heat waves tend to find a threshold temperature beyond which mortality rises rapidly. There may be fewer cold-related deaths as a result of climate change, but scientists expect increases in the number of heat-related deaths to outweigh this positive trend.

Heat waves can be especially deadly in cities, because hot weather accelerates the chemical reactions that produce urban smog, which can cause respiratory distress. Particularly vulnerable are city dwellers in the developing world, where pollution is worse and air conditioning less common.

Another health threat comes from infectious diseases, which may surge as temperatures rise. Such illnesses are already on the rise—emerging from forests cleared for human settlement, being spread by international travel, and mutating to resist existing remedies. (See Anne Platt McGinn, "The Resurgence of Infectious Disease" in Chapter 6.) Climate change could amplify the existing problem. Take malaria, which causes 1 to 2 million deaths annually. The Anopheles mosquito, as well as the malaria-causing parasite it carries, cannot survive in cool weather. But as the mercury rises, Anopheles shifts into high gear, feeding and reproducing more quickly. With the temperature increase scientists expect to see from a doubling of carbon dioxide, the proportion of the world's people living within malarial zones could jump from 45 percent today to 60 percent by the latter half of the next century. Rwanda has already felt this transition on a smaller scale: cases of malaria have more than doubled since the early 1960s, as average temperatures have climbed nearly 1°C. Among Rwandans living in high-altitude areas—cooler zones that previously had seen little or no malaria—the increase was more than fivefold. With further warming, large urban highland populations that are now malaria-free—including millions of people in cities such as Nairobi, Kenya and Harare, Zimbabwe—could be at risk.

Higher temperatures may also help spread dengue fever—called "breakbone fever" by those who know the intense pain it causes in joints. Like the malaria parasite, the dengue virus hitches its ride on a mosquito, usually Aedes aegypti, that thrives in warm conditions. A study sponsored by the Asian Development Bank foresees a four-fold increase in dengue fever cases in Indonesia as projected warming in the next century causes mosquitoes to move into cooler, mountainous areas. Already, since 1993, dengue has been found at higher elevations than ever before: at 2,200 meters in Colombia and 1,700 meters in Mexico. Meanwhile, a hardier dengue vector, the Asian tiger mosquito, has established itself in the Southeast United States, and has begun to extend its range northwards towards Chicago and Washington, DC.

Another scourge closely linked to climate is cholera, a water-borne illness that attacks the human small intestine. The cholera bacterium is thought to originate in South Asia, from which it is carried to Latin America on ships that discharge ballast water near the coast. In 1991, a cholera epidemic struck a 2,000-kilometer stretch of the Peruvian coast. Before the incident ended, 500,000 people fell ill and 5,000 died. A lone ship could have introduced the disease, and poor sanitation was to blame for infecting local populations, but other factors must have been at work to spread the bacterium so far. Scientists tied the outbreak to a climatic event, El Niño, which brings warm sea surface temperatures, heavy rains, and nutrients from the land to the west coast of South America, fostering plankton blooms that carry the cholera bacterium.

People who live near areas of endemic disease will be particularly at risk if the boundaries of tropical diseases are extended by warmer temperatures. As Paul Epstein of the Harvard School of Public Health points out, "rodents and insects carry no passports." Infectious diseases could easily migrate to northern, industrial countries, where natural immunity is low. Nonetheless, these countries are better equipped to suppress disease outbreaks. Hardest hit will be those in developing countries, where infectious disease is already a major cause of illness and death. George Alleyne, director of the Pan American Health Organization, suspects climate change "will be one other phenomenon that widens the health gap between groups of people."

FLOODS AND STORMS

If the planet's average temperature continues to climb, then more water will both evaporate and precipitate. The consequences of this greater cycling of water are still unclear. Some regions may see more intense rains of the kind that devastated Eastern Europe during the summer of 1997. Those rains caused floods that swallowed homes, crops, highways, and factories—and sent national economic advisers in Poland and the Czech Republic scurrying to revise their forecasts for economic growth. Weeks of severe flooding killed at least 100 people and caused billions of dollars worth of damage.

While moderate rains benefit agriculture and water supplies, heavy rains of the sort that drenched Eastern Europe in 1997 allow more water to run off into the sea and are more likely to trigger floods. Meteorologist Thomas Karl and his colleagues at the National Climatic Data Center have found evidence that there is actually a trend towards heavier rains in the United States. While total precipitation has increased by about 10 percent in the United States from 1901 to 1996, there has been little increase in the beneficial moderate rains. Rather, most of the increase has been in the extreme events, such as floods and storms. Karl believes that warmer temperatures may be responsible for the increase in the extremes.

As the atmosphere warms, changes in the intensity and frequency of hurricanes (also called tropical cyclones or typhoons) are likely to vary by region—with some areas deluged and others in drought. A study by Germany's Max Planck Institute suggests that the warmer ocean temperatures expected from a doubling of carbon dioxide will resemble semi-permanent El Niño conditions. El Niño appears every few years when trade winds that push surface ocean currents away from the west coast of Peru weaken or even reverse, allowing warm water to flow back towards South America, bringing heavy rains to the Eastern Pacific while stranding the Western Pacific in a drought. These events set in motion a chain of weather anomalies around the world. While the link between El Niño and climate change has yet to be proven, El Niños have occurred more often since 1977, with an unusually prolonged event from 1990 to 1995. The century's strongest was in 1982–83, but that title is likely to be claimed by the one that began in late 1997. If climate change spurred a semi-permanent El Niño, there would be fewer Atlantic hurricanes in the United States, but more intense tropical cyclones in the Pacific, and more typhoons in Asia.

The effect of climate change on the overall frequency of storms is uncertain. Climate models are not good at replicating these weather extremes. However, the response of oceans to warmer temperatures leads some scientists to believe that storms, whatever their frequency, will be more intense. As the ocean is heated, water expands, raising the average sea level. This, of course, may be hastened by the melting of sea and mountain ice. Warmer sea surface temperatures feed storms, and higher sea levels intensify storm surges.

Today, 46 million people live in areas that are at risk of flooding due to storm surge. If a warmer climate causes the sea level to rise by 50 centimeters, the number of people at risk will double to 92 million—even without accounting for anticipated population growth. In Indonesia, for instance, urban populations are concentrated in low-lying coastal areas; of a total population of 180 million, 110 million live near the shore. Sea level rise is of particular concern in Jakarta, where parts of the city are already subsiding due to the exploitation of ground water.

There is also high risk of flood damage from sea-level rise along the Indian Ocean coast, the south Mediterranean coast, the African Atlantic, the Caribbean coasts, and many small islands. University of Maryland researchers have found that more than 94 million people are at risk from future sea-level rise of 1 meter in Egypt, Bangladesh, China, and Nigeria—mostly around river deltas. Many populated deltas are already affected by land subsidence or sediment starvation by upstream dams. In Bangladesh, the Sunderbans—the largest mangrove forest in the world—would probably be destroyed (it is already threatened by salt intrusion because the flow of the Ganges has been diminished by diversion of water to cities). The U.S. Atlantic and Gulf coasts would also be imperiled; sea level in the Mississippi Delta is already rising faster than the average sea-level rise worldwide.

Regardless of changes in climate, storms will cause more damage as the result of another trend: more people living in coastal cities. Already, two-thirds of the world's population lives within 60 km of a coast, and this number is expected to rise to three-fourths by 2010.

An increase in flood and storm damages, whatever the cause, could bankrupt the insurance industry. Insured property values on the Gulf and Atlantic coasts of the United States alone totaled $2 trillion in 1988. The insurance industry is already suffering from a spate of "billion dollar" storms that have occurred since 1987. In the United States, there has been as much damage from hurricanes in the 1990s as the combined total of the 1970s and 1980s, even after adjusting for inflation. Insurance companies, well-versed in risk assessment, are increasingly concerned about the risks climate change might pose to their business.

ANTICIPATING SURPRISES

Ultimately, the most serious results of climate change may be the hardest to predict. As ecologist Norman Myers explains, when climate change combines with pollution or another environmental problem: "the outcome may be not a double problem, but a super-problem." The climate system itself is full of such "non-linear" possibilities, because it is so complex. A tale from one of the earliest pioneers in chaos theory helps to explain this:

In 1961, as James Gleick, author of the book *Chaos,* tells it, MIT meteorologist Richard Lorenz was playing with his favorite new toy, an early computer model of the weather. When Lorenz entered data for initial weather conditions, his computer—big and clunky by today's standards—solved a batch of physics equations and then spewed out results for future winds, rain, and temperatures. One day, trying to redo part of an earlier run, Lorenz re-entered his data. As he examined the new printout, he expected it to look like the old one. He was surprised. The second time around he had used more rounded numbers (.506 instead of .506127). At first, the second run resembled the first, but then, over time, it began to diverge so sharply that no similarity could be seen.

Lorenz had stumbled into a new field of science now known as chaos. Climate, like Lorenz's model, is chaotic: small changes in important parameters can cause unexpected, non-linear, results. In the words of climate scientist Richard Somerville, "Just as a finger on a trigger can set off an explosion, so a very subtle change in a climate input can have a massive change in a climate output."

So as we push greenhouse gas concentrations to record levels, we are making an important change to one "input" in the Earth's climate system. A leading climatologist writing in the October 1946 *Scientific Monthly* expressed a dominant view of his time: "We can safely accept the past performance as an adequate guide for the future." But as we reach unprecedented levels of carbon emissions, the past may no longer be a good reference. Paleoclimatologist Jonathan Overpeck of the U.S. National Geophysical Data Center recently summed this up in the journal Science: "If the climate system turns out to be highly sensitive to elevated atmospheric trace gas concentrations, then we may be confronted with modes of climate variability without precedent."

What sort of surprises might the climate system have in store? The answer can be found in "positive feedbacks"—the potential for initial climate changes to spur even greater change. Warming, for instance, could cause changes that could in turn lead to the slowing or stopping of the North Atlantic oceanic "conveyor belt." This conveyor, with a flow equal to 100 Amazon Rivers, brings heat from the Gulf Stream to Europe. In the Norwegian Sea, heat from the sea is transferred to the air, so the water becomes saltier and denser and falls to the ocean floor, setting up a current that circulates around the world. Warmer temperatures in the high latitudes could slow the evaporation process; or mountain glaciers and polar ice could melt, infusing the Norwegian Sea with fresh water. In either case, the pool of northern water would not become as dense as it gets today, and the density differential that drives the conveyor would be lessened. Without this transport, fisheries could collapse, and Europe might be plunged into a mini-ice age. Winter temperatures in the North Atlantic could abruptly plummet: within 10 years, Dublin might have the climate of Spitsbergen, which is almost 1,000 kilometers north of the Arctic Circle. University of Bern climate modelers recently found that the rate of greenhouse gas emission is critical, because the strength of the conveyor depends on such subtle density differences. Wallace Broecker, an oceanographer at Columbia University who has extensively studied the conveyor, concludes: "Far from being self-stabilizing, the Earth's climate system is an ornery beast which overreacts even to small nudges."

This scenario points to a problem with our climate models. We have been asking them to tell us what might happen if carbon dioxide concentrations were doubled. But concentrations are not steady and will not necessarily stabilize at that level. It is not unimaginable that concentrations might eventually quadruple. And studies by climate modelers at the National Oceanic and Atmospheric Administration's Geophysical Fluid Dynamics Lab in Princeton, New Jersey indicate that the oceanic conveyor might indeed shut off entirely if that happens.

Furthermore, one climatic surprise may trigger *cascading* surprises. For instance, Princeton researchers have suggested that a weakened conveyor could undermine the oceans' capacity to remove carbon dioxide from the atmosphere. As ocean circulation slowed, the seas would absorb much less carbon dioxide, leaving more of the heat-trapping gas in the atmosphere to feed further warming. Or, if the ocean conveyor were to shut off completely, then the surface air temperature in the Northern Hemisphere could suddenly drop. Such a drop could limit the capacity of the boreal forests to take up carbon dioxide—again, resulting in additional buildup of carbon dioxide in the atmosphere.

Another surprise may come from the response of forests to warming. While forests play a key role in taking up carbon dioxide, some scientists predict a net release of carbon dioxide as rising temperatures change the optimal geographic range of trees. Recall the Yellowstone pines that could die at the southern end of their range and might not be able to quickly take root in cooler climes as the atmosphere warms. The death of such trees could release more carbon dioxide than could be taken up by new tree growth. In any case, much is still unknown about the role that plants play in stabilizing the climate, or about how changes in vegetation will subsequently affect the climate system. For instance, trees and plants tend to absorb more sunlight than does snow or tundra. Thus, forests that spread into formerly barren tundra as temperatures rise may end up absorbing more solar energy than the tundra does, thereby increasing the warming.

In all these cases, the climate may eventually swing back. Not only can complex systems go haywire as a result of positive feedbacks, but also they can be corrected by negative feedbacks. Take the human body, another complex system with countless feedback loops. When a healthy person gets too hot, sweating cools him down. An ill person, however, might sustain a high fever (and perhaps even die) despite the sweating and other such negative feedbacks. Human domination of the earth's ecosystems—from nitrogen overload to increased demand for water to deforestation—is thwarting natural negative feedbacks that could slow global warming. For instance, by cutting down forests that store carbon, we are weakening a negative feedback. Even if the warming is corrected by natural phenomena in the long run, the time scale that climate operates on is far longer than the lifespan of humans. By the time the Earth's "fever" breaks, it may be too late for us. Jerry Mahlman, director of the Princeton lab that has modeled the quadrupling of carbon dioxide, explained to *New York Times* science writer William Stevens: "If you get to where you don't like it, there's not a lot you can do about it—you're wired in for a long time."

MINIMIZING THE RISKS

The point that Mahlman stresses—that a shift to an inhospitable climate could be irreversible on a human time scale—is important. It means that climate change could be a catastrophe from which humans never recover. The nations of the world, in signing the 1992 climate change treaty, acknowledged that the devastating prospects identified by scientists are unacceptable risks. However, in the years since that agreement, emissions of greenhouse gases have continued to rise, and there is still no plan in place to hedge against climate catastrophe. Parties to the climate treaty have a clear choice: to expose the world to further risk by gambling on the status quo or to produce a strategy to minimize the risks.

One proven way to minimize risk is to assemble a diverse "portfolio" of options. This approach was validated in 1952, when a young University of Chicago graduate student showed mathematically that it is risky to put all one's eggs into one basket. Wall Street players quickly canonized his findings: if one stock should fail, a diverse portfolio of investments protects against financial ruin. So too could a diverse portfolio of technologies and policies hedge against the risks of climate change. Just as an investment portfolio contains different types of assets (such as stocks, bonds and mutual funds) a climate portfolio would include three types of actions: further study of the climate system, preparations to respond and adapt to climate changes, and—most urgently—a reduction in the rate at which greenhouse gases build up in the atmosphere.

Sustained scientific research, the first item in the portfolio,

The Risks of Climate Change

Natural and man-made systems alike rely on certain climate parameters. This is just a thumbnail sketch of what's at stake when we gamble with the climate:

AREA	SELECTED RISKS
Ecological Systems	
Forests	Major vegetation changes in one-third of global forests; disappearance of entire forest types; more frequent and intense forest fires.
Terrestrial & aquatic ecosystems	Extinction of certain plants and animals as their range shifts.
Deserts	Hotter but not wetter conditions in some areas. Increased desertification.
Mountains	Extinction of mountain-top plants and animals; loss of one-third to one-half of global glacier mass over the next century.
Oceans & coastal systems	Inundation of coastal wetlands, coral reefs, and river deltas.
Socioeconomic Systems	
Water resources	Large decrease in per capita water availability in some areas.
Agriculture	Hunger and famine in areas dependent on isolated agricultural systems (i.e. in sub-Saharan Africa, parts of Asia, tropical areas of Latin America)
Fisheries	National and local fisheries vulnerable to shift in species mix and production centers. Subsistence and small-scale fishers disproportionately at risk.
Insurance industry	Difficulty in adjusting premiums, due to unpredictable changes in extreme weather events. Bankruptcy of industry from more frequent or larger disasters.
Human Health	
Habitat	Large coastal cities particularly at risk. Damage from coastal storm surges, floods, landslides, windstorms, rapid snowmelt, tropical cyclones, and forest or brush fires.
Disease	More heat-related illness and death. Greater transmission of vector-borne diseases as range and seasons of vectors increase.

Source: IPCC, *Climate Change 1995: Impacts, Adaptations and Mitigation of Climate Change.*

is essential for several reasons. Although the goal of the climate treaty is to avoid "dangerous" concentrations of greenhouse gases, exact threshold levels cannot be predicted with certainty. As scientists get a better idea of how the climate system's many feedback loops operate, they may be able to better gauge the rate and magnitude of projected changes (currently, the estimated range of outcomes is quite large, to account for scientific uncertainty). Important avenues of investigation include, among others, the role that clouds play in both trapping and reflecting solar energy, the various ways in which ecosystems are linked to climate, and the interaction between oceans and atmosphere.

Scientific research is also crucial because it helps inform the second part of the portfolio: strategies to *adapt* to climate change. A key, long-term goal of climate change research is accurate projections of how certain regions will be affected. Such information would allow governments to more cost-effectively implement strategies to adapt to sea-level rise, localized drought, heat waves, and other adverse effects. Water supplies might be better managed, for instance, or farmers might be able to shift to more resilient crops. Development could be restricted in floodplains and wilderness corridors could be created to allow for plant and animal migration. Adaptation measures are important, but the dividends we can expect from this part of the portfolio are necessarily limited. Many effects of climate change would be difficult, if not impossible, to manage: the inundation of coastal zones and small island states, the eradication of species, or a shut-off of the ocean's circulation.

Thus, the centerpiece of the portfolio is slowing the greenhouse gas buildup in the atmosphere. This is the one element that squarely addresses the cause of climate change. Of course, to slow the accretion of greenhouse gases released around the world, national governments will have to cooperate. At Kyoto industrial countries agreed to colleectively reduce their emissions 5.2 percent from 1990 levels between

2008 and 2012. This small cut by itself would not be nearly enough to halt the rising concentration of carbon dioxide in the atmosphere. However, it may be barely sufficient to point the world's energy, transportation, and industrial systems towards a path on which greater emissions cuts could occur.

Fortunately, there are many cost-effective actions that can be taken to reduce emissions. Fossil fuel combustion is the single largest source of carbon dioxide emissions, so a diversification of the world's energy infrastructure could offer the greatest long-term protection. Countries and private investors need not tie their futures to the fuels and technologies that have led the world to the brink of climate disruption. In the 1990s, there are an array of cost-effective alternatives. Energy producers can switch to clean and economical energy sources such as wind and sunlight. And the amount of energy consumed could be greatly reduced by the use of more efficient technologies. Indeed, this is the investment advice espoused by London's Delphi Group, which advises large institutions on investment policies. "Avoid maintaining long term overweight positions in the 'carbon fuel' industry," the group's 1995 report cautioned banks and insurance companies, explaining: "the alternative energy industry offers greater growth prospect than the carbon fuel industry."

New wind turbines, for example, produce emissions-free electricity at a generating cost comparable to that of new coal-fired plants. And the cost continues to fall as the industry expands at a rate of 25 percent per year. The solar power industry is also growing at double-digit rates. Already, solar is the least-cost electricity option for many rural areas; an estimated 400,000 homes far from electricity grids are using solar panels. Also on the market are options to improve the energy efficiency of buildings and vehicles. These include more efficient lights and appliances, small gas turbines that generate both power and heat, and a new generation of light-weight hybrid electric cars. Until now, government policies have hindered such technologies. By removing fossil fuel subsidies and introducing market incentives for the new technologies, governments could help turn this situation around. Of course, to be effective, such technological advances will have to be combined with a stabilization of the human population worldwide.

As climate change negotiations have progressed, coal and oil interests have shown a parochial interest in keeping the world's energy system dependent on them—witness the multimillion dollar, pre-Kyoto media blitz. Certainly, the fossil fuel industry stands to be diminished. But companies can still survive, and even flourish—if they diversify. As opportunities fade in fossil fuels, new ones will open in renewable energy and energy efficiency. There are a host of win-win solutions. An analogous scenario began to play out ten years ago, when nations agreed to the 1987 Montreal Protocol, which curtailed global use of the chlorofluorocarbons (CFCs) and other compounds that destroy the ozone layer. Companies such as Dupont that produced CFCs ended up profiting from the production of ozone-friendly alternatives. And many companies that had been using CFCs developed more efficient, CFC-free production processes that ultimately saved them money.

Still, the fossil fuel lobby continues to deflect attention from the risks of climate change by asserting that the risks to the economy are a greater public concern. But the economic models they use do not allow for policy and technology changes that will make fossil fuel alternatives much less expensive than they are today. Nor do they account for the fact that a cleaner, more efficient energy economy would yield tremendous benefits that are not even related to climate change. For instance, a departure from fossil fuels could significantly lower energy costs. In 1997, a study by a group of energy and environmental organizations found that U.S. carbon emissions could be cut to 10 percent below the 1990 level in 2010 while *reducing* national energy costs by $530 per household and creating nearly 800,000 jobs annually.

Similar research in Canada, Japan, Europe and Australia has found that reductions in carbon dioxide emissions could enhance the economy. Other benefits, not even accounted for in these studies, include less local air pollution and regional acid rain, fewer tanker accidents and strip mines, decreased trade imbalances, and increased national security. This means we would receive dividends from our climate portfolio—even if the catastrophe never occurs.

Along with energy reforms, better forest management could slow carbon dioxide accumulation. Trees take up carbon dioxide from the atmosphere and release it when they decay. Deforestation accounts for as much as a third of the carbon dioxide added to the atmosphere from human activities. But if we halt deforestation and actually increase forest cover—through better conservation, management, and reforestation—then forests may be able to slow the buildup of atmospheric carbon dioxide.

Release of other greenhouse gases, too, could be cut. For instance, many low-cost options exist to reduce methane emissions from industrial sources. The U.S. EPA has found that up to 90 percent of the methane released from landfills can be profitably eliminated, providing side-benefits such as improved air and water quality near dumpsites and less risk of fires and explosions. Another step would be to curb the release of halogenated compounds, primarily perfluorocarbons (PFCs) and hydrofluorocarbons (HFCs), highly potent and long-lived greenhouse gases that are on the rise, as they are increasingly substituted for restricted ozone-depleting chemicals.

In hedging against climate change, a strengthened Kyoto Protocol can guard against a wide range of seemingly unrelated problems. Alteration of the global carbon cycle is just one of the large changes humans have been making to the planet. Others—increasing our population, cutting down forests, using more water, and releasing more toxins—also have profoundly detrimental consequences, which stand to be worsened by climate disruption. By beginning to reduce the risks of climate change, we will be narrowing our risk of exposure in other areas as well.

THE NEXT ENERGY REVOLUTION

By Christopher Flavin

At a small news conference in Landover, Maryland in late 1995, two major U.S. corporations made an announcement that may one day be seen as a big step in launching the energy systems of the twenty-first century. Bechtel Enterprises Inc., once a leading builder of nuclear power plants, and PacifiCorp, a giant utility that operates several huge coal-fired generators in the northwestern United States, announced that they were teaming up to invest in solar energy and other "human-scale energy systems."

The new joint venture, called EnergyWorks, will pursue projects around the world based on wind turbines, biomass generators, industrial energy efficiency, and other technologies that most large energy firms have spurned as puny systems that cannot possibly meet the expanding energy needs of close to six billion people.

But those energy executives who still cast their lot with large oil refineries, nuclear reactors, and the like would do well to remember the lessons of IBM, which discovered too late that personal computers were more than a boutique industry that could never challenge the dominance of mainframes. Once technological change gathers momentum, it can move at lightning speed.

In fact, historians of technology may one day argue that

by the mid-1990s, the world energy economy was already in the early stages of a major transition. One sign, for example, is that relatively small, efficient jet engines are coming to dominate the power industry, sweeping aside less efficient coal-fired models. Another is that advanced electronics have improved the efficiency of lighting by as much as four-fold. Meanwhile, the fastest growing energy market in the 1990s isn't oil, coal, or even natural gas—it is wind power, which expanded from 2,000 megawatts in 1990 to 7,600 megawatts in 1997.

Around the world, advanced electronics, new kinds of synthetic materials, and the techniques of mass production are allowing engineers to substitute clever technologies for brute force. The result is a variety of new modular, mass-produced energy systems that have the potential to be more economical and flexible than the traditional energy systems they replace.

Here, as in the mercurial worlds of computers and telecommunications, it is impossible to predict the future. But the broad outlines of a new energy economy are beginning to emerge. Its chief feature is likely to be a radical decentralization, akin to the computer industry's shift from mainframes to PCs. The new technologies will make it possible to decentralize power generation, even down to the household level, harness the world's most abundant energy resources—solar energy and wind power—and greatly reduce the burden that current energy systems place on the world's atmosphere.

But these changes may add up to more than the sum of their parts. Using technologies such as fuel cells and mass-produced solar generators, it should be possible in the long run to replace virtually all fossil fuels with a hydrogen-based energy system, something that author Jules Verne dreamed of more than a century ago. The hydrogen would be produced using sunlight harnessed on rooftops as well as in remote desert collectors, and would be conveyed to homes and industries via pipeline. Although this vision may sound futuristic, most of the inventions needed to make it real have already been made.

PUNCTUATED EQUILIBRIUM

Technological change has been compared to the evolutionary development that occurs in nature, and the similarities are not all coincidental. Technology is, after all, a systematic extension of human biological capability—an increased capacity to use available energy to do the things that eyes, hands, and legs do, only on a vastly magnified scale. It's not surprising, then, that if there have been longstanding misconceptions about the nature of evolution, the same misconceptions have distorted our vision of technological change.

For nearly a century after Charles Darwin wrote *Origin of Species*, biologists thought of evolution as an exceedingly gradual process, with an almost infinite number of incremental stages between one species and its successor. During the 1970s, Harvard biologist Stephen Jay Gould proposed an alternative theory: that most evolutionary change occurs in sudden bursts—driven in part by changing climates and other environmental influences that force species to change rapidly in order to survive. According to Gould, these bursts may be preceded by long periods of stasis—giving the impression that evolution is glacially slow. Gould's theory, known as "punctuated equilibrium," has since earned broad acceptance among biologists.

In the evolution of technology, the same pattern of punctuated progress can be seen. The telephone, for example, developed rapidly in the late nineteenth century and then changed very little through the middle decades of the twentieth century. Now the telephone is again in a period of explosive transition—simultaneously becoming digital, wireless, and portable, while also becoming a carrier not only of voices but of a wide variety of other kinds of communications—from e-mail to debit card transactions.

To those who make a living out of projecting future energy trends, the current system appears close to immutable. For more than 70 years it has been dominated by big oil refineries, internal combustion engines, and steam-cycle power plants, devices that have become more efficient and larger, but have never been displaced. It is no wonder that these analysts see the future as marked by increasingly small refinements to the existing system.

Reflecting this bias, official energy projections published by the International Energy Agency, the World Energy Council, and various national governments conclude that future energy systems will merely be more efficient versions of the current one. Their studies suggest that our grandchildren will still be driving automobiles powered by internal combustion engines—and using electricity generated by power plants that waste two-thirds of the coal they consume—well into the 21st century.

These prognosticators are mesmerized by how little energy systems have changed in recent decades, but ignore the fact that in the more distant past, energy systems have changed rapidly. The energy economy we have today was created in an explosion of invention between 1890 and 1910. During that short period, many cities were dramatically transformed, with horse-drawn carriages replaced by automobiles, and gas lamps by electric lights.

The carriages and gas lamps had prevailed for centuries, but once the conditions for rapid change were present, the old technologies were replaced with breathtaking speed. Today, we may be at a similar turning point, as revolutionary new energy technologies emerge at the same time that consumers demand a cleaner environment and more flexible, less costly ways of meeting their energy needs. The technological upheavals sweeping so many other industries are unlikely to leave the old energy system intact.

In recent years, even the conservative business press has begun to take such ideas seriously. In its October 7, 1995 issue, *The Economist* magazine stated: "Once [renewable energy] was the province of mad scientists and dreamers. . . No longer. Little noticed, the costs of many renewables have recently been tumbling. Fossil fuels are still almost always cheaper, but a battle has begun on the fringes of the mighty $1-trillion-a-year fossil-fuel industry that could force it into retreat early in the coming century."

ROOFTOP POWER

One of the most neglected "fringes" of the world energy economy is made up of thousands of rural villages that are home to some 2 billion people who lack access to electricity or other modern fuels. Yet these villages are now at the center of one of the most revolutionary new developments: during the past ten years, silicon cells that turn sunlight directly into electricity have been installed on or adjacent to at least 400,000 homes, mostly in remote areas of countries such as Sri Lanka, China, and Mexico.

In Kenya, in 1993, more homes were electrified using solar cells than by extending the grid. In Brazil, utility companies are starting to support solar electrification in the Amazon and other areas where it is impractical to extend power lines. In South Africa, the government has launched a major effort to provide solar power to millions of people. And in Vietnam, where only 14 of the country's 72 million people currently have electricity, the Vietnam Women's Union has launched a solar electrification program.

Solar electric systems are also beginning to appear on the roofs of posh suburban homes in industrial countries. In Sacramento, California, for example, the municipal utility is putting shiny blue solar electric panels on 100 homes each year; their rooftop systems are connected to the utility's electric grid, so that power not needed within the home can be sold to other consumers. Consumers pay for the systems via their monthly power bill, at a rate that is only slightly higher than their neighbors'.

In Switzerland and Germany, more than 1,000 buildings have been outfitted with solar power systems in recent years, with government funding. Thousands more are planned. The Japanese government had installed over 10,000 building-integrated solar generators 1997 and plans 70,000 such systems within the next few years. Although such systems must be subsidized to be affordable today, they could become fully competitive with traditional power sources as large-scale production brings manufacturing costs down.

A product of the electronic revolution, solar cells bypass the mechanical generators now used by virtually all power plants, whether they run on fossil fuels, hydropower, or nuclear energy. First used to power orbiting satellites in the U.S. space program in the 1960s, solar cells are a close relative of the microprocessors that make today's computers possible. The cells consist of semiconductors—usually made of silicon—that emit electrons when struck by sunlight, thereby producing an electric current.

Japanese, Swiss, and U.S. manufacturers have designed experimental "solar tiles" that shelter occupants while also powering their appliances. In Europe, Flachglas, a leading producer of architectural glass, has developed a semi-transparent "curtain wall" that provides filtered light as well as electricity. In a joint venture in the United States, Corning Glass and Siemens Solar are developing a similar product.

The cost of solar cells has declined from more than $70 per watt in the 1970s (in 1994 dollars) to $4 per watt today, and is expected to drop to between $1 and $2 per watt within a decade, according to the National Renewable Energy Laboratory in Colorado. As a result, the potential applications have multiplied. The world market went from 34 megawatts in 1988 to an estimated 125 megawatts in 1997.

Aerial photographs show that even in the cloudy climate of the British Isles, putting solar cells on all the country's existing flat roofs could generate 68,000 megawatts of power on a bright day—about half the United Kingdom's current peak power demand. With a strong push by governments and private investors, it is possible that rooftops alone could provide as much as a quarter of the world's electricity by the middle of the next century.

POWER FROM THE BASEMENT

Another technology that may soon allow individual buildings to produce their own power is the fuel cell. First used to provide electricity for orbiting U.S. spacecraft in the 1960s, fuel cells are battery-like devices that efficiently convert a fuel—usually hydrogen—to electricity. Compared to today's generators, which are mechanical devices, fuel cells produce minimal air pollution and virtually no noise. And because they are small and can be located inside buildings, their waste heat can be productively used, rather than vented to the atmosphere as occurs in most of today's power plants.

The hydrogen that powers fuel cells can easily be obtained by splitting the methane found in natural gas—the most common heating fuel in American and European homes—into hydrogen and carbon dioxide. A number of types of fuel cells are now under development, some with government support.

During the past five years, the imperative to improve urban air quality has produced a surge of investment in fuel cells. Several companies have successfully demonstrated the pollution avoidance benefits of fuel-cell generators by installing them in hospitals and other buildings. Typically, such fuel cells are used to provide around-the-clock electricity, with waste heat captured for water and space heating.

In the United States, the race is on. In 1995, ONSI Corporation, a division of United Technologies, launched the world's first commercial fuel cell factory, with a plan to initially turn out some 50 fuel cells each year, at less than half the cost of earlier fuel cells. Meanwhile, Allied Signal has been working on a 5- to 10-kilowatt fuel cell for home-scale use, relying on technologies it developed in its aerospace business. And IBM announced that it is applying its expertise in multi-layer ceramic substrates to make less-expensive fuel cells in a joint venture with the Dow Chemical Company. In Canada, Ballard Power Systems has teamed with Mercedes and Ford to develop fuel cell-powered automobiles.

Such commitments suggest that a commercial takeoff for fuel cells is likely within the next decade. And as the volume of production grows, costs are expected to plummet. If this technology flourishes, we may soon approach the day when a city that is now served by three or four power plants may have thousands of small networked generators connected to it. In a sign of things to come, the Netherlands already gets one-third of its power from industrial and commercial co-generators. Low cost fuel cells could one day push that figure to two-thirds or more.

Storing Power

Just as buildings of the future are likely to generate their own electricity, they may also be able to store it. During the past few years, at least five companies have begun developing fly-wheels, which function like mechanical batteries. Operating on the same principle as a potter's wheel, a flywheel disc is set to spinning at high speed by an integrated electric motor/ generator. It is contained inside an airless case, almost elimi-nating resistance so that the ensuing long duration of the spin serves as a means of storing kinetic energy—which can then be converted to electricity by the generator as needed.

Although it was invented over a century ago, the flywheel only became practical with the development of strong, light-weight composite materials in the 1970s and 1980s. Modern composites can spin in a vacuum at up to 200,000 revolutions per minute, with the potential to store and release energy at an efficiency of more than 90 percent. Because they have vir-tually frictionless electromagnetic bearings, flywheels can

Two Turns-of-the Century . . .

Horses and carriages, like oil lamps and fire places, had been in use with little change for centuries. The U.S. transportation system in the 1880s was based on 25 million horses, which outnumbered cars by 10,000 to 1.... Yet within 20 years, automobiles—along with electric lights and fossil fuel-burning furnances—had taken over. As the price of the first mass-produced car (the Ford Model T) dropped, production soared.

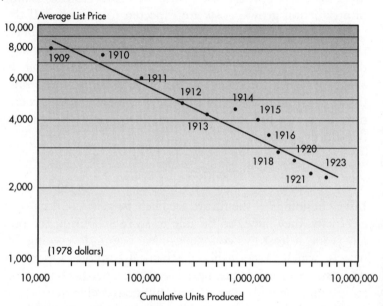

FORD MODEL T: Price Versus Cumulative Production, 1909–23

store electricity for weeks, and last years before wearing out.

At the Lawrence Livermore Laboratory in California, scientists and engineers are developing a mass-produced device half the size of a clothes washer that could sit in a building's basement, storing cheap electricity at night (or solar energy during the day) and releasing it to the grid when needed. Several large and small companies are developing similar devices.

Two Leaps of Energy Technology

Today, the automobiles and the fossil fuel-burning power plants make up the status quo. But these may be overtaken by the next energy revolution, as cleaner, renewable, and decentralized energy systems come on the market. It is striking how closely the current commercial succes of the solar PV module parallels that of the Model T.

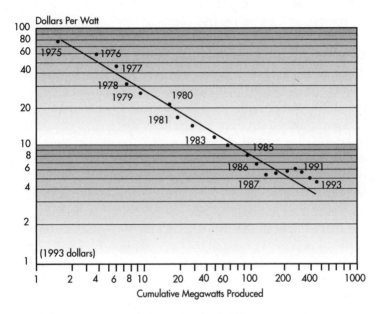

PHOTOVOLTAIC MODULES: Price Versus Cumulative Production, 1975–93

Flywheels would last much longer than chemical batteries, and would not require toxic substances. The materials need-ed to manufacture them are not expensive, and their design readily lends them to mass production, which will yield much lower costs. Because they could be used as storage devices in electric cars as well as in buildings, the ultimate market for fly-wheels could add up to millions of units. It will probably be

10 to 15 years before flywheels are widely available commercially, but after that, their use could grow as fast as that of cellular phones did in the 1990s.

WINDS OF CHANGE

Another modular power technology, the wind turbine, has begun to change the electric power landscape from the northern coasts of Europe to the plains of southern India. The world had more than 30,000 wind turbines operating at the end of 1997, producing about 7,600 megawatts of power. California has 1,700 megawatts, generating enough electricity to supply all of of San Francisco's residents, Germany has more than 2,000 megawatts, and Denmark has more than 1,000 megawatts, which supplies 6 percent of its electric power.

After a slow period in the late 1980s, the world market for wind turbines has exploded since 1990. Following the laws of technological progress and large-scale manufacturing, the cost of wind-generated electricity has fallen by more than two-thirds over the past decade, to the point where it is lower than that of new coal plants in many regions. Within the next decade, it is projected to fall to 3 to 4 cents per kilowatt-hour, making wind the least expensive power source that can be developed on a large scale worldwide.

The new wind turbines aren't the quaint old "wind mills" we remember from past generations; they are sleek, high-tech fiberglass models with gearless, variable speed transmissions and advanced electronic controls. The larger machines have blade spans of 50 meters (160 feet) and more. Unlike large conventional power plants, new wind turbine models enter the market as frequently as new laptop computers do. And, like laptops, they deliver services in small units; the latest wind machines generate 300 to 750 kilowatts per turbine—one-thousandth the size of a typical coal plant.

Europe is now the world's hottest wind power market. Its wind boom is led by Germany, which now has thousands of

gleaming white wind turbines sprinkled across the flat farmland of Lower Saxony and other coastal states. The tenfold
rise in wind power in Germany since 1990 resulted from an
investment boom stirred up by generous tax credits and the
1991 "electricity infeed law" for renewables.

Not far behind are several other European nations, including Denmark, Great Britain, the Netherlands, and Spain. If
development continues at the recent frenzied pace, wind
power could become a major source of European electricity
within the next decade.

In India, a wind energy rush began in 1994 as the government opened up the power grid to independent developers and offered tax incentives for renewable energy development. Indeed, India is now second only to Germany in the
number of annual wind power installations. By early 1995,
some 300 megawatts of wind power were in place, much of it
resulting from joint ventures with European and U.S. manufacturers, some of whom are building assembly plants in
India. Already, land values in windy regions have jumped dramatically. Other countries with sizable wind power projects
underway include Brazil, China, Greece, and Mexico.

Although wind power provides less than 1 percent of the
world's electricity today, it is fast becoming a proven power
option that is reliable enough for routine use by electric utilities. It is not inconceivable that two decades from now, millions of turbines will be spread across windy areas of the
world, providing 20 or 30 percent of the electricity in some
areas. In the United States, three Great Plains states could in
theory supply all the country's electricity, and for China, the
same can be said of Inner Mongolia, which is located within
a few hundred kilometers of Beijing.

The formula used for wind energy—independent developers installing collections of small generators in resource-
rich areas—is proving viable for solar energy as well. In the
Mojave Desert, some 350 megawatts of parabolic dish solar
collectors already provide power for Southern California

Edison's power grid, and similar projects are being eyed in Australia and the Middle East. Similarly, the Houston-based Enron Corporation announced in late 1994 that it planned to build large collections of grid-connected solar photovoltaic generators in the desert regions of China, India, and the United States. As costs fall, these could become a leading source of electricity.

SMART ENERGY?

As regional power systems go from relying on 10 or 20 power plants to networking thousands of small generators, broader changes in the energy system are likely to follow. Recent advances in two-way communications make it possible to precisely monitor and control the power system using microprocessors. With such controls, each solar rooftop, fuel cell, and air conditioner can be linked to a utility's computers via copper or fiber optic lines so that the grid operates as a single "smart" system, turning various devices on and off as needed.

In an experiment in the Chenal Valley neighborhood of Little Rock, Arkansas, the local electric utility, Entergy, has installed unobtrusive, wall-mounted computers that look like fancy thermostats. They provide two-way communication between home and utility and permit on-site optimization of energy use. As demand fluctuates, the utility can provide "real time" pricing to customers, who can program their appliances to turn on when demand is low and electricity is available at less expensive rates. For example, a house can be cooled down just before a period of peak temperatures—and peak power prices.

Entergy projects that real-time pricing, combined with electronic controls, will increase the efficiency of the system by reducing peak power demand and, with it, the need for spare generating capacity. For each new household Entergy hooks up in Chenal Valley, at a cost of $1,050, the utility estimates that it avoids $1,757 worth of power supply costs over the next 20 years. Globally, such systems could eliminate the need to build hundreds of large power plants over the next few decades.

Micro-generators can also be programmed to respond to price signals automatically, so that they provide power to the grid when demand is high, and store it in devices such as flywheels when it is not. A "smart" power system can use price information to balance electricity supply and demand, limit the need for more distribution lines, and thereby reduce costs throughout the electric power system. These advances will greatly facilitate the integration of intermittent wind and solar generators, since they will facilitate the economical deployment of backup generating capacity.

Because energy management typically requires no more than 5 percent of the capacity of a fiber optic cable, energy management systems can be integrated into the high-speed information networks that telecommunications companies are now hooking up to millions of homes and businesses. Alternatively, a utility could install such a line itself and lease excess capacity to companies that provide other information services such as home shopping, travel reservations, and stock quotes.

In 1995, an unusual joint-venture between an electric power company, St. Louis-based UtiliCorp, and the Utah-based software firm Novell announced plans to develop and market an electronic system that allows consumers to optimize the timing of their use of electricity. Unlike the energy management systems being developed by other companies such as Microsoft and TCI, the Novell technology uses existing power lines to transfer data at speeds up to 2 megabits per second while making two-way network communications as simple as plugging a toaster into an electric wall outlet.

The dramatic changes now in prospect for the power industry were acknowledged in a prognosis by *The Financial Times Energy Economist*: "Just as the networking personal computer has replaced the mainframe in the office, so we may be seeing a trend towards the imploding of the centralised, integrated utility in sophisticated economies. . . In short we are at the beginnings of a revolution in power supply."

FORCES OF CHANGE

From some perspectives, the 1990s were a dark time for the world energy system. Oil consumption surpassed the record levels of the late 1970s, with demand in some countries growing at rates as high as 10 percent per year. Even the use of coal continued to expand in many nations, pushing emissions of carbon dioxide, the leading greenhouse gas, to more than 6 billion tons per year. Emissions are still growing rapidly, particularly in China, India, and other developing countries. Even the United States and Japan are failing to hold carbon dioxide emissions steady, not to mention cutting them back as they are supposed to under the Kyoto Climate Protocol.

Although most energy analysts view such trends as convincing evidence that the world energy system won't change anytime soon, the reverse may be true. As Stephen Jay Gould's theory suggests, evolutionary bursts are usually precipitated by strong pressures. Today, three major forces of change are bearing down on the world energy economy— new technologies, industry restructuring, and tougher environmental policies—all of which are likely to be intensified by incipient climate change.

New technologies are the most obvious. As noted earlier, advanced electronics, new materials, and biotechnology are now being put to use in energy systems. The modern automobile, for example, has become virtually a computer on wheels, with electronic controls that provide not only easier steering and breaking but improved fuel economy and lower emissions. Thanks to such developments, spurred by two decades of strong government support for R&D on new energy technologies, it will soon be possible to harness solar and wind energy on a much larger scale.

Industry restructuring is also spurring change. In the past, most electric power systems have been operated as government-owned or controlled monopolies that manage everything from constructing power plants to reading the meters attached to customers' homes. These monopolies have been drawn to giant plants and inefficient, entrenched technologies, and have had little incentive to pursue innovation.

But today, all that is changing. In Brazil, India, Poland, Great Britain, Japan, and the United States, utility systems are being broken up and sold to private investors. In many nations, the generation of electricity is increasingly provided by independent power producers that have no monopoly franchise on the business. Local distribution utilities and industrial users buy power from those producers, using the electricity transmission system as a common carrier, in the same way that railroads and telephone lines are used.

This restructuring has led to an unprecedented wave of innovation, as independent producers find that in order to be competitive, they have to build ever more efficient and less expensive plants. Such producers are pursuing smaller and less environmentally damaging energy sources than did their utility brethren. In the United States, for example, a power plant built in the early 1990s has a capacity of 100 megawatts on average, compared to 600 megawatts less than a decade earlier. Most of the latest plants now are fueled with natural gas rather than coal or nuclear power.

India provides a particularly strong example of the impact of restructuring. As the state utility monopolies were broken in the early 1990s, independent power generation blossomed. Scores of projects are now underway, in a competitive rush to reduce the country's chronic power shortages. Although many of the new plants are coal- and gas-fired, dozens of wind and solar energy projects are also underway, attracting foreign investment and creating a manufacturing boom.

The third force driving rapid change is the growing reach of policies intended to protect the earth's embattled environment. In many countries, emissions and waste-disposal laws have greatly added to the cost of building coal-fired power plants, and nuclear generators have essentially been ruled out as having unacceptably high costs and risks. These changes have boosted the market prospects for efficient natural gas and renewable energy generators.

To help protect the environment, some governments have changed tax and utility laws to level the playing field between dirty and clean technologies. India, for example, allows a full income tax deduction for renewable energy investments, and the United States offers a 1.5 cents per kilowatt-hour subsidy to renewable power. In Germany, renewable power generators have been granted the right to sell power to utilities at a rate of 0.17 DM (12 cents) per kilowatt-hour—about what Germans pay for coal and nuclear power, but well above current prices for the latest natural gas-based power systems—thereby priming the pump for renewables.

As more countries enact similar changes, the boom in renewable energy development now taking place in Germany and India is likely to spread. Japan, for example, has just opened its power grid to independent generators, with special incentives for renewables. Brazil is opening the gates to independents as well, and renewable energy developers are reported to be exploring the coasts and deserts of the country's northeast, which has prime wind and solar sites.

THE HYDROGEN AGE

In elaborate studies churned out by governments and corporations each year, powerful computers are used to project future energy trends. Although the results of such studies are received by many policymakers as gospel, they are generally based on a narrow band of oil price and economic growth assumptions. Indeed, what passes for energy analysis today is dominated by a preoccupation with econometrics and the geopolitics of the Persian Gulf, leaving unquestioned the assumption that we will stay hooked on oil until it is gone, and that coal's role must expand simply because coal is abundant.

Economists who conduct such studies often ignore ongoing technological trends, let alone the broader policy environment. If earlier forecasters had used similar techniques, they would have concluded that we—today—would still be driving around in horse-drawn carriages and writing on typewriters. After all, we never ran out of either hay or paper. Rather, people found ways of meeting their needs more conveniently and economically.

What was true for transportation toward the end of the 19th century and for communications toward the end of the 20th will be no less true for energy at the start of the 21st: when breakthroughs alter the relative competitiveness of a long-dominant resource, its continued abundance becomes suddenly irrelevant. The age of oil, for example, was ushered in not by the discovery of petroleum, which had been found much earlier, but by the development of an internal combustion engine that made oil much more useful. Overnight, 25 million horses were rendered obsolete.

Just as our forefathers at the turn of the last century had a hard time envisioning what was to come, so we now have a hard time seeing what lies beyond the age of fossil fuels. Do all of the changes described above add up to more than an efficient version of the current system? The answer appears to be yes. A number of scientists and other experts have been able to offer at least a glimpse of what we are moving toward: a solar hydrogen economy.

Hydrogen is the simplest of the chemical fuels, and unlike methane, the cleanest fuel used today, is entirely carbon-free. Hydrogen is the lightest of the elements as well as the most abundant. Three-quarters of the mass of the universe consists of hydrogen, which of course is also a principal constituent of water. When the time comes to use the hydrogen as fuel, it is combined with oxygen to produce water, releasing energy but no pollution.

Scientists have foreseen the possibility of a transition to hydrogen for more than a century, and today it is seen as the logical "third wave" fuel—hydrogen gas following liquid oil, just as oil replaced coal decades earlier. The required technology—using electricity to split water molecules through electrolysis—is already being used commercially. (All the world's current energy needs could be met with less than 1 percent of today's fresh water supply, and hydrogen can also be produced from seawater.) Although many people worry that hydrogen is dangerous, if properly handled, it will probably be safer than fuels like gasoline that are widely used today.

The challenge now holding up the transition to hydrogen is finding inexpensive sources of energy to split water. This may seem circular—the need to find cheap energy in order to produce an affordable fuel. But the key to the puzzle lies in the possibility of storage and transportation. Wind and solar energy are often found in the wrong place at the wrong time, but those energy sources can be used to feed the electricity grid when power demand is high, and to produce storable hydrogen when it is not.

In fact, hydrogen may provide the ideal means of storing and distributing these intermittent power sources. Additional hydrogen can be produced in homes and commercial buildings using rooftop solar cells. The hydrogen can then either be stored in a basement tank for later use in a fuel cell or conventional boiler, or be piped into a local hydrogen distribution system.

In either case, a decade or two from now, hydrogen could begin to enter the markets now dominated by oil and natural gas—including home heating, cooking, industrial heat, and transportation. In fact, scientists, have determined that in the early stages, hydrogen fuel can be derived from natural gas, and that during the transition, consumers may use a mixture of hydrogen and methane gas. Experimental hydrogen-powered cars have already been developed by Mazda and Mercedes. With the advent of small fuel cells, such cars may become highly efficient and affordable. By the middle of the next century, oil and coal could be phased out.

Although renewable energy sources are more abundant in some areas than others, they are far less concentrated than oil, since two-thirds of proven petroleum reserves are in the Persian Gulf. Moreover, the coming solar-hydrogen economy is likely to be based on a diverse array of renewable resources, with the mix varying by region. The hydrogen can be carried to where it is needed through pipelines similar to those used to carry natural gas.

Over time, solar- and wind-derived hydrogen could transform the way energy is produced and used virtually everywhere. All of the world's major population centers are within reach of sunny and wind-rich areas. The Great Plains of North America, for instance, could supply much of Canada and the United States with electricity and hydrogen fuel. For Europe, solar power plants could be built in North Africa, with hydrogen transported along existing gas pipeline routes. In China, hydrogen could be produced in the country's vast western deserts and shipped to population centers on the coastal plain.

Many people assume that producing sufficient hydrogen from solar and wind energy requires huge swaths of land, but these technologies actually use less than one-fifth as much land to produce a given amount of energy as does hydropower, which now supplies nearly a third of the world's electricity. Moreover, while much of the land used for hydropower has to be condemned for flooding (often of prime cropland), the tracts used for wind farms can still be used for crops and grazing.

What then would a solar-hydrogen energy system look like? One of its chief advantages is that it would be largely invisible. Fuel cells and flywheels would be hidden in peoples' basements; solar rooftops would be nearly indistinguishable from conventional rooftops; and hydrogen pipelines would be buried underground, as are today's natural gas pipelines.

Some rural farming areas may be sprinkled with wind turbines, but most of the larger wind and solar power plants are
likely to be located in remote areas such as India's Thar
Desert or Mexico's La Ventosa, where people rarely visit.

On first reflection, such an energy system may seem fanci-
ful. But two decades ago, the idea of desktop computers and
an ubiquitous digital Internet would have seemed equally far-
fetched. And arguably, what is most inconceivable is that an
information-age economy will be powered by a primitive
industrial age energy system.

As corporate and government decision makers begin to
understand just how economical and practical a zero-emis-
sion, carbon-free energy system can be, and just how inefficient and dirty the current system is, they may finally summon
the sort of effort that made the last great energy transition
possible—a hundred years ago.

2

Oceans in Distress

IT COMES DOWN TO
THE COASTS

By Peter Weber

W hat is a view of the ocean worth? The price of a night at an expensive hotel, or the purchase of a beachfront bungalow? Enduring a biting winter wind, or a beach-bound traffic jam on a sultry day in August? For many, the answer is: whatever it takes. Every year, half of the world's vacationers head for the sea.

But for many more people, being close to the shore is worth something more than an annual pilgrimage. It is worth the cost of leaving better-paying jobs, or ancestral ties, or friends, and moving their homes to the coast. Fully half the world's people live within 50 miles or so of saltwater. And their ranks are growing. In 25 years, some 5.5 billion people—equivalent to the entire population of the world in the mid-1990s—are expected to live in the coastal zone.

What is the attraction? The meeting of land and sea works a kind of magic that is more powerful than that of just scenic beauty. The soil on the coastal plain, laid down when the land was covered by the ocean, and subsequently replenished by sediments washed down from the mountains, tends to be particularly fertile. About 2 percent of the world's agricultural land, including some of its most intensively and productively cultivated land, was actually taken from the sea by people.

Offshore, the same nutrients promote the growth of

aquatic plants, which in turn feed fish that now provide humankind's largest single source of animal protein—larger, even, than beef or chicken. The world's primary fishing grounds are in these fertile coastal waters, from which 90 percent of the marine catch is taken. Farming and fishing are major coastal industries that employ hundreds of millions of people worldwide.

Coastal dwellers can also make a good living from international trade, 80 percent of which is carried by ship. That's one reason why nine of the world's 10 largest cities and 33 of the top 50 are near the coasts. And of course there are the vacationers bringing their portion of the more than $2 trillion annually spent on tourism worldwide. Although there are no estimates for coastal tourism alone, the Madrid-based World Tourism Organization estimates that tourism accounts for nearly one-tenth of the global economic output and is one of the fastest growing industries. The attraction of the coasts is as much economic as aesthetic.

It's not surprising, then, that the narrow ribbons of land and water that outline the world's continents and islands are widely used as development zones. The phenomenon is nowhere more vividly illustrated than in The Netherlands, whose crowded populace lives with the sea literally in its back yard. In fact, one-third of The Netherlands is land that used to be under the North Sea or its tributaries; because coastal land is so valuable to the Dutch, they have been diking and draining it continuously for over a thousand years. Their sea-hugging cities are now thriving centers of commerce and culture, and their farms are some of the most productive in the world.

All this activity may churn out money, but it is also churning up the coasts—as the Dutch have become acutely aware in recent decades. Draining wetlands has reduced the natural habitat for wildlife and has driven the Dutch national symbol, the stork, from the country.

But the problem is more than just a few endangered

species. By choosing to concentrate its swelling population along the coasts, humanity is locating the ecological damage of its activities precisely where the world's most productive ecosystems are concentrated. The coastal zone, extending from the beginning of the coastal plain to the end of the continental shelf, accounts for only 8 percent of the world's surface area, but hosts 26 percent of the earth's primary (plant) productivity, the world's major spawning and nursery grounds, and one of the earth's most diverse ecosystems, the coral reefs. As a result, coastal areas, which are approximately twice as productive on average as the inland areas, suffer roughly nine times more damage because of the number of people living there.

HAZARDS AT THE CROSSROADS

Having chosen to live where land meets sea, humanity has greatly increased the difficulty of achieving a stable relationship with the Earth's environment. The intersection between human and biological activity has already scarred the coastal landscape by altering and destroying large portions of some of its most fertile habitat.

Not all coastal habitat is highly productive; about half of the world's 440,000 kilometers of coastline are lined by cliffs and ice, and another 20 percent are beaches, which have relatively low biological activity. However, wetlands and estuaries, where rivers turn brackish as they enter the sea, are among the most productive of all ecosystems. There, nutrients from land feed plant growth so abundant that mangrove forests, for instance, which cover only 0.4 percent of the world's surface area, account for 2.3 percent of plant productivity. That fecundity makes mangroves, other coastal wetlands, and estuaries particularly important as nurseries for marine species. Some two-thirds of all commercially caught fish spend their first and most vulnerable stages in estuaries and wetlands, and many more species go to these coastal ecosystems to feed.

These are also some of the most endangered ecosystems in the world. Estuaries are particularly vulnerable because they are naturally sheltered harbors, and therefore tend to be heavily used and polluted. Wetlands have traditionally been regarded as wasteland, and therefore are targets for city expansion. All over the world, there are coastal cities that have degraded nearby estuaries and wetlands through the combined effects of direct habitat destruction and pollution. Commercially burgeoning Singapore, for example, has removed almost all of its mangrove wetlands and reduced off-shore water visibility from eight meters prior to 1960 to an average three meters in 1992. San Francisco Bay, the largest estuary in the western United States, has lost 60 percent of its water area to land reclamation over the past 140 years.

It is agriculture, however, not urbanization, that causes the most extensive destruction. The Dutch impound coastal wetlands with dikes, then pump them dry with windmills, primarily for the fertile farmland. The Chinese have been draining coastal wetlands for the rich soils they yield for 6,000 years. The densely populated delta country of Bangladesh has impounded at least 30,000 square kilometers of wetland for agriculture; it is no coincidence that Bangladesh has the world's highest population density for a mainland country, as well as the largest area of impounded farmland.

Other causes of extensive coastal habitat destruction include the rapidly expanding fish farming industry, timber extraction and civil engineering projects that alter the flow of sediments and fresh water. The wetlands at the mouth of the Mississippi River are eroding away at a rate of 150 square kilometers per year, largely due to flood control and channeling projects in the delta and upstream. Worldwide, about half of all saltmarshes and mangrove swamps have been cleared, drained, diked, or filled, and few estuaries remain unpolluted or unaltered.

Offshore, coral reefs, kelp forests, seagrass beds, and other shallow water habitats are endangered by the combination of direct destruction and pollution from land. Coral reefs are of particular concern. They line more than 100,000 kilometers of coast and harbor a large portion of the coasts' biological wealth. Unfortunately, they are highly vulnerable to changes in their environment. If the normally clear tropical waters they form in are clouded by pollutants, for example, the corals can't photosynthesize to produce their food. They also recover slowly when damaged. Other offshore habitats, likewise, suffer from such habitat degradation. The pollution and harbor development off Singapore, for instance, has degraded the majority of the seagrass beds and all but 5 percent of the coral reefs.

The unique ecology of coral reefs makes them one of the world's most diverse ecosystems, second in density of unique species only to tropical rain forests; thus the widespread damage to these reefs constitutes a major blow to the Earth's overall biological diversity. Yet, 5 to 10 percent of the planet's coral reefs have essentially been ruined by pollution and direct destruction, and another 30 percent could be lost in the next 10 to 20 years. The most graphic examples are the extensive portions of reef that have been mined for construction materials in places like southern India and Sri Lanka, and the damage caused by fishers using explosives to kill and catch fish. But globally, pollution from burgeoning developments onshore is the more extensive and intractable threat to these and other coastal habitats.

THE DEMOGRAPHIC SQUEEZE

Without closer attention to the management and protection of these coastal ecosystems, the destruction is bound to accelerate. Because of steady coastward migration, coastal populations—and the environmental pressures they bring—may be growing even faster than the global population, which is climbing by some 80 million people a year.

One of the forces driving the trend is rural poverty. Like a pied piper, the promise of employment in cities draws people from depressed agricultural areas. The United Nations estimates that 20 to 30 million of the world's poorest people annually migrate from rural to urban areas, especially to Third World mega-cities, which are usually on the coasts. Rural coastal populations may also be increasing for similar reasons. In the Philippines, the coastal population is growing faster than that of the rest of the country in part because people who give up on farming often move to coastal areas to try fishing. While land is scarce, open access to fishing grounds gives poor people at least the hope of making a living.

In China, the coastal population may be increasing by 10 percent or more per year, though the country's overall growth rate is only 1.2 percent. Already the population density along the China coast is three times as high as the national average, and this region accounts for 70 percent of the country's gross national product. While the economic success along the coast will inevitably attract more Chinese, the government is encouraging this coastward migration by placing special economic development zones there.

In Southeast Asia, where marine biodiversity is particularly high, more than two-thirds of the population lives within the coastal zone. Coastal populations are also particularly high in southern Asia, Europe, southeastern Africa, and portions of North and South America. And as the global trend of rural flight and urbanization progresses, the challenge to protect the world's coasts will become more severe.

More Than Coastal Living

As if this pattern of human habitation weren't damaging enough, the thin ribbons of coast are also subject to devastating environmental assaults from both far inland and out at sea. Pollution from human activity outside of the coastal zone funnels into estuaries and coastal waters, while in an almost mirror image, the impacts of fishing and shipping become more concentrated closer to shore.

A surprising proportion of the pollutants entering coastal waters originates not from the adjacent coastal land but from more distant sources. Of the polluting nutrients, about half come from inland. In the eastern United States, for instance, the Chesapeake Bay has been overwhelmed by nutrients from inland sources. Farms contribute one-third and air pollution another one-quarter of the nitrogen pollution that has caused eutrophication, algal blooms, and oxygen depletion in this estuary—once one of the most productive in the world. The oyster catch in the Chesapeake fell from 20,000 tons in the 1950s to under 3,000 tons in the late 1980s, at least partly as a result of this pollution.

In a study of samples from 42 of the world's major rivers, Jonathan J. Cole and his colleagues at the Institute of Ecosystem Studies at the New York Botanical Garden found that the level of pollution correlates uncannily with the level of human activity in the watershed. The Rhine, for example, has 10 times the population density of the Mississippi, and dumps 10 times more nutrients into the sea, even though the Mississippi drains an area 14 times as large.

About one-third of the pollutants entering the marine environment come from air emissions, a large portion of which settle into coastal waters. For many heavy metals and volatile organic chemicals, air is the primary route to the sea. In the North Sea, about a quarter of the pollution, including the majority of PCBs and other chlorinated organic chemicals, comes from the air. In the Persian Gulf, the 4 to 12 million barrels of oil that the Iraqi army deliberately spilled during the 1991 Gulf War turned out to be only part of the total amount of oil estimated to have entered the Gulf as a result of the war. Another 4 to 5 million barrels are thought to have been carried into the Gulf by oil-laden smoke. Worldwide, about 10 percent of the oil that reaches the oceans is airborne.

Ironically, human industries and settlements are choking coastal waters with the very rivers that make these waters productive. The excess nutrients, sediments, pathogens, and persistent toxins come mostly from land-based sources. Even oil pollution, which is typically associated with accidents at sea such as that of the Exxon Valdez, is as likely to have flowed into the water directly from a car or factory on land as from a barge or boat.

On the ocean side of the coastal zone, overfishing has depleted some of the world's major fish stocks, along with the health of their ecosystems. There is a growing crisis in the world fisheries, as epitomized by the collapse of North Atlantic cod stocks off Canada. Although pollution and habitat destruction have played a role in this crisis, the main problem is simply that the capacity of the fishing industry—in numbers of people and in the efficiency of their high-tech equipment—has grown too large for the regenerative capacity of the oceans. Of the world's 17 major fishing grounds, all of which are primarily coastal, every one has been fished to its limits or beyond, according to the United Nations Food and Agriculture Organization (FAO), which tracks global fishing trends. Nine are now in serious decline because of overfishing.

As high-tech factory boats and traditional fishers alike have extracted larger and larger proportions of the biomass from coastal waters, whole ecosystems have begun to break down. In the Shetland Islands, Arctic terns, puffins, and other nesting birds failed to breed in the mid- and late 1980s, apparently due to overfishing of the sand eel, a small shoaling fish caught for fish meal and oil. The birds normally feed young sand eels to their chicks, but the fish's population declined with the commercial catch, which peaked at 56,000 tons in 1982 and then plunged to 4,800 tons in 1988. In a similar disaster, off the coast of Peru, guano birds abandoned their young when the Peruvian anchovy fishery collapsed. In Kenya, researchers found that heavy fishing of triggerfish on coral reefs allowed the proliferation of rockboring sea urchins, which were endangering the entire ecosystem.

GLOBAL IMPLICATIONS

What happens to the coasts has effects that reach far beyond their local aquatic and human communities, however. Though they are among the most vulnerable of Earth's ecosystems, the coasts house biological processes and diversity that are essential to the health and stability of the biosphere as a whole.

The oceans, which are the *largest* ecosystems, rely disproportionately on the coasts for food. Although the coastal waters over continental shelves cover only 10 percent of the ocean surface, they account for 20 percent of the marine plant production. The energy captured in these waters' prolific plant growth feeds into the oceanic food chain, starting with small marine organisms such as copepods and other zooplankton, and moving out to sea with currents and migratory species. Unlike on land, animal life makes up the majority of biomass in the oceans, and its movement into the open ocean redistributes some of the disproportionate productivity of coastal waters.

This coastal productivity also helps to drive the oceans "biological pump," the process by which the oceans help to regulate global climate. Scientists have found that the marine food chain moderates the atmospheric concentration of carbon dioxide, the primary heat-trapping gas. Carbon dioxide enters the churning upper layer of the oceans, where phytoplankton and other marine plants use it in photosynthesis to make simple sugars. While 90 percent of this carbon is recycled through the food chain, some falls into the deeper layers of the oceans as the detritus of decaying phytoplankton and other sea plants or animals. There, the carbon is stored in deep ocean currents that take about 1,000 years to bring it back to the surface as carbon dioxide.

The high biological diversity of the coasts helps to stabilize these global systems. Organisms ranging from bacteria to great blue whales play key roles. Copepods, for instance, are minute crustaceans that eat phytoplankton and are thought to be the most numerous animals in the oceans. They fill a critical link between the primary producers and the rest of the marine food chain. If ecological conditions change in a way that no longer permits copepods to perform this function, their disappearance could have devastating consequences

But there's another dimension, as well, to the extraordinary diversity of coastal organisms. About 90 percent of the history of life on earth has taken place in salt water, making the oceanic gene pool an invaluable resource. Its species are the descendants of the 3 to 3.5 billion years of evolution that predated the appearance of plant life on dry land some 450 million years ago. Therefore, many coastal species have no evolutionary counterparts on dry land. These unique species make irreplaceable contributions to food production, medicine, and scientific research.

A large proportion of these species are housed in coral reefs. Only the deep ocean floor, which covers half the earth's surface, is thought to contain more. Within coastal waters, a general rule of diversity is that shallow waters harbor more diversity than deeper waters, rocky areas more than sandy or muddy ones, and the tropics more than temperate or polar zones. Coral reefs—shallow, rocky, and tropical—are believed to contain the highest density of unique species in the oceans.

Researchers are increasingly turning to these coastal waters in their search for medical cures and unique compounds. They have derived anti-leukemia drugs from sea sponges, bone graft material from corals, chemicals from red algae, and anti-infection compounds from shark skin.

Because marine life is relatively unstudied compared to terrestrial life, the oceans and coasts are a vast new frontier for research.

SHORING UP THE SEA

Under the current international regime, protecting the coastal zone is up to coastal nations. Nearly two decades ago, international negotiations over the Law of the Sea, a United Nations-mediated treaty on the management of the oceans, gave rise to international acceptance of the concept of a 200-nautical-mile coastal area—called the Exclusive Economic Zone (EEZ)—within which the coastal country has exclusive rights to the natural resources. By 1976, 60 countries had claimed EEZs of their own and the notion became an accepted part of customary oceans law.

The recent ratification of the Law of the Sea formalized the EEZ construct and put in force the treaty provisions that encourage coastal states to conserve and protect these waters. But the language is vague and probably unenforceable because of long-standing concerns over national sovereignty—the same issue that blocked international standards for coastal zone management at the 1992 Earth Summit in Rio de Janeiro. The delegates acknowledged the growing coastal crisis, but they shied away from infringing on national jurisdiction.

Of the three major threats to the coasts—coastal development, pollution from inland, and overfishing of coastal waters—it is development that warrants the highest priority for major changes in policy. The direct destruction and pollution of essential ecosystems is steadily undermining the coastal zone on every continent, and the surging of coastal populations means that these threats are worsening.

The single most effective change that could be made to slow the juggernaut of coastal development would be to eliminate subsidies such as government-sponsored insurance and funding for ocean-altering roads, dikes, and dams. The Netherlands, for instance, spends $400 million a year just to pump water and repair inland dikes, and new seawalls and dikes can cost hundreds of millions of dollars. These investments have come under domestic scrutiny, not only because they contribute to the loss of coastal habitat for the stork and other wetland-dependent species, but also because they may not be cost-effective. Some of the impounded agricultural land is often too wet to farm, and the Dutch don't need all of it because they are already producing more food than they can either use or sell abroad. As a result, expenditures on draining coastal land for farming can lead, absurdly, to still more expenditures on farm subsidies to cover excess production.

To save money and begin rehabilitating the coastal ecosystem, the Dutch government has made an extraordinary and courageous decision to return 150,000 hectares of farmland (15 percent of the total converted area) to rivers and estuaries over a period of 25 years. Although the Dutch will continue diking and developing other parts of the coastal zone, this reversal reflects their growing concern over the degradation of their coasts.

In the early 1900s, the Dutch built a 30-kilometer-long earthen seawall across the mouth of the Zuider Sea in the northwest to protect the impounded farmland in the estuary from flooding. The barrier against the sea completely altered the original ecosystem, turning the giant brackish water estuary into a fresh water lake, now known as Lake Ijssel. The country has continued to pursue this strategy of "coastal defense," but recent projects have been more ecologically sensitive. For instance, rather than building a similar earthen seawall across all of the estuaries in the rich coastal region of Zeeland in the southwest, the Dutch built mechanical seawalls that can be opened to allow relatively natural water flow, and closed in case of a strong coastal storm that threatens flooding.

As the Zeeland projects demonstrate, coastal development can be made less destructive. But the methods don't have to be high-tech engineering solutions. Natural buffer zones, for instance, can protect coastal habitat from nearby development. Wetlands trap toxins, pathogens, and excess nutrients and sediments as they move seaward, while also protecting coastal communities from coastal storms and sea surges. Coral reefs act as natural seawalls, reducing the erosive action of the ocean by absorbing the impact of waves.

Simple guidelines can make a significant difference. In Thailand's Ban Don Ba for instance, the provincial government instituted building restrictions to protect the region's primary tourist attraction, the coral reefs. Developers now must build back from the beach and cannot use coral for construction material.

In Ecuador, which has lost 144,000 hectares of mangrove forests to shrimp ponds, the government is sponsoring a national program to manage coastal resources so that local communities can continue to profit from them without destroying them. Starting with a U.S. Agency for International Development pilot project, the Ecuadorean government has formed six special coastal management zones, with management committees composed of local and government people. In the case of the shrimp industry, which constitutes a sizable portion of Ecuador's exports and economy, shrimp farmers were given special training on how to protect the coastal environment while maintaining their livelihoods.

Even if well-managed, however, coastal development could turn the world's coastlines into continuous strings of cities, farms, and resorts. Aside from the catastrophic ecological impacts, such an eventuality could take a heavy toll on those who live and invest there. As is becoming increasingly evident in places like the Eastern seaboard of the United States, coasts are dynamic. Portions are always eroding or shifting, and over the course of tens of thousands of years, changes in sea level can alternately expose and inundate the coastal zone. In the 10,000 years since the last ice age, the sea level has been rising as the result of melting ice and glaciers and thermal expansion of the oceans. Most of the world's low coasts continue to retreat due to the recent rate of sea level rise of 1 to 2 millimeters per year, or 10 to 20 centimeters per century.

With the increase in greenhouse gases and the threat of global warming, coastal living in the coming century will become more precarious. Sea level is projected to rise by 60 centimeters in the next 100 years, and storms are likely to grow stronger. Governments may need to consider restricting or even prohibiting further coastal development altogether.

DYING SEAS

By Anne Platt McGinn

During the last four thousand years, the part of our past that we think of as the history of civilization, human settlements have tended to cluster around land-enclosed seas, rivers, and lakes. People in these settlements have been able to supply themselves with food, security, and community to a degree that would have been far more difficult in the vast inland territories—drylands, mountains, scrub forests, deserts, and steppes—that make up the bulk of the terrestrial world.

Whether it was the ancient Aegeans on the Mediterranean, the Persians on the Caspian, or the Chinese on the Yellow Sea, civilizations rose in places where small boats could exchange knowledge and goods, trade was easily conducted, fish were abundant, and the land was rich with the topsoil carried downstream by rivers.

For these reasons, the basins of the great seas were also more highly valued than other landforms, and controlling them became central to human notions of security. Security meant military control of homelands and trade routes. It has also meant, increasingly in the past few centuries, control of the water itself—by damming tributaries, digging irrigation ditches, dredging shipping channels and harbors, and constructing breakwaters.

In just the last few decades, however, a new kind of stress has crept into the historic relationship between humans and the seas. While civilizations have continued to develop most rapidly around the coasts and rivers that feed the seas, that growth has accelerated to a point that is now dangerously unstable. Various side effects of human activity that passed unnoticed until this century have begun to ravage the very qualities that make the seas valuable—depleting both sea-based and land-based food production, fouling the human nest, and evidently even beginning to alter weather patterns for the worse.

Today, most of the world's seas are suffering from a wide range of human-caused assaults, in various lethal combinations: their ecological links to the land blocked by dams; their bottoms punctured and contaminated by oil drilling; their wildlife habitats wiped out by coastal development; and their water contaminated—or turned anoxic—by farm and factory waste. And what fish remain after these assaults are being decimated by overfishing. In the world's most biologically productive and diverse bodies of water, ecosystems are on the verge of collapse—and in some cases have already collapsed. The levels of damage and progress toward protection vary from sea to sea. But in general, compared to the open oceans, semi-enclosed seas tend to be damaged more severely and quickly because water circulation is limited and there is less dilution of pollutants.

Today, the seas are as strategically important as they ever were in the days of Kublai Khan's armada or the Greek trading ships, but for new reasons. The old preoccupation with controlling key military positions, ports, and trade routes is now rivaled by a more urgent priority: to rescue and protect the more fundamental assets that made the seas worth living near in the first place, but which are now being dangerously damaged.

To set up this protection means establishing a new paradigm for security, in which shared responsibility for sustaining the vitality of these seas becomes the basis for a mutual, rather than competitive, effort. This is something that national governments may find difficult, since it necessarily overrides traditional concepts of sovereignty and control. But most of the great seas are shared in too many ways for anything but a mutual vigilance—and coordinated defense against our own human excesses—to work. Cooperative solutions have begun to emerge in a few regions, such as the Mediterranean and the Baltic. But on other seas, conflicts are escalating—suggesting that cooperation is not likely to prevail without a fuller understanding of just what is at stake.

There are about 35 major seas in the world, some coastal and some enclosed by land. Of these, seven—the Baltic, Mediterranean, Black, Caspian, Bering, Yellow, and South China Seas—illustrate the panoply of ills that now afflict, in varying degrees, all 35. Each of these seven carries different wounds. One, the Black, is a microcosm of them all.

BLACK SEA: A SEA OF TROUBLES

In ancient times it was valued for its abundance of fish, its relatively temperate climate, and its strategic location: the city of Constantinople was the gateway between East and West, capital of the Byzantine Empire, and one of the great hubs of human civilization. During the past century, the Black Sea became famous for its beach resorts where wealthy Russians and Ukrainians built their *dachas*. But in recent decades, this beautiful place has been ravaged. First, and most tragically, there has been the onset of a disease that is now endemic to enclosed or semi-enclosed bodies of water worldwide: an immense excess of marine nutrients. Like a compulsive eater who becomes increasingly obese, immobile, and finally moribund, the Black Sea has been overloaded with nutrients—fertilizer washing downstream from farms, human waste from the cities. The result has been massive eutrophication—a burgeoning growth of algae and bacteria, creating thick floating

mats so dense that they block sunlight and destroy the natural ecological balance.

To this cancer-like process, other complications have been
added. While the Black Sea was serving as a playground for
elite Soviets during the Cold War, it was also being used as a
convenient sink for all sorts of industrial activity—in an era
when Soviet industries were driven by production quotas
with little concern for their environmental impact. Toxic pollutants from plants ran uncontrolled down the three main
tributary rivers, and growing quantities of municipal waste
mingled with industrial and agricultural waste. The contaminated waters weakened the fish populations, which were further destroyed by heavy overfishing.

In this morass of biological decline, the most visible blight
is the vast greenish mass that now lies over much of the water.
What was once a rich, diverse ecosystem has been replaced by
a monoculture of opportunistic weeds and algae. Gradually,
as the dissolved oxygen supply is depleted by the algae and
bacteria, the water becomes anoxic—incapable of supporting
oxygen-dependent plants or animals. When the algae dies, it
settles to the sea bottom, releasing hydrogen sulfide, which is
poisonous to aquatic species.

A key source of the trouble can be found along a 350 kilometer stretch of northwestern shoreline where three major
rivers, the Danube, the Dniester and the Dnieper, drain into
the sea. The Danube delivers much of the fertilizer runoff,
detergent waste, and human sewage produced by the 81 million people in the Central and Eastern European drainage
basin. Each year, it dumps an estimated 60,000 tons of phosphorus and 340,000 tons of inorganic nitrogen on the shallow waters of the Black Sea shelf, which is approximately one-
fourth of the sea's entire area.

In the past 25 years, the Danube's concentrations of
nitrate and phosphate (stable compounds that form when
nitrogen and phosphorus react with oxygen) have increased
six-fold and four-fold respectively. Concentrations from the

Dniester, which flows across the Ukrainian breadbasket region, have increased threefold for nitrate and sevenfold for phosphate since the 1950s. The Dniester has also brought heavy loads of pesticides, after flowing through the fields of Ukrainian and Moldovan farmers. On the southern end of the Kremenchug reservoir, about 250 kilometers south of Kiev, the algae covering the Dnieper river is so thick that landsat images reveal boat tracks across the river. Heavy industry also contributes to the stresses: an estimated one billion tons of mine tailings, coal ash, slag heaps, and other mineral wastes are dumped each year in the Dnieper River watershed area. And the Dnieper still suffers from the radioactive fallout of the Chernobyl nuclear disaster in 1986.

Today, 90 percent of the volume of the Black Sea is anoxic. All of the deep layers of water in the central and southern parts of the basin are anoxic, and the dead water is expanding steadily upward from the bottom. The upper tenth, while still biologically productive, is deteriorating. "I know of no other inland sea under such pressure," said Stanislav Konovalov, director of the Soviet Institute for Biology of the Southern Seas at Sevastopol, Ukraine, in 1992. Since then, conditions have worsened.

Extreme eutrophication has repercussions through the food web, causing a decline in the number of species and economic losses in both fisheries and seaside tourism. Populations of the jelly fish-like ctenophore *Mnemiopis leidyi*, first noticed in 1982, have erupted—consuming zooplankton, shellfish, and eggs and larvae of fish. At times, up to 95 percent of the Black Sea biomass consists of these gelatinous pests.

The problem is exacerbated by the long time needed for biological recovery in inland seas even under the best of conditions. It takes 167 years for water to flow from the Danube river delta southward through the sea's basin and out through the Bosporus Strait to the Mediterranean—and far longer, of course, to reach the Atlantic Ocean. Anoxic conditions in the deep bottom waters were recorded as early as

1912; today, much of the sea is oxygen-deprived. With limited freshwater supplies and virtually no flushing, the Black Sea
is essentially choking to death. Some scientists say it has 10 to
15 years to live; others give it 40 years. Most fishermen and
tourists say it is already dead.

To effectively reduce nutrient loads will require major
changes in industrial and agricultural practices, updating of
sewage treatment facilities, and reduced detergent use.
Unfortunately, the needed changes seem to be neither economically nor politically realistic, given the desperate economic situations in the former Soviet and Eastern European
countries. Yet, the dilemma for these countries is that if they
do not invest in such changes, their resources and economics
will only decline further.

Moreover, the pall of eutrophication is not the only problem confronting the Black Sea community of nations. Toxic
pollution from industries in the Black Sea drainage basin, oil
spills from intensive shipping, direct dumping of waste, and
the disruptions of marine or coastal habitats by mineral exploration and river alteration have all added to the blight.

Between 1986 and 1992, the Black Sea's total fish catch
dropped from 900,000 to 100,000 metric tons per year.
Dolphin, caviar, sturgeon, anchovy, and mackerel populations
have all plummeted. Altogether, the cumulative effects of
dead water, poisoned water, and overfishing have already cost
more than 150,000 fishing jobs. Another 2 million people
who make their living from fishing and fishery-related industries are at risk. Direct economic losses have mounted to
more than $250 million per year in the fishing industry, and
the costs to related industries could push the figure over $1
billion. At the same time, the tourism industry has lost $300
million each year because of beach closings, unsanitary conditions, algae-clogged swimming areas, and outbreaks of
cholera on both the Romanian and Ukrainian sides of the
Danube Delta. "The Black Sea is on the brink of extinction,"
the Russian newspaper *Tass* reported in 1994.

YELLOW SEA: HEAVY METALS

Six thousand kilometers east-southeast, between northern China and Korea, the Yellow Sea suffers its own version of the Black Sea's dysfunctional relationship with its tributary rivers. And here, too, the result has been a disaster for fisheries. But whereas the Black Sea region is moderately populated, the Yellow Sea coastal region is densely populated and growing rapidly. Here, as a result, the decline of fisheries has gone beyond the economic sphere, into overt military confrontation. And here, perhaps more than anywhere else, the fundamental dilemma—and irony—of the human relationship with the seas is illustrated in its simplest form: the more people there are to depend on the seas for food and jobs, the more pollution there is to make those assets scarcer. In China, pollution takes on a broader meaning as well—it includes huge quantities of silt from the intensive farming that takes place on every available hectare of the drainage basin.

In fact, the Yellow Sea gets its name from the ochre-colored soil that washes down the Yellow River (Huang He) out to the Bohai Sea (the large bay linking Beijing and the Yellow Sea) at a rate of 2.4 billion tons per year. Today, a more accurate name for the Yellow Sea might be the *Brownish-Red* Sea. And the problem with this silt is that it is no longer just topsoil, but is now laced with heavy metals. Just as the sea has absorbed silt for thousands of years, it now absorbs the pollution and wastes from China's rapidly industrializing coastal areas.

Currently, there are more than 670 million Chinese living on or near the coast. With an estimated 40 percent of the industrial plants located along the coast, more workers and their families are tempted to move to coastal areas every year in search of jobs. In fact, of all the migratory movements in the world today, this internal movement of rural Chinese to the coast may be the largest. Population densities along China's 13 coastal provinces average more than 600 people per square kilometer. And in the rapidly growing city of

Shanghai, more than 2,000 people crowd into each square kilometer of land along the sea. These pressures are only going to get worse: most Chinese coastal cities are growing at rates fast enough to more than double their populations in just 14 years.

To keep up with demand for housing and buildings, coastal land that used to be cultivated is now developed at a rate of 3,400 square kilometers per year. This leaves aquatic and terrestrial habitat areas at an even greater disadvantage: not only are they losing ground, but they are being forced to absorb increasing volumes of runoff from more industries and more people. Not surprisingly, the coasts of China and Korea are showing signs of extraordinary stress.

Pollution from heavy metals "may be among the highest in the world" in China's coastal areas (including the Yellow Sea, East China Sea, and South China Sea), according to Fan Zhijie of the State Oceanic Administration in Dalian, China and R.P. Côté of the Dalhousie University School for Resource and Environmental Studies in Halifax, Nova Scotia. One reason is that rapid industrialization in the region has occurred with few or no pollution control measures.

According to the Chinese *Annual of Environment Quality in Offshore of China, 1989,* the Yellow River dumped 751 tons of cadmium, mercury, lead, zinc, arsenic, and chromium, along with 21,000 tons of oil, into the Bohai Sea in 1989. The Yellow Sea itself received more than twice that quantity of heavy metals. This study also found that the greatest concentrations of toxic metals occurred in the top layer of sediment—in some cases more than 1,000 times greater than those in the water.

The contamination is thus heavily concentrated in the seabed where many species live and feed. And indeed, monitoring between 1981 and 1984 showed that the concentrations of cadmium in crustaceans (such as crabs) increased three-fold, while lead and copper in fish and mollusks (such as mussels) increased two- to four-fold. Data from 1989 found that mercury in bivalves (clams and oysters) was over 10 times acceptable levels.

In addition to the contamination flowing in from rivers, the Yellow Sea is being contaminated by atmospheric pollution, particularly from coalburning plants and smogbound cities, and by direct dumping from coastal industries. The Qingdao Soda Plant on Kiaochow Bay, for example, has dramatically altered the condition of sediments. Chromium levels in sediments near the plant have been recorded at levels as high as 430 mg per kilogram—enough to dramatically discolor a beach near the discharge point. In 1963, 141 types of marine animals—mollusks, crustaceans, echinoderms, and the like—were living in these sediments; by 1988, only 24 remained.

In addition to excess numbers of vessels and fishers, most of the estuaries, bays, and wetlands bordering the Yellow Sea have been polluted enough to have serious effects on fisheries—the decline of which has been drastic enough to make them targets for military intervention. North Korea declared a 50-nautical-mile military warning zone to protect its remaining fisheries from pirates and foreign fleets. Chinese fishers in the Yellow Sea have been attacked and fired at by North Korean vessels, while South Korea has arrested fishers who stray too close to its depleted grounds. In the East China Sea and South Yellow Sea, Chinese patrol boats' attacks on Russian fishing vessels have slowed only because Russia deployed a navy flotilla there and threatened to "blow pirates out of the water."

BALTIC SEA: ORGANOCHLORINES

In Scandinavia, the numerous rivers and fjords coming out of Sweden and Norway into the Baltic Sea have a very different look; instead of wending across wide, intensively cultivated and heavily populated valleys like so many of the world's sea-feeding tributaries, they wind through quiet, seemingly pristine forests. But these forests are also the sites—and resources for—another kind of sea-endangering industry: pulp and paper mills. In the 1940s, most of these mills began using elemental chlorine or chlorine compounds to bleach the paper— to make it white enough to satisfy consumers, publishers, and especially advertisers.

The bleaching processes release substantial amounts of organochlorine compounds into the environment. These compounds do not dissolve in water, but are lipid-soluble and accumulate readily in the fatty tissues of animals and fish. With the pulp and paper industries of Sweden and Finland now accounting for 10 percent of the world's total output, some 300,000 to 400,000 tons of chlorinated compounds are released each year—much ending up in the Baltic Sea.

What happens when these compounds find their way up the food chain into humans and other higher animals has become a subject of intense scientific scrutiny in the past decade—with the weight of evidence linking them not only to cancer but to reproductive and endocrine diseases.

Among the early inklings of these effects were reports of die-offs in sea eagles, seals, and minks, first observed on the shores of the Swedish coast in the late 1950s. Since then, these species have suffered severe declines and are now almost extinct. Studies of other species in decline—including both marine mammals and such fish as herring, cod, sprat, and salmon—show that they too contain high levels of organochlorines. Compared to fish in the neighboring North Sea, fish in the Baltic have been found to contain concentrations of these chemicals three to ten times greater.

In addition to the population declines or collapses, marine biologists report a disturbing increase in birth defects in populations with high organochlorine levels. Among Baltic gray seals, half the females observed in one study were incapable of breeding because of deformed uteri horns. Among baby seals, eggshell-fragile skulls and skull bone lesions were believed to be caused by the immune suppression effects of exposure to PCBs. Unfortunately, these trends were not well documented until the late 1980s. Now the effects are so far along and pollution is so great that it is "almost too late to do anything about it," according to Susan Shaw, Executive Director of the Marine Environmental Research Institute in New York City, who works with marine biologists in Sweden.

For epidemiologists, the witches' brew of organochlorines (11,000 have been identified) is trouble enough. But in the Baltic, other ingredients are being added to the mix as well. For years, this sea served as a receptacle for the untreated sewage and industrial wastewater generated by areas under Communist rule, such as Upper Silesia in Poland and Ostrava in the Czech Republic. A 1991 *Ambio* article, for example, indicates that atmospheric metal input is the most important source of metal contamination in the Baltic area. Metal concentrations in the region have increased five-fold over the last 50 years, largely as a result of burning fossil fuels. Fish from many coastal areas are now blacklisted, because they contain too much mercury. But with the sources of Baltic pollution so diffused, it is difficult—with one major exception—to detect and monitor the polluters.

The exception is the pulp and paper mills. In the last few years, the European community has moved to impose new restrictions on chlorine bleaching. How well they succeed may go a long way toward determining the health of the Baltic for future generations—both of marine life and of the people who depend on it.

CASPIAN SEA: THE CONTROL OF RIVERS AND RESOURCES

A majority of the major seas are only partially enclosed, which gives them at least some—albeit very limited—opportunity to recover. With the Black Sea, there is at least a narrow channel to the Mediterranean. But about 500 kilometers east of the Black, the smaller Caspian Sea is entirely enclosed and its riverine lifelines have been more manipulated—and strangled.

Surveying the Damage

SEA	Baltic	Bering	Black	Caspian	Mediterranean	South China	Yellow
THREAT							
Over-fishing	●	●	●	●	●	●	●
Eutrophication	●	○	●	●	●	●	●
Dams	●	○	●	●	●—●	●	●
Organo-chlorines	●	●	●	●	●	●	●
Heavy Metals	●	●	●	●	●—●	●	●
Oil Drilling	●	●	●	●	●	●	●
Population (millions)	80	1.4	465	45	360	517	250
Area (thousands of sq.km.)	370	420	2,292	371	2,500	3,685	404

Source: Various reports and articles

KEY	
● High	● Low
● Medium	○ Negligible

As a consequence, it has even less absorptive capacity. Yet, it too has had to serve as a receptacle for massive amounts of waste. And that collision of interests has produced an outcome of ironic and tragic simplicity: the Caspian's most valued product—its caviar—has been virtually wiped out.

Perhaps nowhere else is the human bent for controlling and manipulating—and its effects on nature—so pronounced as in the Caspian. Over the centuries, powerful rivals have fought to control this sea's strategic rivers and ports. In the late down nineteenth century, an oil boom in Azerbaijan gave birth to a major industrial center on the Caspian's western shore, in the area around Baku; during World War II, the Soviet war effort was powered almost entirely by Baku's oil. And since the breakup of the Soviet Union, there have been ongoing discussions among Azerbaijan, Russia, Kazakhstan, Turkmenistan and Iran, as well as Western oil companies, about access to oil supplies.

If the southern part of the Caspian drainage area is strategically important for oil, the north is strategic for its agricultural resources and hydro-electric power. It produces one-fifth of the former Soviet countries' total crop yield, and one-third of their industrial output. In the last forty years, a string of dams and hydropower plants has been built along the Volga River, to supply electric power to the industries and to irrigate the crops. These uses have lowered water levels enough to severely impair the Volga's capacity to dilute waste and runoff, upsetting the natural balances of salinity, temperature, and oxygen in water stream.

The Volga is the Caspian's major source of contamination. Draining the area from north of Leningrad to south of Tehran, it was forced to accept more than one-fourth of all the wastewater disgorged by Russia. From petrochemical factories alone, some 67,000 tons of wastes flush into the sea each year. Further south, Azerbaijan cities and industries dump an estimated 250 and 300 million cubic meters of sewage and waste into the sea each year.

As a result, here too, fisheries have collapsed. The catches of pike and perch, for example, have dropped by 96 percent in the past three decades. But the biggest shock to this region has been the fate of its caviar—or sturgeon's eggs. The Caspian Sea used to produce 90 percent of world's supply of this prized delicacy, still known as the "black pearls of the Caspian." But the number of sturgeon returning to the Caspian from the Volga River has declined drastically, primarily because of obstructed migratory paths, overfishing, and pollution.

In the 1970s, it was not uncommon to find a specimen that was 60 years old and weighed 900 pounds. Today, an estimated 90 percent of the sea's sturgeon are killed before they are mature enough to reproduce—and the typical adult is just 18 years old and weighs 77 pounds. In the Iranian Sefid Rud River delta in the southern Caspian, the commercial catch of sturgeon dropped from 6,700 tons in 1961 to less than one-half ton in 1993. The World Conservation Union (IUCN) listed Caspian Sea sturgeon as endangered in its 1996 Red List of threatened and endangered species.

This pattern of accelerating decline is being played out in virtually every fishery of every sea in the world. As supplies dwindle, fish are captured at earlier stages of their life cycle. With fewer fish available, fishers turn to more desperate measures to capture them. A vicious circle, already hastened by contamination from human and industrial waste, river diversion projects, and sheer growth in human population, accelerates still further. One result is to drive the search for food farther afield, to parts of the planet where supplies have not yet been exhausted.

BERING SEA: TO THE ENDS OF THE EARTH

In the far northern reaches of the Pacific Ocean, enclosed by the Aleutian island chain and the Russian Kamchatka peninsula, the Bering Sea receives nutrient-rich ocean currents and replenishing water from the south to support its abundant marine mammals, plants, and fish. In gulfs, bays, and ocean waters that are relatively free of pollution and habitat destruction, marine life thrives. One might suppose that this sea, at least, is safe. But it is not.

Unlike the other seas discussed here, the Bering Sea has not supported a large human population. But as demand for food has risen, and with it the technology of extraction, the Bering is proving an asset of central importance to the food security of the human world at large.

The Bering Sea is "perhaps the richest marine region in the world ocean, as evidenced by the number of species and their biomass," according to economist Natalia Mirovitskaya of Russia's Institute of World Economy and International Relations and marine scientist J. Christopher Haney of the Woods Hole Oceanographic Institution in Massachusetts.

The Northwestern Pacific as a whole (including the Sea of Okhotsk, Sea of Japan, Yellow Sea and East China Sea) has an exceptionally high marine productivity—yielding up to 917 kilograms per square kilometer each year, compared to an average world ocean productivity of less than 189 kilograms.

Yet, despite its geographic remoteness, some species in the the Bering Sea are already being ravaged by overfishing and mismanagement. Wasteful fishing practices in the groundfish industry, for example, have contributed to annual losses of $250 million in the Bering Sea and Gulf of Alaska crab fisheries. The Alaskan pollack industry took off in the 1960s, with dramatic increases in catch attracting new investment in the industry. Between the early 1970s and the late 1980s, the United States and Canada increased their catches in this region four-fold—and were joined by an influx of fishers from Russia, Korea, China, and Japan.

Alaska or walleye pollack is now one of the world's biggest catches. In 1994, 4.3 million metric tons of it was taken, worldwide. But in the central Bering Sea, catches of pollack crashed from a peak of nearly 1.5 million metric tons in 1989 to 11,000 in 1992—a 99-percent decline in just three years primarily because of overfishing in the "Donut Hole," an area of international water outside the bounds of the Russian and American Exclusive Economic Zone (EEZ) jurisdictions, where Russian, American, Japanese, Korean, Chinese, and even Polish fishing vessels all compete in the search for pollack.

SOUTH CHINA SEA: "A DISASTER WAITING TO HAPPEN"

Some 6,000 kilometers down the Pacific Rim from the Bering Sea, the South China Sea serves a region as heavily populated as the Bering is sparse—yet some of its troubles are uncannily similar. It's a region where virtually all of the problems afflicting seas worldwide are being further exacerbated by political conflict—over fisheries, oil fields, military control, and the competing interests of commercial and local economies. But what in the Bering Sea is described as a "donut hole" might be better compared in the South China Sea to a Charybdis—the treacherous whirlpool of Greek mythology.

China, the largest of the South China's many antagonists, has claimed exclusive domain over a large part of this sea, including the Spratley Islands, ever since Chinese merchants first took to its waves in the 15th century. The claim is rejected by other countries because it limits access to fisheries, seabed oil and minerals, shipping lanes, and navigational rights. The disagreement is particularly contentious between China and Vietnam, and in areas around Taiwan, Brunei, Malaysia, and the Philippines where EEZ boundaries overlap.

China is now expanding its claims to include coveted oil fields—further escalating the disputes. Oil was first discovered in the area in 1976, and there are now an estimated 80 to 100 oil wells in the South China Sea. The Philippines, Vietnam, Taiwan, and the United States all have interests there, and tensions have been rising over who owns what. The United States began funding Indonesia's war in East Timor around the time of that discovery, partly to protect its oil interests in the region. And in the 1980s, China tripled the size of its South China naval fleet—suggesting that it, too, may be willing to wage war over these resources.

A 1991 newspaper article from Bandung, Indonesia describes the South China Sea as "a disaster waiting to happen." It warns of the potential for ecological disaster caused by uncontrolled commercial activity, but its message is no less applicable to the burden of environmental degradation the sea is already carrying. And the fact that the South China Sea serves as a strategic military zone complicates the picture—and raises tensions—even further. Military bases are located throughout the region, navy ships patrol the waters, and spent nuclear fuel is shipped through the area.

MEDITERRANEAN: TANKERS AND TOURISTS

Few seas have played more vital roles in the rise of human civilizations—and the support of their rapidly growing populations over the past four millennia—than the Mediterranean. Providing access to three continents, it played key roles in the rise of Aegean, Egyptian, Phoenician, Greek, and Roman empires, and to the development of historic exchanges of information and culture between places as far-flung as China, Britain, and Ethiopia. Today, it is bordered by 18 countries, all of which are as dependent on the sea as their predecessors were. Yet, the Mediterranean, like the other seas, is being subjected to heavy degradation—with the prospect of irreversible losses to its dependent human communities.

Concern about this degradation began to emerge in the 1960s and 1970s, with a series of tanker spills and severe chemical leaks. The heart of the Mediterranean, the Lake of Santa Gida near Cagliari, Sardinia, was a fertile breeding area for 10,000 water birds. But it was also a repository for mercury effluent from petrochemical factories. Mercury contamination was so severe in the fall of 1976 that the regional government had to block off the entrance to the lake, remove all the shellfish, and dredge the bottom to remove any traces of the metal.

While marine scientists had warned for many years of marine degradation, it was not until fishers were banned from contaminated waters, beachgoers were forced to go home early, and oil-covered seals and dolphins made the nightly news, that—with tourist revenue at stake—the first actions were taken. Tourism is critical to the Mediterranean economy; each summer, the seasonal population on the sea's coasts almost doubles, adding 100 million visitors each year to the region's more than 160 million residents.

The Mediterranean is especially vulnerable to pollution because it is a major shipping and transport route between the Middle East and Europe—meaning that there is heavy traffic of oil tankers. It also has naturally low levels of rainfall, nutrients, and species diversity, which, combined with increasing levels of urban and coastal pollution, leave the sea with little leeway. Luckily, in the 1970s, developing and industrialized countries around the region realized that the sea was sick, and for environmental reasons and self-interest they joined together to try to prevent it from getting worse.

In 1975, Mediterranean countries were the first to approve a UNEP sponsored regional sea program—and today, arguably, the condition of the Mediterranean is not as bad as it would have been without the Mediterranean Action Plan (MEDAP). The first issue MEDAP tackled was marine dumping, in the Barcelona Convention. A Regional Oil Center was established on Malta in 1976 to provide training, information, emergency management programs, and waste retention facilities in ports. But the problems did not stop: in the 1980s, one fifth of the world's oil spills occurred in the Mediterranean Sea.

With growing concern for regional environmental issues, the debate and discussions moved beyond the issues of oil pollution and dumping, to a more comprehensive definition and understanding of marine pollution. Likewise, the action plan itself evolved from a general framework to specific substance- and media-based limits and controls. The Land-Based Protocol, signed and finalized in 1980, was a significant achievement because it set limits on industrial, agricultural, and municipal emissions into the Mediterranean in addition to controlling wastes in rivers and air—thus establishing clear links between land pollution and marine pollution. In November 1995, member states of MEDAP agreed, in principle, to turn the Mediterranean basin into a trade-free zone by 2010. In response, the European Union pledged $6 billion in aid to help its less developed coastal neighbors clean up pollution, combat poverty, and improve environmental protection and enforcement.

RE-SETTING THE COMPASS

The world's seas, crucial to both human economies and the planet's life systems, have been gravely injured. Human actions have done most of the damage, some of it now irreversible. Even so, few agreements have been reached on how joint efforts can be made to save these shared resources.

Existing agreements are staked on archaic claims of rights to extraction and control. When no claims exist, as in the Bering Sea "Donut Hole," or when claims overlap, as in the South China Sea, a gold rush mentality has brought growing tensions.

Among the Earth's sea-dependent populations, there appears to be little or no money for marine protection, or in many cases even for basic sanitation services and sewage treatment. Subsistence fishers, seasonal dockworkers, small-scale farmers, and migrant workers are encountering growing hardship. As resources become scarce and tensions rise, the fishing industry, tourist resorts, oil and gas developers, and shipping facilities are all taking losses.

To reverse these losses will require at least three politically difficult but ecologically essential steps. The first is to reduce and restrict the use of damaging chemicals: chlorine in paper bleaching, and phosphates, nitrates, and chlorine in detergents and pesticides. These are chemicals that persist in the environment, bioaccumulate in animal tissues, cause direct damage to individual species and entire aquatic ecosystems, exacerbate anoxia, and disrupt the earth's carbon cycle. Banning or limiting their use will allow ecosystems to slowly re-establish their natural equilibrium.

The second step is to secure financial commitments from industrial countries and private companies, to invest in basic infrastructure to handle the sewage and waste from cities. This is already being done in the Baltic where Finland, Sweden, Denmark, and Germany are helping eastern Baltic countries to pay for sewage treatment plants. Recently, the

European Bank for Reconstruction and Development committed $67 million to construct a sewage treatment plant in Tallinn, the capital of Estonia.

The third, and most critical, step is to secure cooperation—commitment to joint management in lieu of preoccupation with extraction and control—at all levels of community and government. On the international level, an instructive model is the Ronneby Declaration, signed in 1990 by all of the Baltic Sea countries, members of the European Union, and four multilateral banks. This agreement identifies 132 pollution hot spots in the Baltic region, most of them in the former Eastern bloc countries. To clean up the hot spots, a 20-year, $25.6 billion Joint Comprehensive Environmental Action Program underwrites investments in sewage treatment, the refitting of pulp and paper plants, and other pollution control efforts. Similarly, environment ministers from Bulgaria, Georgia, Romania, Russia, Turkey, and Ukraine signed the Black Sea Strategic Action Plan in October 1996. The agreement calls upon Black Sea states to reinforce regulations and fines for polluters, introduce a regional fisheries licensing and quota system, ban disposal of all municipal solid waste, install waste reduction plans in 10 designated "hot spots," improve wetlands management, and expand conservation areas in estuaries and coastal zones. At the community level, a successful example can be found in the Gulf of Thailand, where several Buddhist and Muslim fishing villages are working with local activists and the U.S.-based Earth Island Institute to close the inner reaches of Kuntulee Bay to pushnets and trawlers. Each of these cases shows how action and change can happen even in the absence of political agreement.

Finally, we need a philosophical change of heart to reconnect ourselves with the seas that have supported our civilizations since the dawn of history. We may not need to restore the seas to their original pristine conditions—that may no longer be possible. But we urgently need to rehabilitate and protect whatever ecological and economic value can still be salvaged.

3

Biological Instabilities

BIO-INVASIONS

By Chris Bright

Earlier generations of Americans thought the Florida Everglades required a cure. The immense marsh at the tip of the peninsula—a hot, unwholesome expanse of mosquito-infested sawgrass—was an obstacle to the advancing fronts of civilization and industry. So around the turn of the century, officials of the U.S. Department of Agriculture (USDA) began distributing seeds of the melaleuca tree *(Melaleuca quinquenervia)*, a thirsty, fast-growing native of Australia. The tree had already been planted to drink up "fever swamps" elsewhere—and there was the possibility of timber production. Melaleuca took root in the popular imagination; by the 1930s, nurserymen weren't able to grow enough to satisfy demand. One forester even took to broadcasting melaleuca seed over the Everglades from his airplane.

But the melaleuca's only product has been a spreading thicket of trouble. Its impenetrable stands displace virtually all other vegetation. Its dense root mat oozes substances poisonous to other plants. Its airborne secretions are poisonous to people: they can cause severe respiratory and skin irritation. And the melaleuca is "fire adapted"—it spreads by burning. Its inner bark is a wet, insulating sponge, while its outer bark is tinder-dry and its leaves are laced with a flammable oil. So even though it sucks up water four times as fast as the native sawgrass, it burns with explosive force. A few days afterwards, the tree sprouts new growth and rains millions of seeds onto the burnt-over land. Germination begins in three days and a seedling may reach six feet in its first year. The melaleuca may already have invaded as much as 600,000 hectares of Florida wetland and if it is not controlled, says Ronald Myers, an expert on the problem, "the Everglades will be no more."

The melaleuca's rampage fits a pattern typical of exotic species—species introduced into ecosystems in which they are not native. Freed from the diseases, predators, and other factors that keep them in check in their native habitats, exotics can wreak ecological havoc. And as they spread, they displace ever greater numbers of rarer species, whose ranges are more circumscribed. About 30 percent of the creatures on the official U.S. Endangered and Threatened List, for example, are there at least in part because of exotics.

Of course, the migration of species into new habitat has always been a part of nature, but human interference has so greatly amplified the process as to make it, taken globally, a phenomenon without precedent in the history of life. In Hawaii, where exotic invasions have reached epidemic proportions, an average of 18 new insects or other arthropods have established themselves every year over the past half century or so. That's more than a million times the natural rate of invasion for that group of organisms. Hawaii may be an extreme case, but all over the world, exotics are accounting for an ever larger share of the biota—the local assemblage of living things. Yet little is being done to stop this process, largely because it's bound up with so many economic activities—everything from intentional introductions of exotic grasses for grazing cattle, to accidental releases of shrimp viruses from aquaculture shipments.

Like other forms of environmental degradation, exotic invasions exact a price. In 1957, for example, the Nile perch (*Lates niloticus*) was released into Africa's Lake Victoria to improve the fishing. But the perch, a voracious predator, eliminated nearly half the lake's 400 native fish species. And it proved an inferior food fish. Its oily flesh must be smoked, so nearby forests were logged. Now the perch itself appears to be in decline, due to lack of prey, overfishing, and the deoxygenation of algae-choked waters provoked by the loss of the herbivorous fish. Uganda, Kenya, and Tanzania—the countries surrounding the lake—must endure the loss of both fisheries and forests, even as their populations continue to grow.

The full costs of a disruptive invasion are beyond reckoning, but the immediate costs may be clear. In the United States, the USDA estimated losses and control expenses during the 1981 outbreak of the gypsy moth *(Lymantria dispar)*, a forest pest native to Europe, at $764 million. (About 40 percent of all serious insect pests in the United States are exotic; so are at least half the weeds.) The zebra mussel *(Dreissena polymorpha)*, a shellfish from the Caspian region that is spreading throughout eastern North America, could increase the cost of U.S. power production. Since it breeds prolifically and encrusts almost any available surface, including powerplant water pipes, the mussel could force the power industry to spend $800 million redesigning its plants plus $60 million annually on maintenance. Exotics can pose serious public health threats as well. Over the last decade, the Asian tiger mosquito *(Aedes albopictus)*, already widespread in Asia, established itself in Brazil, southern Europe, South Africa, and the continental United States. This mosquito is known to carry dengue fever, yellow fever, and encephalitis.

THE DOMINO EFFECT

Not every exotic is a monster, of course—the ginkgo tree on the lawn will probably never take over the countryside. It's likely that only a small percentage of exotics even manage to survive in their new homes. And according to many ecologists, an exotic that does establish itself will not necessarily do measurable harm. But at present, there is simply no way to identify the serious troublemakers—the invasive exotics—until the damage is done.

Part of the reason for this is that the invaders do their damage in so many different ways. Sometimes they cause a kind of ecological domino effect. The zebra mussel, for instance, is stripping the plankton out of more and more North American lakes and rivers, forcing an abrupt shift in the basic community food source—from plankton to bottom sediment. Over the long term, that shift may suppress plankton-feeding fish species, and increase bottom-feeding organisms like aquatic worms and crawfish. Such effects can extend far beyond the immediate ecosystem. In the 1960s and 1970s, for example, the U.S. state of Montana introduced the exotic opposum shrimp *(Mysis relicta)* into the state's Flathead River. It was hoped that the shrimp would serve as an additional food for a species of salmon, also exotic, that had been introduced as a game fish. But the shrimp proved a formidable predator of the local zooplankton—the main food of juvenile salmon. The salmon population collapsed, taking with it a wide spectrum of terrestrial species that had come to depend on the fish. Among the wildlife the shrimp has displaced are eagles, gulls, otters, coyotes, and bears.

The "food web"—the network of predator-prey relationships—is not the only ecological process that is vulnerable. Fire-adapted exotic grasses are changing the role that fire plays in natural areas of the American west, Hawaii, and Australia. Other effects are more complex. Why, for example, should the arrival of the Argentine ant *(Iridomyrmex humilis)* threaten the Cape Floral Kingdom, an extremely diverse and unique South African plant community? Because some 1,300 plant species depend on native ants for seed burial, and the native ants are being displaced by the invader.

But the damage can also be direct. Sometimes, for instance, the intruders simply eat the natives. Rats are the most important exotic predators of island birds, which have often evolved in the absence of any predators. This lack of evolutionary defenses explains what happened in 1964, when rats arrived on New Zealand's Big South Cape Island: five bird and one bat species disappeared. (More than 80 percent of the world's major islands now have exotic rat populations.)

Sometimes exotics out-compete natives for an essential resource. On the prairies of the western United States, Eurasian cheat grass *(Bromus tectorum)* has proven a stronger competitor for water than the once dominant native wheat grass *(Agropyron spicatum)*; cheat grass now carpets more than 40 million hectares.

Sometimes an invader brings along its diseases or para-sites. The Chinese grass carp *(Ctenopharyngodon idella)*, widely used for aquatic weed control, has infected freshwater fish in Europe and North America with an Asian tapeworm *(Bothriocephalus opsarichthydis)*.

But perhaps the most insidious form of damage occurs when exotic and native merge. Interbreeding can swamp a native gene pool in foreign genes, thereby eliminating its dis-tinctiveness and eroding the species' genetic diversity. In the U.S. Pacific Northwest, massive releases of hatchery-bred salmon are believed to be diluting endangered salmon popu-lations in this way. Interbreeding may even create new, hybrid species, as when crosses between crop and wild potatoes pro-duced the Bolivian weed potato *(Solanum sucrense)*.

Although the damage that invasive exotics do is well doc-umented, the key to their success is still a mystery. For decades, ecologists have been compiling lists of invasive char-acteristics, then rejecting them as having no predictive value. But one useful approach to the problem is a concept called "weediness." A text book case of weediness can be found in the red fire ant *(Solenopsis invicta)*, a viciously aggressive stinging ant from Brazil that is now widespread in the U.S. southeast. The fire ant thrives in disturbed areas, like plowed fields. It disburses widely, by mating swarms or by clumping together to form floating mats during floods. Its reproductive abilities are amazing even by insect standards—no other ant species produces as high a proportion of sexually active individuals. Its colonies also grow very dense: they may contain hundreds of queens (most ant species form only single-queen colonies) and command over an acre (four-tenths of a hectare) of territory. And fire ants will eat just about anything. In the United States, they have killed off as much as 40 percent of all native insect species in some areas. Preference for disturbed habitat, efficient dispersal, rapid population growth, and opportunistic feeding—these hallmarks of weediness appear to some degree in a huge assortment of other widespread exotics. Ragweed, rats, and starlings are all weeds.

Another approach to the problem seeks common features among the areas invaded. Here too, every theory invites a host of exceptions, but many ecologists argue that small ecosystems—islands and lakes, for example—are more readily invaded than large ones. Their vulnerability may be due to evolutionary isolation, which tends to foster small assemblages of rather narrowly adapted species. And previous disturbance is also commonly seen as a factor: unhealthy ecosystems may be more hospitable to exotics.

To date, the study of exotics could be summed up in three negative statements: it's impossible to predict where an exotic will establish itself, or what it will do afterwards, or when it will do it. The collared dove *(Streptopelia decaocto)*, for example, was brought into southern Europe more than 200 years ago by the Ottoman Turks. Why did it wait until around 1930 to begin an invasion that has now nearly covered the continent? Climate change and a preference for urban settings have been suggested as causes, but no one really knows if they are. In the U.S. midwest, several previously well-mannered garden shrubs have recently become invasive, apparently because they have adapted to their new surroundings. Invasive exotics often adapt readily to new environments. Since its arrival in North America in the mid-1980s, for instance, the Asian tiger mosquito has already fine-tuned its daylength sensitivity to suit various locations on the continent.

A CULTURAL CONSTANT

Moving other creatures around is a deeply ingrained human habit. Exotics are an ancient and constant cultural effect—a fact of life for the neolithic farmers who watched the spread of Europe's first weeds nearly 10 millennia ago; a fact of life for the people who brought the dingo *(Canis familiaris dingo)* to Australia perhaps 3,000 years later. Some ancient introductions were made over great distances, but the general pattern was a fairly gradual intermingling within regional biotas. That began to change about 500 years ago, with the spreading ascendancy of European cultures, beginning in the Americas. Sometimes the New World proved better ground for European plants and animals than for Europeans themselves. When French colonists arrived in Florida in 1560, the native peoples supplied them with pork from well-established herds of feral pigs—a legacy of earlier explorers. By the 17th century, an extensive Old World agricultural assemblage was available throughout the colonies of eastern North America.

With the intentional introductions came the unintentional ones, some of them disastrous. The arrival of European and African pathogens in the New World was one of the greatest calamities in human history; it is estimated that during the course of the 16th century, 30 million native Americans, perhaps two-thirds of the hemisphere's population, died from Old World diseases. Other invasions were less catastrophic but no less permanent. In the same century, Spanish agriculture in what is now Chile released a massive invasion of Mediterranean weeds.

In later centuries, the coalescence of a global trading network, with Europe at its hub, drew much of the world into the biotic mixing bowl. In seaports all over the globe, exotic flora sprouted in ballast heaps unloaded from ships. Rats made their way throughout the Pacific and into Australia.

And more and more organisms became objects of trade themselves. In the 1830s, the "Wardian case," a kind of traveling terrarium that looked like a miniature greenhouse, revolutionized the introduction of American and Asian plants into European gardens. Throughout the 19th century, "acclimatization societies" in North America and Australia dedicated themselves to haphazard releases of exotics for various reasons—usually on the assumption that the local fauna was inferior to that of Europe. The starling *(Sturnus vulgaris)*, for example, owes its conquest of North America to a society bent on bringing to the New World every bird mentioned in the plays of William Shakespeare. Railroad "fish cars" were trundled all over the American landscape to introduce exotic fish, with the choice of stream often left to the whim of the crew. In Australia, the rabbit, which still plagues that continent, was released to stock an unfamiliar land with familiar game.

Today the pattern has shifted again, into a kaleidoscopic network of movement in which practically any point on the globe can send or receive material. The complexity of movement defies full description, but a look at a few major "pathways" (the mechanisms through which exotics are introduced) offers a perspective on it.

Trade remains the most important factor overall, and among its many pathways, one is of special concern. Shipping containers, the big metal boxes that can be stacked on ships, then offloaded onto trucks or trains, have revolutionized shipping and may do the same thing for the movement of exotics. World container traffic now stands at around 100 million 20-foot units a year, and it's growing. In 1980, container ships accounted for 1.6 percent of world shipping tonnage; by 1993, that share had more than tripled to 4.9 percent. (A good two-thirds of the world's shipping consists of such noncontainer commodities as minerals, grain, and oil.)

That may not sound like a lot, but it's more than enough to make the shipping container the Wardian case of our era—

except that some of its contents are accidental. The Asian tiger mosquito arrived in the United States in containers of used tires imported from Japan. "The safe, protected environment of the sealed container," writes George Craig, Jr., one of the mosquito's observers, "provides a splendid mobile pram between continents." Craig notes that container traffic has also broken the old link between invasion and seaport: containers may not be unloaded until they reach their final destination and that could be anywhere a road or railroad leads.

Ballast water has proven a more effective pathway than the solid ballast it replaced—though for different classes of organisms. Ships carry immense quantities of ballast water from sea to sea, pumping it in or out as cargo is loaded or unloaded. A single bulk carrier may have a ballast capacity of nearly 50 million U.S. gallons; the total capacity of the 1,625 bulk carriers in the world's major fleets might therefore approach 80 billion gallons—about 300,000 cubic meters. And in terms of tonnage, bulk carriers make up only about a third of the world's shipping.

Ballast water exchange has become a manmade overlay to the globe's natural currents—a network of artificial rivers running through the oceans. Myriad small creatures—fish, worms, plankton, crabs, and clams, to name a few—ride these new currents all over the world. In Coos Bay, Oregon, a study cataloged the ballast water release of more than 400 exotic species from 1988 to 1991. At least 14 of the more than 100 exotics known to have been released into Australian ports have become established. In North America, the zebra mussel arrived in ballast water. And that's how the comb jelly *Mnemiopsis leidyi* found its way into the Black Sea. The jelly has devastated local fisheries and sometimes accounts for as much as 95 percent of the sea's wet weight biomass.

From time to time, a brown tree snake *(Boiga irregularis)* is found on the runway of a Hawaiian airport, where it has fallen from a wheel well or cargo bay of an airplane arriving from the Pacific island of Guam. The snake was inadvertently introduced into Guam from the Papua New Guinea region; it has overrun the island and eliminated nine of Guam's 18 native bird species. Thus far, the snake is not known to have established itself in Hawaii, but every new find leaves Hawaiian ecologists wondering whether any stowaways survived a flight undetected. Air traffic is another rapidly broadening global pathway. In 1989, only three airports received more than a million metric tons of cargo; by 1995 that number had risen to at least 10. The speed of air transport may help spread pathogens and other organisms that would probably be detected in the course of ship passage.

But the pathways themselves don't tell the full story; entire economic sectors depend on or actively promote the spread of exotics. Agriculture, for instance, molds landscapes to suit exotic crops and livestock, which must then be defended against exotic pests. Forestry razes native forests to grow exotic timber which, when cut, can transport exotic forest pests. Aquaculture dumps exotic fish into rivers and streams. just one aquaculture species, the Mozambique tilapia *(Oreochromis mossambicus)*, is now established in nearly every tropical and subtropical country. And dozens of smaller industries—horticulture and the aquarium trade, for example—are moving all sorts of creatures from place to place. The aquarium trade is the source for 65 percent of the exotic fish species known to have become established in the United States.

A young industry, biotechnology, may force the process into yet another quantum leap. An entirely new dimension of pathways has opened up with the development of transgenic organisms—creatures whose genetic complement contains DNA from other species with which they could not possibly have interbred. Many of these organisms are already in the field testing stage—insect viruses, crop plants, and fish among them. Critics of the industry point out that a transgenic organism's "exotic" genes could move into wild populations through ordinary interbreeding—and that such an event might have serious consequences. Crop plants, for example, often have wild relatives with which they interbreed. Crops engineered to be especially tolerant of herbicides or salt might confer their new traits on their wild relatives, allowing them to invade a salt marsh—or a heavily sprayed wheat field.

Of course, a transgenic organism could be extremely disruptive even without releasing its unusual genes. Last year, two Oregon State University scientists discovered in laboratory tests that a soil bacterium they had engineered to produce the fuel ethanol also cut soil populations of mycorrhizal fungi by more than half. These fungi are essential to nutrient uptake in higher plants. "So if the bacterium had been released," one of the scientists dryly observed, "it could have been a real problem. If the organism survived readily and spread widely, very likely we would be unable to grow crops without a control measure for this organism." Thus far, there have been at least 2,258 experimental releases of genetically engineered organisms in the United States alone. By 1997, Monsanto, the leading company in the effort to commercialize engineered plants, had nearly 8 million hectares planted to transgenic crops worldwide.

Whether it's an intermingling of chromosomes or oceans, this blurring of ancient biological boundaries is frequently a matter of policy. Too often, exotics are a specious "easy way out" for natural resource managers. It's much easier to introduce a fish that will tolerate a dirty river than it is to clean the river up so that its native fish can thrive. It's easier to plant quick-growing exotic timber than it is to manage a natural forest for sustainable production. And it's not just a matter of rivers and forests—the local people may lose out as well. The introduction of exotics is often an ingredient in activities that undermine local cultures and economics. In agriculture, for instance, when mass-market crops replace traditional varieties, they encourage a dependence on international suppliers and buyers. In forestry, a preference for exotic timber can lead to situations like the one in Chile, where a subsidized reforestation program promotes the planting of exotic pines and Eucalyptus species. Major landowners, trying to bring as much land as possible into the program, are reported to have displaced large numbers of small farmers. The process affects fisheries too: Lake Victoria's Nile perch has fed an export-oriented fish processing industry much more effectively than it has fed the families of local fishers.

UNSCRAMBLING THE EGG

Coming to grips with the exotic menace will require a degree of ecological realism. Current technology does not generally permit the wholesale removal of an exotic once it has established itself in an ecosystem. As one ecologist puts it, "getting it out of that system is like trying to unscramble an egg." But there are some exceptions to the rule. It is often possible to eradicate an exotic during the initial phase of its invasion, while it is still just "settling in." And there are some instances of later success. Perhaps the most remarkable of these was the eradication of the malaria mosquito *(Anopheles gambiae)* from Brazil in the 1930s, a feat achieved by the liberal use of arsenic against a creature that, fortunately, proved poorly adapted to its new environment.

But more typical is the stalemated effort to rid the western hemisphere of the yellow fever mosquito *(Aedes aegypti)*, beginning at the turn of the century and continuing sporadically today. Even the United States, which spent $100 million dosing this mosquito with DDT in the 1960s, has failed to dislodge it. Among the factors that usually doom such efforts are an inability to locate all habitat—every tree hole, empty beer can, or junked tire, in the case of the yellow fever mosquito. High reproduction rates are another obstacle; "weedy" species usually bounce back fast even after enormous losses. A policy that insists on total eradication may actually make things worse, as in the USDA's $200 million war on the fire ant in the 1950s and 1960s. The Department's pesticides hurt native ants more than the fire ant, giving the invader an edge in occupying the newly emptied habitat.

Luckily, complete eradication isn't usually necessary. Most exotics need only be "controlled"—reduced to the point of ecological insignificance. Sometimes this can be done by physical or chemical means. In the western United States, some small natural areas have been cleared of tamarisk trees (*Tamarix* species) simply by repeated cutting. But even where such techniques succeed, they must be continually renewed, and the use of chemicals often has serious ecological or political liabilities. During the 1980s, California's spraying programs against the Mediterranean fruit fly *(Ceratitis capitata)*, a serious agricultural pest, sparked considerable public opposition, despite a major publicity campaign. The program was perhaps a greater biological success than a political one: the fruit fly was eradicated, but left in its wake no clear public consensus on how to respond to future infestations. Damage claims against the state totaled more than $2 billion, of which some $3.7 million were actually paid.

Another strategy, biological control, pursues the offending exotic by introducing other exotics to attack it. In crude form, biocontrol has been around for centuries, but in early instances of its use, the cure often proved worse than the disease. In 1762, for instance, a Jamaican sugar planter introduced an aggressive Cuban ant *(Formica omnivora)* onto his plantation, because the ant attacked rats—already a well-established pest in the Caribbean. The ants flourished, but didn't much bother the rats. So an enormous South American toad *(Bufo marinus)* was introduced to control both. It flourished as well—it's now called the cane toad for its success in infesting sugar plantations. The rats remained, however, so the small Indian mongoose *(Herpestes auropunctatus)* was introduced; by 1898, 26 years after it arrived, the mongoose had decimated the island's bird and reptile fauna, along with much of the islanders' livestock.

Modern biocontrol seeks more decisive results, generally

by using the culprit organism's native predators. Solid successes have been achieved this way, as with the control of the water fern *Salvinia molesta*, in Papua New Guinea's Sepik River. By 1980, a decade after it first appeared, the fern had made the Sepik unfishable and impassable, starving out local villages in the process. By 1990, the infestation had been largely cleared by the introduction of a weevil, one of a group of insects that regulates the fern's growth in its native Brazil. And so far, at least, its new setting hasn't tempted the weevil away from its exclusive diet of water fern.

But the technique has important limitations. Sound biocontrol requires "host specificity"—the ideal biocontrol agent preys exclusively on the target organism and pursues it to the edge of oblivion. Neither target nor agent is expected to die out entirely, but any increase in the target's population is met by an increase in the agent's. It's possible to find candidate agents among the insects that approach this ideal, but even with insects, careful testing is necessary. Several wasp species introduced into Hawaii for crop pest control apparently caused the extinction of native moths. Many insects—and many other types of invertebrates—have diets too broad for biocontrol. For the same reason, the use of any vertebrate invites serious trouble. One of the field's biggest debacles has been the introduction of mosquitofishes (*Gambusia* species) all over the world for mosquito control. The effect on the mosquitoes is generally negligible, but the mosquitofish have extirpated native fish by eating their larva and fry. Of course, many pathogens are host specific, and some diseases have been successfully employed as biocontrols, notably myxomatosis virus, a rabbit disease. But concerns that microbes could mutate and attack nontarget organisms have greatly limited their use thus far.

The principles of biocontrol have often led resource managers to assume that for every pest, there's an ideal predator that can reduce it to insignificance. Unfortunately, this does not appear to be true. For 35 years, researchers have been seeking biocontrols for the balsam woolly adelgid *(Adelges piceae)*, a European insect that has infested North American fir trees *(Abies* species). The adelgid has nearly eliminated a variety of balsam fir *(A. balsamea var. phanerolepsis)* and is on its way to destroying the Fraser fir *(A. fraseri)* but so far, no effective biocontrol agents have been found.

Even though it's no panacea, biocontrol may be the best remedy available in many cases. Certain Australian insects may, for instance, be Florida's best bet against the melaleuca. In any case, there are few other options. Some promising new technologies could prove useful against particular classes of exotics—artificial pheromones may confuse mating reflexes in certain insects, for example, and it's possible to engineer oral vaccines that cause infertility in mammals. But at present, no emerging technology works against as broad a range of exotics, in as many different environments, as biocontrol.

EXOTIC POLITICS

The greatest challenges in dealing with exotics are not biological, however; they are political. On an international level, exotics usually get inadequate coverage in treaties that regulate important pathways. They do figure in the International Plant Protection Convention, which requires cooperation on agricultural pest control. But the Convention on Biological Diversity contains only a vague resolution to control dangerous exotics "as far as possible and appropriate." Marine exotics get more thorough treatment in the Convention on the Law of the Sea, but this treaty only went into effect last year, so it's too soon to gauge the results. Within their own jurisdictions, most countries seem to give serious attention to exotics only when they disturb a major industry or become an important public health threat.

It's not hard to find weak points in this legal framework. In response to the arrival of the Asian tiger mosquito, for instance, the United States imposed disinfection standards on tire imports—but not on tire exports. Gordon Craig, the mosquito authority, argues that if U.S. tire shipments bring the mosquito to the Caribbean, the region's disease burden could be greatly aggravated. Dengue fever is already well established in the region, but it lacks an effective rural vector. The Asian tiger mosquito could readily perform that service.

Biological pollution, as invasions are sometimes called, is a policy nightmare because it results from so many disparate—and important—economic activities. Yet the same can be said of chemical pollution, and there is widespread acceptance of complicated regulatory shields against dangerous chemicals. One of the reasons for this is the publicity surrounding some major instances of chemical pollution, like the Bhopal disaster in India, in which a gas leak from a Union Carbide plant killed thousands of people. Few people probably view exotics with similar alarm, but an education campaign publicizing some worst cases—actual or potential—could change that. Widespread American interest in forest conservation, for instance, usually focuses on logging as the primary threat. But in much of the country, exotic forest pests may be at least as dangerous to the forests as poor management. Once a consensus for action has begun to take shape, it should be directed at the following goals.

Quarantine officials, ecologists, agronomists, and others who deal with exotics should be invited to pool their findings in a set of databases accessible to anyone with an interest in the subject. Such a project would be a logical extension of many efforts already underway; ultimately it could provide a far more effective basis for policy advocacy—and for action—than exists today.

Planned imports and releases of exotics should be regulated by a "clean list" approach, in which an organism must be explicitly approved as harmless—"clean"—before it can be legally introduced. (The more common approach uses a "dirty list," which catalogs organisms that have been banned because they are known to be harmful, and admits unlisted organisms.)

Importers should be required to accept liability for any damages their imports cause. This requirement should apply to first-time imports of exotics, and to releases of both exotics and genetically engineered organisms. The same principle of liability should be extended to importers of commodities known to be important pathways for dangerous exotics.

When a government funds an introduction—whether it's a new fish for aquaculture or a forage plant for livestock—it should require the studies necessary to determine the ecological effects of the new arrival. This policy should apply to both domestic introductions and to foreign ones which may, for instance, be carried out in the course of a foreign aid project.

Unfortunately, no single set of regulations will slow the rate of inadvertent introductions. That task will require an array of specific technologies and procedures built around the pathways involved. For example, alternative ballast water systems have been designed to reduce the rate of ship-borne introductions. The principal political task here will be to build a broad public mandate for the development and application of these responses. In the process, the public should be acquainted with the possibility that some forms of commerce may never be worth the risks they entail—Siberian timber imports into the United States, for instance. (The spruce bark beetle *(Ips typographus)*, one of the forest pests associated with Siberian timber, has already killed millions of trees in Japan and Europe.)

Uninvited exotics that get past these barriers should be subjected to immediate evaluation and, where warranted, control. Since exotics are most vulnerable in the incipient stages of an invasion, protocols for responding should be as free from red tape as possible—and tied as firmly as possible to a scientific evaluation of the threat.

Finally, governments should adopt a general policy favoring the use of native species—and wherever possible, the use of native *populations*—in government activities that involve the release of organisms. Such activities include landscaping, roadside planting, erosion control, forestry, range management, fish and game stocking—even some foreign aid programs. The policy could be combined with a clean list approach to permit the use of exotics when no suitable natives can be found. By pushing industries towards the use of natives, such a policy could help to shape them into more environmentally benign forms, just as the U.S. federal commitment to recycled paper helped boost the use of recycled fiber in paper production. The policy could also advance ecological research, educate the public about exotics, and speed up landscape restoration programs. In developing countries, it could be a tool for helping local economies and indigenous peoples. A couple of examples show how broad the payoffs could be:

In the U.S. southeast, the Asian sawtooth oak *(Quercus acutissima)* has been widely introduced as a wildlife food plant—despite the fact that native oaks appear to be in decline. But in the state of Illinois, foresters can care for both wildlife *and* native forests by planting the 15 native oaks now grown at state nurseries. The Illinois Department of Conservation now uses plants native to the state almost exclusively for its planting programs—a precedent that other land management agencies would do well to consider.

In Honduras, the Inter-American Development Bank is funding a reforestation project for the ruined watershed around the immense El Cajon Dam. Plans call for the introduction of Eucalyptus species and other exotic trees which critics fear could disrupt what is left of the area's ecosystem. Yet in Costa Rica, a number of local nurseries are doing a brisk business selling thousands of mostly native tree species for reforestation there.

Both cases come down to conserving particular local resources—the things that make a community distinct. These are the resources that are most vulnerable to exotic invasions. And in both cases, a knowledge of those resources could be an important weapon against invasion. For as exotics spread from one community to the next, homogenizing millions of years of intricate variety, they challenge our ability to value diversity—and to use it wisely. If we are to stem the rising tide of biological pollution, we must do more than just keep exotic species out; we must recognize the value of the species that belong where they are.

THE DECLINE OF PRIMATES

By John Tuxill

The little apes would hardly have dominated the patchwork of forest and savanna in which they lived. Two million years ago, east Africa was home not just to lions and leopards, but to saber-toothed cats, giant baboons, and wild pigs as big as buffalo. The apes must have invested a good deal of effort in just trying to stay out of the way. But if we could have watched them foraging in small bands, feeding on fruits and nuts or scavenging meat when they could, we would instantly have recognized several unusual abilities: a preference for walking upright, a high degree of cooperative behavior, and a penchant for using tools—sticks, stones, or bones—in their daily search for food. Those small, vulnerable hominids had embarked on a unique evolutionary experiment—a line of development that would one day confer on their descendants a power without precedent in the entire history of life.

Two million years is only a brief moment in evolutionary time, but the rift that has opened since then between ourselves and our fellow primates—modern apes, monkeys, lemurs, and lorises—is momentous on any scale. We humans share 98.4 percent of our gene pool with chimpanzees; only 1.6 percent of our genome is uniquely ours. But that seasoning of distinctly human DNA has, in a sense, catalyzed a reversal of our ecological role. We are no longer molded by the ecosystems in which we live—we mold them. Increasingly, however, we are learning that there is a price to pay for our ecological dominance—and no one is paying more heavily than our closest relatives.

THE DEMOGRAPHIC GAP

Consider the arithmetic of our success. When our species first emerged some 100,000 to 150,000 years ago, hominids (the group containing us, our direct ancestors, and their closest relatives) were still a minor branch on the primate family tree. Some primates—particularly little ones like the marmosets of South America—can number in the tens of millions. But for many thousands of years, the early human population probably totaled no more than 5 to 8 million widely-dispersed souls. As our ancestors moved into new regions and learned how to exploit natural resources more intensively, our numbers slowly expanded. By the end of the last Ice Age 10,000 years ago, the human population might have reached 10 million. As consummate hunter-gatherers, we had become the most widespread primate—the only one to colonize both hemispheres. But there was still at least one other group of large primates that outnumbered us: the adaptable baboons of Africa, whose natural densities and range suggest a prehistoric population on the order of 20 to 40 million.

The total number of humans probably remained in the tens of millions for several more millennia, until agriculture had become a major social force. But by the time of Christ, humans had probably become the most numerous primate species, when our population passed 250 million, on its way to 1 billion by the early 1800s. Our numbers likely eclipsed all other primate species combined by 1930, when the human population climbed past 2 billion.

Since then, the demographic gap between ourselves and the 232 other known primate species has widened even more dramatically. As our population has soared to nearly 6 billion, other primate populations have dropped sharply, and the continued survival of many species is now in doubt. According to the World Conservation Union (IUCN), primates are now the most imperiled major order of mammals. Nearly half of all primates are already threatened with extinction, and the IUCN considers another one-fifth "near-threatened." In general terms, the reasons for the declines are no mystery: they all relate, directly or indirectly, to human actions. But we will need to understand the relationship between ourselves and our closest relatives in detail, if we are to secure the safe passage of primates—and the rest of our planet's biodiversity—across the human demographic explosion.

THE HOMELESS

In general, primates are an adaptable bunch. Some, like the hamadryas baboon of the Arabian peninsula, forage in deserts, while others, like Tibetan macaques, thrive on cold mountain slopes. But most species retain a strong affinity for the habitat in which primates first evolved: the verdant belt of tropical forest that hugs the Earth's equator. The fate of these forests will therefore largely determine the fate of most primates. And more and more of these forests are losing their ecological integrity, as they are logged, colonized, and cleared for agriculture. All told, forest loss and other forms of habitat degradation are a factor in the decline of nearly 90 percent of threatened primate species, making this the single biggest problem they face.

Not surprisingly, the highest concentrations of endangered primates occur in "hotspots" of tropical forest loss— the places where forest communities are disappearing most rapidly. In south and east Asia, the IUCN has classified a full 90 percent of all primate species as threatened or near-threatened. In Indonesia and Malaysia, orangutans—the most arboreal of the great apes and, therefore, the most dependent on trees—have lost over 80 percent of their forests in just 20 years ("orangutan" is Malay for "man of the forest"). Vietnam's Tonkin snub-nosed monkey may now be the rarest primate in the world. Hunting and the loss of nearly 90 percent of its lowland rainforest habitat since 1950 have reduced it to a handful of populations totaling fewer than 200 individuals, all of them living in forest patches outside the country's national parks and nature reserves.

In Madagascar, another hotspot, the odds of extinction are rising not just for individual species, but for an entire evolutionary lineage millions of years in the making. Madagascar's long geologic isolation allowed evolution to take a separate course there: instead of monkeys or apes, the island's primates consist entirely of lemurs. (Lemurs look a little like a cross between a monkey and a raccoon.) Of all the primates alive today, lemurs are thought to be the most "ancient"—the group that most closely resembles the earliest primates. All of Madagascar's primates are endemic to Madagascar and to the nearby Comoros Islands (that is, they are found nowhere else). Since the arrival of humans roughly 1,000 years ago, Madagascar has lost at least 80 percent of its old growth forest. Even before the first Europeans set foot on the island in 1500, at least 15 primate species had gone extinct—including the giant *Megaladopsis*, which was as large as a female gorilla. Of the surviving 30 or so species, fully two-thirds are threatened with extinction, primarily because of forest loss. One of the highest primate conservation priorities in Madagascar today is the aye-aye, a bat-eared, bug-eyed nocturnal creature that fills the ecological role of a woodpecker, extracting grubs from decaying wood with its long, crooked middle finger. It was once thought to be on the threshold of extinction, but scientists now believe several thousand aye-aye may remain in widely scattered locations.

Even Madagascar's forests are in better shape than the forest along the coast of southeastern Brazil, where only vestiges remain of a rich biome that once blanketed nearly a million square kilometers. Centuries of colonization and agriculture have reduced Brazil's unique Atlantic forest to little more than a few tattered patches; only 1 to 5 percent of the original forest still stands. Collectively, the Atlantic forest monkeys form the world's most endangered primate assemblage: 11 of the forest's 12 endemic species are right on the edge of extinction. For example, the 12- to 15-kilogram muriqui, the largest of all New World primates, has an estimated population of only around 500. The Atlantic forest is also home to the tiny lion tamarins, four closely related species whose striking manes and buoyant mannerisms seem so incongruous in the face of their dwindling numbers; their populations range from 250 to 2,500.

But lemurs, tamarins, and other endemics are not the only primates threatened by habitat loss. Even the generally more adaptable widespread species are suffering. The red colobus monkey, for example, is distributed across the entire equatorial waist of Africa, from Senegal to eastern Kenya. Yet according to the IUCN's Primate Specialist Group, it is declining everywhere, and nine of its 14 recognized subspecies are threatened with extinction. One of the most endangered subspecies occurs only along the lower Tana River in eastern Kenya, where a large-scale hydroelectric project financed by international aid agencies is threatening the riverine forests upon which the colobus depends.

In Japan, the macaques find themselves in a similar plight. These monkeys are at home in both the warm temperate forests of southern Japan and the snow-bound northern mountains, where some troops are famous for congregating in natural hot springs to ward off the winter cold. In recent decades, however, Japanese macaques have steadily lost habitat to urban development, agricultural expansion, and the spread of monoculture Japanese cedar plantations. Deprived of natural food supplies, the macaques have turned to raiding orchards and fields, earning the wrath of local farmers. Of the roughly 50,000 macaques remaining in Japan, about 5,000 are captured or killed each year in what some researchers have called a "civil war" between wild monkeys desperate for food and farmers determined to protect their produce. Japan has a land area smaller than California's, but its population (126 million) is more than four times as large. Unless the country forges a stronger consensus on the need to restore its native forests, the math doesn't look good for the macaques.

THE HUNTED

Even where primates still find ample habitat, they often face heavy hunting pressure—a serious threat to at least one in every three threatened species. Primates are usually hunted for the cooking pot: we are the primate clan's leading predator and, except for chimpanzees, the only primate that routinely hunts other primates for food. While some cultures have a long history of subsistence hunting, the expansion of many rural populations is radically increasing the ecological pressures that the hunting creates. Ecologist Carlos Peres has documented how over a one-and-a-half year period, a single family of Brazilian rubbertappers in rural Amazonia killed 380 large primates—wooly monkeys, spider monkeys, and howler monkeys. With that kind of hunting effort, it doesn't take all that many people to empty a forest.

And it's not just the number of hunters that is increasing; the growing use of guns is increasing the efficiency of the hunting as well. Even in remote regions, hunters who once relied upon nets, snares, and blowguns now have access to powerful shotguns, which are often introduced by traders, miners, or loggers. Scientists have combined field data like that collected by Carlos Peres, with computer models to show that the introduction of shotguns into a community can lead to local extinctions of the larger, more slowly reproducing primates in only 20 to 30 years.

But subsistence hunting is overshadowed in many areas by unregulated commercial hunting. In much of central Africa, a deadly synergism between market hunters and the trade in tropical hardwoods is pushing primate and other wildlife populations into rapid decline. Selective logging practices are not themselves a major problem for most primates. They may even benefit certain species like gorillas, which prefer foods found in secondary forest patches. Logging *roads*, however, are a different story. By providing access to formerly isolated forests, the roads offer a short-term bonanza for hunters who pursue wild game to supply the growing trade in "bush meat." The numbers of primates, antelope, forest hogs, civets (a cat-like animal), and other creatures killed for bush meat in central Africa are staggering. In Gabon, a country of about 1.2 million people, some 8 million pounds of bushmeat are consumed annually, half of it in urban areas. Primates are a large component of this total—in neighboring Equatorial Guinea they constitute up to 25 percent of the bushmeat marketed. In many areas, the trade in bushmeat is now the main source of income for rural residents.

The complicity of logging operations in the bushmeat trade is blatant and widespread. In one study in the Republic of Congo (not the former Zaire, but the country to the west of it), researchers found that logging company employees supplemented their income by supplying local hunters with weapons, ammunition, and transport in exchange for a share of the meat. According to some experts, bushmeat hunting in central Africa may even outrank habitat loss as a threat to primates and many other forest animals.

Overhunting damages more than just the primate populations themselves. Hunters tend to target the big primates—and big primates usually have big ecological roles. The collapse of their populations may trigger a cascade of ecological effects throughout an entire natural community. In the American tropics, for instance, spider and wooly monkeys consume large quantities of wild fruit while foraging over wide areas of forest. Many tree species rely heavily on these monkeys to disperse their seeds. When the monkeys are hunted out of a forest, some types of trees may not be able to "sow" their seeds properly. If no more seeds land in suitable sites, then the next generation of those tree species is in trouble—and so is the next generation of the birds, mammals, insects, fungi, and various other creatures that the trees support.

Some trees may depend entirely on this dispersal mechanism for survival. In central Africa, for instance, lowland gorillas feed on the fruits of the moabi tree. (So do the people, and other parts of the tree are valuable too: the seed oil is used for cooking, the bark for medicine, and the lustrous wood for furniture.) Moabi seeds are huge—as are the seeds of certain other central African trees. But Melissa Remis, an anthropologist who has studied the gorilla, says the gorilla's guts can accommodate seeds up to 12 centimeters long. "If it weren't for them and for elephants," she says, "trees like moabi might not exist."

Some hunters are pursuing primates not for bush meat, but for the pet trade. Most nations have enacted laws to restrict or ban the trade in wild primates, and most countries that have wild primate populations are party to the Convention on International Trade in Endangered Species of Flora and Fauna (CITES), which essentially bans international trade in endangered species. But the regulations are unevenly enforced, and illegal trade continues within and between many countries, especially in Asia. As recently as 1995, vendors in the Pramuka market in Jakarta, Indonesia were offering dozens of live primates for sale, and a researcher visiting the market was told that live orangutans could be purchased nearby. Orangutans and the other apes—gibbons, chimps, and gorillas—are especially charismatic; they are so much like us that there is a virtually insatiable demand for them. Wild-caught infant apes are continually being sought by unscrupulous carnivals, by restaurants and bars to entertain their customers, and by people who just think they would make great pets.

One of the most egregious episodes of ape-smuggling occurred in Taiwan during the late 1980s, when a popular

Taiwanese television show featured a live orangutan as a main character. The show led many viewers to want young orang-utans as pets, and ape smugglers, with little to fear from Taiwan's poorly enforced wildlife protection laws, were happy to oblige. As many as 1,000 orangutans may have illegally entered the country, and were subsequently sold through newspaper advertisements. That's the equivalent of 3 to 5 percent of the entire wild orangutan population. But the full toll was certainly far higher, since the capture of an infant pri-mate invariably involves killing its mother, and many captured infants would have died in transit. By the early 1990s, accord-ing to a recent World Wide Fund for Nature report, "the cap-ital of Taiwan, Taipei, was reputed to have more orangutans per square kilometer than the species' natural habitat." Most of these orangutans have since been abandoned by their own-ers because they have matured and become unmanageable. The twice-orphaned orangs are probably destined to spend the rest of their lives in facilities designed to care for apes in this predicament. They have not learned the skills necessary for life in the wild and many now carry human diseases, so it is unlikely that they could ever be returned to their forest homeland.

PROTECT THE MONKEY AND YOU PROTECT THE FOREST

There are a few bright spots in our relationship with our fel-low primates. Biomedical research, for example, has made a great deal of progress in reducing its impact on wild primates. Each year, some 40,000 monkeys and apes are used in this kind of research; we owe a great debt to these laboratory pri-mates, since many important medical studies would have been simply impossible without them. The South American owl monkey, for instance, has been one of the most valuable animal models for malaria research. And because the owl monkey has such large eyes—it's one of the world's few fully nocturnal primates—it has also been important for research on eye diseases such as glaucoma.

Most biomedical research is done in the industrialized countries, and the labs have long been fed by an extensive international trade in wild-caught primates. (The United States, Britain, and Japan are the leading primate importers and virtually all of their imports are now for research.) The biomedical trade in wild primates reached its peak during the 1950s and 1960s, when it swallowed up hundreds of thousands of animals. The total for chimpanzees alone is believed to be somewhere between 40,000 and 90,000, from the late 1960s to the late 1980s. By way of comparison, the total wild chimp population is presently thought to be 200,000 at most, and possibly only half that.

But beginning with Latin American nations in the 1970s, most primate-source countries have clamped down on the export of wild-caught primates, and researchers have turned increasingly to captive-bred animals. The establishment of CITES in 1973 also helped slow the trade; the number of monkeys imported into the United States, for instance, declined from 113,714 in 1968 to 13,148 in 1983. By the early 1990s, between 50 and 80 percent of the remaining trade was being supplied by only two countries, Indonesia and the Philippines. In 1994, these countries also banned exports. That leaves only a handful of countries, such as Guyana, still exporting wild-caught primates.

Another form of progress involves primates' cultural importance. In some cases, we may be able to forge a healthier relationship with our closest relatives by looking anew at traditional attitudes in cultures that developed alongside primates. In some societies, primates are granted sacred status or considered taboo to hunt or eat. In such cultures, the idea of primate bush meat would be just about as appalling as cannibalism. Throughout south and east Asia, for example, temples and sacred forest groves provide refuge for langurs and macaques, who are viewed as living emblems of the resident gods or spirits. In Africa, some villages protect pygmy chimpanzees (also called "bonobos") and refuse to hunt them, holding them to be too much like humans. Villagers in parts of Java maintain a taboo against hunting gibbons for the same reason. And in Madagascar, there are taboos against hunting certain species of lemur.

Sacred status alone, however, may not always be enough to guarantee a species' survival. In India, hanuman langurs are revered by devout Hindus—indeed, the species takes its name from the Hindu monkey god Hanuman, dedicated servant of the mythical King Rama. The langurs are the most common monkeys in India, and in many towns their presence has not simply been tolerated—it has been encouraged. Yet increasingly intensive land use is gradually squeezing the langurs out of the forests, fallow lands, and other habitats they need. And the langurs' popularity often fades quickly when they turn to raiding crops after losing their wild food sources. Despite their sacred status, India's hanuman langurs are in long-term decline. Without effective habitat conservation, even highly esteemed species like the langurs will be gradually reduced to a collection of isolated populations on temple grounds and little patches of forest. Without room to forage, they will have to rely on people for food; essentially they will become zoo animals.

But it doesn't have to turn out that way. In a sense, primates can be their own best friends when it comes to conserving their habitat. Conservationists have found that primates make excellent "flagship" species for ecosystems. They can be used to attract public attention and generate support for natural areas protection—all of the less conspicuous plants and animals in the community can benefit from their charisma as well. In Brazil, for instance, endangered primates have helped catalyze efforts to save the few remaining areas of Atlantic rainforest. Brazilian scientists' efforts to conserve the golden lion tamarin—a project now nearly three decades old—is one of the longest-running primate conservation programs in the world. It's also one of the most successful, since most remaining areas of healthy forest within the species' range now contain resident lion tamarins. And since more tamarin habitat is needed, the monkey is now being used to focus public attention on the importance of restoration ecology.

INCLUDING PRIMATES IN
THE SOCIAL CONTRACT

It would be easy to typecast poor rural people as the villains in the tragedy of primate loss, because of their role in overhunting and converting habitat. But there is growing evidence that the same people, given the right conditions, can make effective primate conservationists. In the Central American nation of Belize, for instance, a town called Bermudian Landing has mobilized to protect native black howler monkeys. Following discussions with researchers studying the monkeys during the mid-1980s, about a dozen community members—mostly poor farmers—donated small areas of land bordering a nearby river as a reserve for the howlers. Eventually, nearly a hundred other landowners followed their lead, and the sanctuary expanded. The howlers make for good neighbors because they feed mostly on leaves and do not bother the farmers' crops. The reserve has also produced economic benefits for the community, since tourists and Belizean schoolchildren now visit to view the monkeys. The reserve's howler population has grown from 800 to 2,400—enough to allow some monkeys to be moved to other parts of the country, where the species had disappeared.

Community-oriented primate conservation is also keeping hopes alive for primates in far more difficult conditions. The rarest of all great apes are Africa's famed mountain gorillas, which live high on the cloud-forest slopes of the Virunga volcanoes, an area shared by Rwanda, Uganda, and the Democratic Republic of Congo (the former Zaire). Between 1960 and 1981 the Virunga gorilla population declined steadily from 450 to a mere 250, but at that point the tide began to turn. International conservation organizations joined forces with the Rwandan government to launch the Mountain Gorilla Conservation Project. A public education program helped Rwandans understand the uniqueness of gorillas and the value of their forest habitat for water catchment. Certain groups of gorillas were habituated to the presence of humans, and gorilla ecotourism soon began earning Rwanda as much as $10 million annually. In addition, well-trained and equipped Rwandan park guards began effective anti-poaching patrols. By the late 1980s the Virunga population had rebounded to nearly 320. Just as important, says the eminent zoologist George Schaller, is the fact that "the people of Rwanda became proud of their apes. The gorillas became part of Rwanda's identity in the world, a part of the nation's vision of itself."

Rwandans' social pact with their gorillas seems to have weathered even the recent civil war. Tutsi rebels commandeered the gorillas' habitat in 1991. By the time full-scale war erupted in 1994, all expatriate conservationists had been evacuated, and military forces were operating throughout the gorillas' mountain home. Yet despite the horrific human violence, Rwanda's gorillas emerged virtually unscathed. Only two are known to have died in Rwanda as a result of the fighting. The first, a silverback male named Mrithi, was shot in 1992 by soldiers who mistook him for the enemy. The second, a male named Mkono, was killed by a land mine in 1994.

What kept gorilla deaths to a minimum was the remarkable dedication and concern of many Rwandans for the gorillas' welfare throughout those terrible days. Even though they had pledged to topple the Hutu regime, rebel leaders promised to honor the anti-poaching laws. Park guards continued to patrol without pay, risking their lives to continue monitoring the gorillas. After the war, as park administrators and researchers gradually returned to find their offices ransacked and looted, they pledged to rebuild and continue their conservation work.

Nsengiyumva Barakabuye, one of those officials, put it this way: "Gorillas are our only renewable resource. Some have said, 'Give the park to returning refugees!' But we will never do that. The gorillas are too valuable."

Although the courage of the Rwandan park staff speaks volumes about what conservation can accomplish, time is running out for many primates and even the mountain gorilla is far from secure. At the same time they were weathering the chaos in Rwanda, the gorillas were falling to poachers' spears and snares just across the border in Uganda and what was then Zaire, where eight gorillas died during a seven-month period in 1995. Last May, four more were reported killed there, when they were caught in a crossfire between the army of Laurent Kabila, who became the country's new president, and an expatriate force of dissident Rwandan Hutus.

MAKING A GLOBAL COMMITMENT

The Mountain Gorilla Conservation Project shows how much can be achieved under even the grimmest conditions. But as with other types of environmental work, primate conservation efforts will have to be scaled up drastically if we are to turn the global trends around. Fortunately, we already have an agenda to point us forward. The IUCN's Primate Specialist Group and other organizations have compiled a set of Conservation Action Plans that identify the priorities. The first challenge is to better manage existing protected areas that shelter primates—to turn "paper parks" into on-the-ground realities. That will mean giving rangers, naturalist guides, and other park personnel the training and resources they need to do their jobs; it will also mean finding ways to let the parks benefit the people who live around—and sometimes within—park boundaries. In some cases, park systems may need to be expanded to cover habitats or species that are not yet protected, such as Vietnam's Tonkin snub-nosed monkey.

To function effectively, the parks will need to be carefully integrated into both the landscapes and the societies in which they are situated. Many studies have also shown that over the long term, parks cannot be managed successfully as isolated units in a sea of intensively modified landscape. Instead, natural areas need to be organized into regional networks that allow for large-scale ecological processes, such as migrations and range shifts in response to environmental change. And ultimately, if we are to give other primates the space they need, we will have to use less space ourselves—or at least, use it less intensively. Either way, the long term success of the parks will depend on our success in stabilizing our own population. We can no longer afford to think of natural areas conservation and family planning as separate issues.

Other social challenges include the need to expand environmental education efforts, like Rwanda's, which emphasize the values of both the primates themselves and their habitats. A related challenge is to increase the economic benefits that living wild primates bring to local residents, through such means as carefully designed ecotourism programs. Finally, conservation will also require additional field research on primates—particularly by scientists from the primates' home countries—to provide a more solid basis for field management and policy decisions.

To be sure, this is an ambitious agenda, but the price tag may still be fairly modest, in comparison with other types of development projects. For example, the IUCN Lemur Specialist Group has estimated that all conservation activities recommended for Madagascar's primates between 1993 and 1999 would cost just over $7 million, or about $1.2 million per year. This sum is puny by the standards of the major lending agencies—World Bank projects, for example, typically run in the tens of millions at a minimum. Yet lemur conservation would yield enormous benefits, since it would help insure the health of entire ecosystems. Even so, the cost is still too great a burden for a lower-income country like Madagascar to shoulder alone. Primate conservation must remain a global cause, one that will continue to require the support of wealthy societies like the United States, Japan, and the members of the European Community.

In the end, the struggle to save primates is no different from the struggle to conserve any other aspect of the planet's biological wealth. But what primates do better than other kinds of wildlife is to capture and return our gaze in kind, communicating the past, present, and future bonds we share with all life on earth. George Schaller, renowned for his many studies of large mammals (including gorillas), explains that this bond is not purely a matter of science. "No one who looks into a gorilla's eyes—intelligent, gentle, vulnerable—can remain unchanged," he writes, "for the gap between ape and human vanishes; we know that the gorilla still lives within us." We humans, the most adaptable of primates, might be able to survive in a world with no room for our closest relatives, but we would find it a far poorer and lonelier place.

NATURE'S "FREE" SERVICES

By Janet N. Abramovitz

During the last half of 1997, massive fires swept through the forests of Sumatra, Borneo, and Irian Jaya, which together form a stretch of the Indonesian archipelago as wide as all of Europe. By November, almost 2 million hectares had burned, leaving the region shrouded in haze and more than 20 million of its people breathing hazardous air. Tens of thousands of people had been treated for respiratory ailments. Hundreds had died from illness, accidents and starvation. The fires, though by then out of control, had been set deliberately and systematically—not by small farmers, and not by El Niño, but by commercial outfits operating with implicit government approval. Strange as this immolation of some of the world's most valuable natural assets may seem, it was not unique. The same year, a large part of the Amazon Basin in Brazil was blanketed by smoke for similar reasons. The fires in the Amazon have been set annually, but in 1997 they destroyed 28 percent more forest than the year before, which in turn had recorded five times as many fires (some 19,115 fires during a single six-week period) as in 1995.

For the timber and plantation barons of Indonesia, as for the cattle ranchers and frontier farmers of Amazonia, setting fires to clear forests has become standard practice. To them, the natural rainforests are an obstruction that must be sold or burned to make way for their profitable pulp and palm oil plantations. Yet, these are the same forests that for many others serve as both homes and livelihoods. For the hundreds of millions who live in Indonesia and in the neighboring nations of Malaysia, Singapore, Brunei, southern Thailand and the Philippines, it became painfully apparent that without healthy forests, it is difficult to remain healthy people.

The fires in Southeast Asia generated enough smoke to be visible from space for many months. Some relief came with the arrival of the seasonal rains, but those rains were later and lighter than normal—in part because of an unusually strong El Niño effect. Along with the trees, the region's large underground peat deposits caught on fire, and such fires are perniciously difficult to put out; they can continue smoldering for years.

When the smoke finally cleared, Southeast Asia—and the world—attempted to tally the costs. There were the costs of impaired health and sometimes death, from both lung diseases and accidents caused by poor visibility. There was the productivity that was lost as factories, schools, roads, docks, and airports were shut down (over 1,000 flights in and out of Malaysia were cancelled in September alone); there were the crop yields that fell as haze kept the region in day-long twilight, and the harvests of forest products that were wiped out. Timber (some of the most valuable species in the world) and wildlife (some of the most endangered in the world) were consumed by flames. Over three-fourths of the world's remaining wild orang-utans live inn the fire-ravaged provinces of Sumatra and Kalimantan. Some of them, caught fleeing the flames, became part of the illegal trade. Because of their location, the Indonesian fires, like those in the Amazon, dealt a heavy blow to the biodiversity of the earth as a whole.

As the smoke billowed dramatically from Southeast Asia, a much less visible—but similarly costly—ecological loss was taking place in a very different kind of location. While the Indonesian haze was being photographed from satellites, this other loss might not be noticed by a person standing within an arm's length of the evidence—yet, in its implications for the human future, it is a close cousin of the Asian catastrophe. In the United States, more than 50 percent of all honeybee colonies have disappeared in the last 50 years, with half of that loss occurring in just the last 5 years. Similar losses have been observed in Europe. Thirteen of the 19 native bumble-bee species in the United Kingdom are now extinct. These bees are just two of the many kinds of pollinators, and their decline is costing farmers, fruit growers, and beekeepers hundreds of millions of dollars in losses each year.

What the ravaged Indonesian forests and disappearing bees have in common is that they are both examples of "free services" that are provided by nature and consumed by the human economy—services that have immense economic value, but that go largely unrecognized and uncounted until they have been lost. Many of those services are indispensable to the people who exploit them, yet are not counted as real benefits, or as a part of GNP.

Though widely taken for granted, the "free" services provided by the natural world form the invisible foundation that supports all societies and economies. We rely on the oceans to provide abundant fish, on forests for wood and new medicines, on insects and other creatures to pollinate our crops, on birds and frogs to keep pests in check, and on forests and rivers to supply clean water. We take it for granted that when we need timber we can cut trees, or that when we need water we can find a spring or drill a well. We assume that clean air will blow the smog out of our cities, that the climate will be stable and predictable, and that the mounting quantity of waste we generate will continue to disappear, if we can just get it out of sight. Nature's services have always been there, free for the taking, and our expectations—and economies— are based on the premise that they always will be. A timber magnate or farmer may have to pay a price for the land, but assumes that what happens naturally on the land—the growing of trees, or pollinating of crops by wild bees, or filtering of fresh water—usually happens for free. We are like young children who think that food comes from the refrigerator, and who do not yet understand that what now seems free is not.

Ironically, by undervaluing natural services, economies unwittingly provide incentives to misuse and destroy the very systems that produce those services; rather than protecting their assets, they squander them. Nature, in turn becomes increasingly less able to supply the prolific range services that the earth's expanding population and economy demand. It is no exaggeration to suggest that the continued erosion of natural systems threatens not only the continuing viability of today's human enterprise, but ultimately the prospects for our continued existence.

Underpinning the steady stream of services nature provides to us, there is a more fundamental service these systems provide—a kind of self-regulating process by which ecosystems and the biosphere are kept relatively stable and resilient. The ability to withstand disturbances like fires, floods, diseases, and droughts, and to rebound from the shocks these events inflict, is essential to keeping the life-support system operating. As systems are simplified by monoculture or cut up by roads, and the webs that link systems become disconnected, they become more brittle and vulnerable to catastrophic, irreversible decline. We are being confronted by ample evidence, now—from the breakdown of the ozone layer to the increasingly severity of fires, floods and droughts, to the diminished productivity of fruit and seed sets in wild and agricultural plants—that the biosphere is becoming less resilient.

Unfortunately, much of the human economy is based on practices that convert natural systems into something simpler, either for ease of management (it's easier to harvest straight rows of trees that are all the same age than to harvest carefully from complex forests) or to maximize the production of a desired commodity (like corn). But simplified systems lack the resilience that allows them to survive short-term shocks such as outbreaks of diseases or pests, or forest fires, or even longer-term stresses such as that of global warming. One reason is that the conditions within these simplified systems are not hospitable to all of the numerous organisms and processes needed to keep such systems running. A tree plantation or fish farm may provide some of the products we need, but it cannot supply the array of services that natural diverse systems do—and must do—in order to survive over a range of conditions. To keep our own economies sustainable, then, we need to use natural systems in ways that capitalize on, rather than destroy, their regenerative capacity. For humans to be healthy and resilient, nature must be too.

Resiliency is destroyed by fragmentation, as well as by simplification. Fires in healthy rainforests are very rare. By nature, they are too wet to burn. But as they are opened up and fragmented by roads and logging and pasture, they become drier and more prone to fire. When fire strikes forests that are not adapted to fire (as is the case in the rainforests of both Brazil and Indonesia), it is exceptionally destructive and tends to kill a majority of the trees. The fires in Southeast Asia's peat swamp rainforests bring further disruption, by releasing long-sequestered carbon into the atmosphere.

The fires in Indonesia were not started by poor slash-and-burn peasants, but by "slash-and-burn industrialists"—owners of rubber, palm oil, rice, and timber plantations who took advantage of a dry year to clear as much natural forest as they could. Though it issued a law forbidding the burning, the government of Indonesia is in fact pushing for higher production levels from these export sectors. In both the rainforests and the peat swamps, it gave the plantation owners large concessions to encourage continued "conversion" to one-crop commodities. And the government continues to push costly agricultural settlements into peat forests ill-suited to rice. After the fires became a serious regional problem (and international embarrassment), the government revoked the permits of 29 companies, but such actions were too little, too late.

The fires in 1997–1998 are not the first to ravage parts of Southeast Asia; extensive logging in Indonesia and Malaysia led to a major conflagration in 1983 that burned over 3 million hectares and wiped out $5 billion worth of standing timber in Indonesia alone. After 1983, fires that had once been rare became a common occurrence. The 1997–1998 fires will likely turn out to have been the most costly yet, with estimated losses of some $20 billion. Unless policies change, the fires will be reignited each year.

WHAT FORESTS DO

Around the world, the degradation, fragmentation, and simplification—or "conversion"—of ecosystems is progressing rapidly. Today, only 1 to 5 percent of the original forest cover of the United States and Europe remains. One-third of Asia's forest has been lost since 1960, and half of what remains is threatened by the same industrial forest activities responsible for the Indonesian fires. In the Amazon, 13 percent of the natural cover has already been cleared, mostly for cattle pasture. In many countries, including some of the largest, more than half of the land has been converted from natural habitat to other uses that are less resilient. In countries that stayed relatively undisturbed until the 1980s, significant portions of remaining ecosystems have been lost in the last decade. These trends have been accelerating everywhere. As the natural ecosystems disappear, so do many of the goods and services they provide.

That may seem to contradict the premise that people want those goods and services and would not deliberately destroy them. But there's a logical explanation: governments and business owners typically perceive that the way they can make the most profit from an ecosystem is to maximize its production of a single commodity, such as timber from a forest. For the community (or society) as a whole, however, that is often the least profitable or sustainable use. The economic values of other uses, and the number of people who benefit, added up, can be enormous. A forest, if not cut down to make space for a one-commodity plantation, can produce a rich variety of nontimber forest products (NTFPs) on one hand, while providing essential watershed protection and climate regulation, on the other. These uses not only have more immediate economic value but can also be sustained over a longer term and benefit more people.

In 1992, alternative management strategies were reviewed for the mangrove forests of Bintuni Bay in Indonesia. When nontimber uses such as fish, locally used products, and erosion control were included in the calculations, the researchers found that the most economically profitable strategy was to keep the forest standing with only a modest amount of timber cutting—yielding $4,800 per hectare. If the forest was managed only for timber-cutting, it would yield only $3,600 per hectare. Over the longer term, it was calculated that keeping the forest intact would ensure continued local uses of the area worth $10 million a year (providing 70 percent of local income) and protect fisheries worth $25 million a year—values that would be lost if the forest were cut.

The variety and value of goods produced and collected from forests, and their importance to local livelihoods and national economies, is an economic reality worldwide. For instance, rattan—a vine that grows naturally in tropical forests—is widely used to make furniture. Global trade in rattan is worth $2.7 billion in exports each year, and in Asia it employs a half-million people. In Thailand, the value of rattan exports is equal to 80 percent of the legal timber exports. In India, such "minor" products account for three fourths of the net export earnings from forest produce, and provide more than half of the formal employment in the forestry sector. And in Indonesia, hundreds of thousands of people make their livelihoods collecting and processing NTFPs for export, a trade worth at least $25 million a year. Many of these forests were destroyed in the fire.

Even so, non-timber commodities are only part of what is lost when a forest is converted to a one-commodity industry. There is a nexus between the two catastrophes of the Indonesian fires and the North American and European bee declines, for example, since forests provide habitat for bees and other pollinators. They also provide habitat for birds that control disease-carrying and agricultural pests. Their canopies break the force of the winds and reduce rainfall's impact on the ground, which lessens soil erosion. Their roots hold soil in place, further stemming erosion. In purely monetary terms, a forest's capacity to protect a watershed alone can exceed the value of its timber. Forests also act as effective water-pumping and recycling machinery, helping to stabilize local climate. And, through photosynthesis, they generate enough of the planet's oxygen, while absorbing and storing so much of its carbon (in living trees and plants), that they are essential to the stability of climate worldwide.

Beyond these general functions, there are services that are specific to particular kinds of forests. Mangrove forests and coastal wetlands, notably, play critical roles in linking land and sea. They buffer coasts from storms and erosion, cycle nutrients, serve as nurseries for coastal and marine fisheries, and supply critical resources to local communities. For flood control alone, the value of mangroves has been calculated at $300,000 per kilometer of coastline in Malaysia—the cost of the rock walls that would be needed to replace them. Protecting coasts from storms will be especially important as climate change makes storms more violent and unpredictable. One force driving the accelerated loss of these mangroves in the last two decades has been the explosive growth of intensive commercial aquaculture, especially for shrimp export. Another has been the excess diversion of inland rivers and streams, which reduces downstream flow and allows the coastal waters to become too salty to support the coastal forests.

The planet's water moves in a continuous cycle, falling as precipitation and moving slowly across the landscape to streams and rivers and ultimately to the sea, being absorbed and recycled by plants along the way. Yet, human actions have changed even that most fundamental force of nature by removing natural plant cover, draining swamps and wetlands, separating rivers from their floodplains, and paving over land. The slow natural movement of water across the landscape is also vital for refilling nature's underground reservoirs, or aquifers, from which we draw much of our water. In many places, water now races across the landscape much too quickly, causing flooding and droughts, while failing to adequately recharge aquifers.

The value of a forested watershed comes from its capacity to absorb and cleanse water, recycle excess nutrients, hold soil in place, and prevent flooding. When plant cover is removed or disturbed, water and wind not only race across the land, but carry valuable topsoil with them. According to David Pimentel, an agricultural ecologist at Cornell University, exposed soil is eroded at several thousand times the natural rate. Under normal conditions, each hectare of land loses somewhere between 0.004 and 0.05 tons of soil to erosion each year—far less than what is replaced by natural soil building processes. On lands that have been logged or converted to crops and grazing, however, erosion typically takes away 17 tons in a year in the United States or Europe, and 30 to 40 tons in Asia, Africa, or South America. On severely degraded land, the hemorrhage can rise to 100 tons in a year. The eroded soil carries nutrients, sediments, and chemicals valuable to the system it leaves, but often harmful to the ultimate destination.

One way to estimate the economic value of an ostensibly free service like that of a forested watershed is to estimate what it would cost society if that service had to be replaced. New York City, for example, has always relied on the natural filtering capacity of its rural watersheds to cleanse the water that serves 10 million people each day. In 1996, experts estimated that it would cost $7 billion to build water treatment facilities adequate to meet the city's future needs. Instead, the city chose a strategy that will cost it only one-tenth that amount: simply helping upstream counties to protect the watersheds around its drinking water reservoirs.

Even an estimate like that tends to greatly understate the real value, however, because it covers the replacement cost of only one of the many services the ecosystem provides. A watershed, for example, also contributes to the regulation of the local climate. After forest cover is removed, an area can become hotter and drier, because water is no longer cycled and recycled by plants (it has been estimated that a single rainforest tree pumps 2.5 million gallons of water into the atmosphere during its lifetime.) Ancient Greece and turn-of-the-century Ethiopia, for example, were moister, wooded regions before extensive deforestation, cultivation, and the soil erosion that followed transformed them into the hot, rocky countries they are today. The global spread of desertification offers brutal evidence of the toll of lost ecosystem services.

The cumulative effects of local land use changes have global implications. One of the planet's first ecosystem services was the production of oxygen over billions of years of photosynthetic activity, which allowed oxygen-breathing organisms—such as ourselves—to evolve. Humans have begun to unbalance the global climate regulation system, however, by generating too much carbon dioxide and reducing the capacity of ecosystems to absorb it. Burning forests and peat deposits only makes the problem worse. The 1997–1998 fires in Asia sent about as much carbon into the atmosphere as did all of the factories, power plants, and vehicles in Western Europe. For carbon sequestration alone, economists have been able to estimate the value of intact forests at anywhere from several hundred to several thousand dollars per hectare. As the climate changes the value of being able to regulate local and global climates will only increase.

WHAT BEES DO

If we are often blind to the value of the free products we take from nature, it is even easier to overlook the value of those products we don't harvest directly—but without which our economies could not function. Among these less conspicuous assets are the innumerable creatures that keep potentially harmful organisms in check, build and maintain soils, and decompose dead matter so it can used to build new life, as well as those that pollinate crops. These various birds, insects, worms, and microorganisms demonstrate that small things can have hugely disproportionate value. Unfortunately, their services are in increasingly short supply because pesticides, pollutants, disease, hunting, and habitat fragmentation or destruction have drastically reduced their numbers and ability to function. As Stephen Buchmann and Gary Paul Nabhan put it in a recent book, *The Forgotten Pollinators*, "nature's most productive workers [are] slowly being put out of business."

Pollinators, for example, are of enormous value to agriculture and the functioning of natural ecosystems. Without them, plants cannot produce the seeds that ensure their survival—and ours. Unlike animals, plants cannot roam around looking for mates. To accomplish sexual reproduction and ensure genetic mixing, plants have evolved strategies for moving genetic material from one plant to the next, sometimes over great distances. Some rely on wind or water to carry pollen to a receptive female, and some can self-pollinate. The most highly evolved are those that use flowers, scents, oils, pollens, and nectars to attract and reward animals to do the job. In fact, more than 90 percent of the world's quarter-million flowering plant species are animal-pollinated. When animals pick up the flower's reward, they also pick up its pollen on various body parts—faces, legs, torsos. Laden with sticky yellow cargo, they can appear comical as they veer through the air—but their evolutionary adaptations are uncannily potent.

Developing a mutually beneficial relationship with a pollinator is a highly effective way for a plant to ensure reproductive success, especially when individuals are isolated from each other. Spending energy producing nectars and extra pollen is a small price to pay to guarantee reproduction. Performing this matchmaking service are between 120,000 and 200,000 animal species, including bees, beetles, butterflies, moths, ants, and flies, along with more than 1,000 species of vertebrates such as birds, bats, possums, lemurs, and even geckos. New evidence shows that many more of these pollinator species than previously believed are threatened with extinction.

Eighty percent of the world's 1,330 cultivated crop species (including fruits, vegetables, beans and legumes, coffee and tea, cocoa, and spices) are pollinated by wild and semi-wild pollinators. One-third of U.S. agricultural output is from insect-pollinated plants (the remainder is from wind-pollinated grain plants such as wheat, rice, and corn). In dollars, honeybee pollination services are 60 to 100 times more valuable than the honey they produce. The value of wild blueberry bees is so great, with each bee pollinating 15 to 19 liters (about 40 pints) of blueberries in its life, that they are viewed by farmers as "flying $50 bills."

Without pollinator services, crops would yield less, and wild plants would produce few seeds—with large economic and ecological consequences. In Europe, the contribution of honey bee pollination to agriculture was estimated to be worth $100 billion in 1989. In the Piedmont region of Italy, poor pollination of apple and apricot orchards cost growers $124 million in 1996. The most pervasive threats to pollinators include habitat fragmentation and disturbance, loss of nesting and over-wintering sites, intense exposure of pollinators to pesticides and of nectar plants to herbicides, breakdown of "nectar corridors" that provide food sources to pollinators during migration, new diseases, competition from exotic species, and excessive hunting. The rapid spread of two parasitic mites in the United States and Europe has wiped out substantial numbers of honeybee colonies. A "forgotten pollinators" campaign was recently launched by the Arizona Sonoran Desert Museum and others, to raise awareness of the importance and plight of these service providers.

Ironically, many modern agricultural practices actually limit the productivity of crops by reducing pollination. According to one estimate, for example, the high levels of pesticides used on cotton reduce annual yields by 20 percent (worth $400 million) in the United States alone by killing bees and other insect pollinators. One-fifth of all honeybee losses involve pesticide exposure, and honeybee poisonings may cost agriculture hundreds of millions of dollars each year. Wild pollinators are particularly vulnerable to chemical poisoning because their colonies cannot be picked up and moved in advance of spraying the way domesticated hives can. Herbicides can kill the plants that pollinators need to sustain themselves during the "off-season" when they are not at work pollinating crops. Plowing to the edges of fields to maximize planting area can reduce yields by disturbing pollinator nesting sites. Just one hectare of unplowed land, for example, provides nesting habitat for enough wild alkali bees to pollinate 100 hectares of alfalfa.

Domesticated honeybees cannot be expected to fill the gap left when wild pollinators are lost. Of the world's major crops, only 15 percent are pollinated by domesticated and feral honeybees, while at least 80 percent are serviced by wild pollinators. Honeybees do not "fit" every type of flower that needs pollination. And because honeybees visit so many different plant species, they are not very "efficient"—that is, there is no guarantee that the pollen will be carried to a potential mate of the same species and not deposited on a different species.

Many plants have developed interdependencies with particular species of pollinators. In peninsular Malaysia, the bat *Eonycteris spelea* is thought to be the exclusive pollinator of the durian, a large spiny fruit that is highly valued in Southeast Asia. The bats' primary food supply is a coastal mangrove that flowers continuously throughout the year. The bats routinely fly tens of kilometers from their roost sites to the mangrove stands, pollinating durian trees along the way. However, mangrove stands in Malaysia and elsewhere are under siege, as are the inland forests. Without both, the bats are unlikely to survive.

Pollinators that migrate long distances, such as bats, monarch butterflies, and hummingbirds, need to follow routes that offer a reliable supply of nectar-providing plants for the full journey. Today, however, such nectar corridors are being stretched increasingly thin and are breaking. When the travelers cannot rest and "refuel" every day, they may not survive the journey.

The migratory route followed by long-nosed bats from their summer breeding colonies in the desert regions of the U.S. Southwest to winter roosts in central Mexico illustrates the problems faced by many service providers. To fuel trips of up to 150 kilometers a night, these bats rely on the sequential flowering of at least 16 plant species—particularly century plants and columnar cacti. Along much of the migratory route, the nectar corridor is being fragmented. On both U.S. and Mexican rangelands, ranchers are converting native vegetation into exotic pasture grasses for grazing cattle. In the Mexican state of Sonora, an estimated 376,000 hectares have been stripped of nectar source plants. In parts of the Sierra Madre, the bat-pollinators are threatened by competition from human bootleggers, who have been overharvesting century plants to make the alcoholic beverage mescal. And the latest threat comes from dynamiting and burning of bat roosts by Mexican ranchers attempting to eliminate vampire bats that feed on cattle and spread livestock diseases. The World Conservation Union estimates that worldwide, 26 percent of bat species are threatened with extinction.

Many of the disturbances that have harmed pollinators are also hurting creatures that provide other beneficial services, such as biological control of pests and disease. Much of the

wild and semi-wild habitat inhabited by beneficial predators
such as birds has been wiped out. The "pest control services"
that nature provides are incalculable, and do not have the
fundamental flaws of chemical pesticides (which kill beneficial
insects along with the pests and harm people). Individual bat
colonies in Texas can eat 250 tons of insects each night.
Without birds, leaf-eating insects are more abundant and can
slow the growth of trees or damage crops. Biologists Paul and
Anne Ehrlich speculate that without birds, insects would have
become so dominant that humans might never have been
able to achieve the agricultural revolution that set the stage
for the rise of civilization.

It is not too late to provide essential protections to the
providers of such essential services—by using no-till farming
to reduce soil erosion and allow nature's underground economy to flourish, by cutting back on the use of toxic agricultural chemicals, and by protecting migratory routes and nectar corridors to ensure the survival of wild pollinators and
pest control agents.

Buffer areas of native vegetation and trees can have
numerous beneficial effects. They can serve as havens for resident and migratory insects and animals that pollinate crops
and control pests. They can also help to reduce wind erosion,
and to absorb nutrient pollution that leaks from agricultural
fields. Such zones have been eliminated from many agricultural areas that are modernized to accommodate new equipment or larger field sizes. The "sacred groves" in South Asian
and African villages—natural areas intentionally left undevel-
oped—still provide such havens. Where such buffers have
been removed, they can be reestablished; they can be added
not only around farmers' fields, but along highways and river
banks, links between parks, and in people's back yards.

People can also encourage pollinators by providing nesting
sites, such as hollow logs, or by ensuring that pollinators have
the native plants they need during the "off-season" when they
are not working on the agricultural crops. Changing some

prevalent cultural or industrial practices, too, can help. There is the practice, for example, of growing tidy rows of cocoa trees. These may make for a handsome plantation. But midges, the only known pollinator of cultivated cacao (the source of chocolate), prefer an abundance of leaf litter and trees in a more natural array. Plantations that encourage midges can have ten times the yield of those that don't.

Scientists have begun to ratchet up their study of wild pollinators and to domesticate more of them. The bumblebee, for example, was domesticated ten years ago and is now a pollinator of valuable greenhouse grown crops.

THE OTHER SERVICE ECONOMY

Natural services have been so undervalued because, for so long, we have viewed the natural world as an inexhaustible resource and sink. Human impact has been seen as insignificant or beneficial. The tools used to gauge the economic health and progress of a nation have tended to reinforce and encourage these attitudes. The gross domestic product (GDP), for example, supposedly measures the value of the goods and services produced in a nation. But the most valuable goods and services—the ones provided by nature, on which all else rests—are measured poorly or not at all. The unhealthy dynamic is compounded by the fact that activities that pollute or deplete natural capital are counted as contributions to economic wellbeing. As ecologist Norman Myers puts it, "Our tools of economic analysis are far from able to apprehend, let alone comprehend, the entire range of values implicit in forests."

When economies and societies use misleading signals about what is valuable, people are encouraged to make decisions that run counter to their own long-range interests—and those of society and future generations. Economic calculations grossly underestimate the current and future value of nature. While a fraction of nature's goods are counted when they enter the marketplace, many of them are not. And nature's services—the life-support systems—are not counted at all. When the goods are considered free and therefore valued at zero, the market sends signals that they are only economically valuable when converted into something else. For example, the profit from deforesting land is counted as a plus on a nation's ledger sheet, because the trees have been converted to saleable lumber or pulp, but the depletions of the timber stock, watershed, and fisheries are not subtracted.

In 1997, an international team of researchers led by Robert Costanza of the University of Maryland's Institute for Ecological Economics, published a landmark study on the importance of nature's services in supporting human economies. The study provides, for the first time, a quantification of the current economic value of the world's ecosystem services and natural capital. The researchers synthesized the findings of over 100 studies to compute the average per hectare value for each of the 17 services that world's ecosystems provide. They concluded that the current economic value of the world's ecosystem services is in the neighborhood of $33 trillion per year, exceeding the global GNP of $25 trillion.

Placing a monetary value on nature in this way has been criticized by those who believe that it commoditizes and cheapens nature's infinite value. But in practice, we all regularly assign value to nature through the choices we make. The problem is that in normal practice, many of us don't assign such value to nature until it is converted to something manmade—forests to timber, or swimming fish to a restaurant meal. With a zero value, it's easy to see why nature has almost always been the loser in standard economic equations. As the authors of the Costanza study note, "...the decisions we make about ecosystems imply valuations (although not necessarily expressed in monetary terms). We can choose to make these valuations explicit or not...but as long as we are forced to make choices, we are going through the process of valuation."

The study is also raising a powerful new challenge to those traditional economists who are accustomed to keeping environmental costs and benefits "external" to their calculations.

While some skeptics will doubtless argue that the global valuation reported by Costanza and his colleagues overestimates the current value of nature's services, if anything it is actually a very conservative estimate. As the authors point out, values for some biomes (such as mountains, arctic tundra, deserts, urban parks) were not included. Further, they note that as ecosystem services become scarcer, their economic value will only increase.

Clearly, failure to value nature's services is not the only reason why these services are misused. Too often, illogical and inequitable resource use continues—even in the face of evidence that it is ecologically, economically, and socially unsustainable—because powerful interests are able to shape policies by legal or illegal means. Frequently, some individuals or entities get the financial benefits from a resource while the losses are distributed across society. Economists call this "socializing costs." Stated simply, the people who get the benefits are not the ones who pay the costs. Thus, there is little economic incentive for those exploiting a resource to use it judiciously or in a manner that maximizes public good. Where laws are lax or are ignored, and where people do not have an opportunity for meaningful participation in decision-making, such abuses will continue.

The liquidation of 90 percent of the Philippines' forest during the 1970s and 1980s under the Ferdinand Marcos dictatorship, for example, made a few hundred families over $42 billion richer. But 18 million forest dwellers became much poorer. The nation as a whole went from being the world's second largest log exporter to a net importer. Likewise, in Indonesia, the "benefits" from burning the forest enrich a relatively few well-connected individuals and companies but tens of millions of others are bearing the costs. Even in wealthy nations, such as Canada, the forest industry wields heavy influence over how the forests are managed, and for whose benefit.

We have already seen that the loss of ecosystem services can have severe economic, social, and ecological costs even though we can only measure a fraction of them. The loss of timber and lives in the Indonesian fires, and the lower production of fruits and vegetables from inadequate pollination, are but the tip of the iceberg. The other consequences for nature are often unforeseen and unpredictable. The loss of individual species and habitat, and the degradation and simplification of ecosystems, impair nature's ability to provide the services we need. Many of these changes are irreversible, and much of what is lost is simply irreplaceable.

By reducing the number of species and the size and integrity of ecosystems, we are also reducing nature's capacity to evolve and create new life. Almost half of the forests that once covered the Earth are now gone, and much of what remains is in fragmented patches. In just a few centuries we have gone from living off nature's interest to spending down the capital that has accumulated over millions of years of evolution. At the same time we are diminishing the capacity of nature to create new capital. Humans are only one part of the evolutionary product. Yet we have taken on a major role in shaping its future production course and potential. We are pulling out the threads of nature's safety net even as we depend on it to support the world's expanding human population and economy.

In that expanding economy, consumers now need to recognize that it is possible to reduce and reverse the destructive impact of our activities by consuming less and by placing fewer demands on those services we have so mistakenly regarded as free. We can, for example, reduce the high levels of waste and overconsumption of timber and paper. We can also increase the efficiency of water and energy use. In agricultural fields we can leave hedgerows and unplowed areas that serve as nesting and feeding sites for pollinators. We can sharply reduce reliance on agricultural chemicals, and improve the timing of their application to avoid killing pollinators.

Maintaining nature's services requires looking beyond the needs of the present generation, with the goal of ensuring sustainability for many generations to come. We have no honest choice but to act under the assumption that future generations will need at least the same level of nature's services as we have today. We can neither practically nor ethically decide what future generations will need and what they can survive without.

4

Bread and Water

WHERE HAVE ALL THE
RIVERS GONE?

By Sandra Postel

In 1922, American naturalist Aldo Leopold journeyed by canoe through the great delta of the Colorado River. What he reported seeing there was a verdant waterscape, where for millennia the river had been depositing its rich silt and building up a diverse ecosystem before entering the Sea of Cortez—known north of the border as the Gulf of California. He saw deer, quail, raccoon, bobcat, vast fleets of waterfowl, and even the great jaguar, el tigre—"the despot of the Delta." The meandering river, slowing as it spread out through countless green lagoons, led Leopold to muse, "for the last word in procrastination, go travel with a river reluctant to lose his freedom in the sea."

Leopold never returned to the Delta for fear of finding this "milk-and-honey wilderness" badly altered. His fears were justified; today, the Colorado's freedom has been lost to a degree even the prescient Leopold could scarcely have imagined. Except in years of unusually high precipitation, the Colorado River no longer reaches the sea at all—it literally disappears into the surrounding desert. Much of the abundant wildlife is gone. Off the coast to the south, the once-productive fisheries in the Sea of Cortez have declined dramatically. In striking contrast to Leopold's experience, this author experienced the delta as a dessicated place of mud-cracked earth, salt flats, and murky pools.

What has happened to the Colorado is but an extreme example of a disturbing worldwide trend: more and more rivers are running dry as dams and diversions siphon water off for burgeoning cities and thirsty farms. In Arizona, the Salt and Gila rivers used to converge west of Phoenix; but now they dry up east of the city because of extensive diversions for irrigated farms in the region. In California, some 35 kilometers of the San Joaquin River have been so permanently dewatered that thickets of trees have sprung up in the dry riverbed, sand and gravel are mined from it, and developers have even proposed building houses in it. In China, about 50 kilometers south of Beijing, villagers say the Heaven River dried up 20 years ago. And in the water-deprived Middle East, where surface streams are extensively overtapped, the lower stretches of the Jordan River have dwindled to a salty trickle.

It is the arresting decline of the world's larger rivers, however, that most graphically conveys the magnitude of the problem. The Nile, the Ganges, the Amu Dar'ya and Syr Dar'ya, the Huang He (or Yellow River), and the Colorado are each now so dammed, diverted, or overtapped that for parts of the year, little or none of their freshwater reaches the sea. Their collective diminution portends not only worsening water shortages and potential conflicts over scarce supplies, but mounting ecological damage. That damage, in turn—from degraded river deltas and species on the brink of extinction to shrinking inland lakes and disappearing wetlands—places the economies and people who depend on them at growing risk.

Many regions have now fallen into a zero-sum game—in which increasing the water supply to one user means taking it away from another. More water devoted to human activities means serious and potentially irreversible harm to natural support systems. With population and consumption levels rising at record rates in many parts of the world, it is a dilemma with far-reaching consequences—one that calls for a wholly new approach to valuing and managing rivers.

RIVERS AT RISK

Human efforts to control rivers date back thousands of years. The Assyrian Queen Sammu-Ramat, who ruled during the late 9th century B.C. in what is now northern Iraq, is reputed to have had inscribed on her tomb: "I constrained the mighty river to flow according to my will and led its water to fertilize lands that had before been barren and without inhabitants." In Zhengzhou, China, about 700 kilometers southwest of Beijing, stands a statue of the emperor Yu, under whose reign the Chinese people were said to have prospered from the building of dikes and irrigation canals to control the mighty Yellow River.

But it was not until this century that engineering schemes began to alter natural water courses on a massive scale. The construction of dams to store water and diversion canals to transport it to cities and farms has been central to the economic growth of regions wet and dry alike. A controlled supply of water for irrigation became critical to boosting food production as population and consumption grew. Large-scale hydroelectric power fueled urban and industrial expansion. And the taming of flood waters allowed farms and towns to situate on fertile soils and near shipping channels.

Indeed, for a time, river basin "development" became the *sine qua non* of economic advancement. Winston Churchill, noting the Nile's importance to the entire northeast Africa region, after a military campaign on that river in 1908, prophesied that "One day, every last drop of water which drains into the whole valley of the Nile ... shall be equally and amicably divided among the river people, and the Nile itself ... shall perish gloriously and never reach the sea." He was not speaking sardonically. Four years later, a California engineer, Joseph Lippincott, foresaw a similar fate for the Colorado

River: "We have in the Colorado an American Nile awaiting regulation, and it should be treated in as intelligent and vigorous a manner as the British government has treated its great Egyptian prototype."

The construction of the great Hoover Dam on the lower Colorado in the 1930s broke all engineering records up to that time. Some 220 meters high and able to store 1.7 years' worth of the river's average flow, Hoover Dam presaged an engineering frenzy that was to tame many of the world's rivers over the ensuing decades. Around the world, the number of "large" dams (those more than 15 meters high, and backing up months' or years' worth of their rivers' flows) climbed from just over 5,000 in 1950 to about 40,000 today. More than 85 percent of large dams have been built during the last 35 years.

Hoover Dam was also the first of a generation of structures that became known as "superdams"—those more than 150 meters high. Today, there are more than 100 of these megaliths, most of them built during the past four decades. Besides Hoover, they include such giants as the Bhakra Dam in India and the Itaipú in Paraguay, as well as such familiar U.S. dams as Glen Canyon on the Colorado and Grand Coulee on the Columbia.

Worldwide, dams collectively store on the order of 6,000 cubic kilometers of water—equal to 15 percent of the earth's annual renewable water supply. Thousands of kilometers of diversion canals siphon water out of rivers and reservoirs and deliver it where and when needed to expanding cities and farming regions. Globally, water demand has more than tripled since mid-century, and the rising demand has been met by building ever more and larger water supply projects. Many rivers now resemble elaborate plumbing works, with the timing and amount of flow completely controlled by planners and engineers so as to maximize the rivers' benefits to human activity.

But if the intended triumph of such plumbing was to

bring rivers as neatly into the service of human convenience as a bathroom faucet, it hasn't worked out that way. Rivers are central to the planet's ecology; turning them on and off at will damages other parts of the system. And because aquatic organisms cannot live long without water, large reductions in streamflow—even for short periods of time—can be damaging or deadly to them. In addition, most water-based animals are well-adapted for living either in the flowing waters of rivers and streams or in the standing waters of lakes and ponds; relatively few thrive in both. When rivers are dammed, and flowing water is replaced by a permanent reservoir, many river species are placed at risk.

In short, the manipulation of river systems is wreaking havoc on the aquatic environment and its biological diversity. Fresh waters contain extraordinary concentrations of animal life—including, for example, about 40 percent of the 20,000 recognized fish species. According to some estimates, the total diversity of animal life per unit area of rivers is 65 times greater than that of the seas.

In North America, the American Fisheries Society lists 364 species or subspecies of fish as threatened, endangered, or of special concern—the vast majority of them at risk because of habitat destruction. Many are found in arid regions where intensive water demands and rising salinity are destroying vital habitat. More than a third of the desert fish species of the American Southwest, for instance, are now listed as threatened or endangered. As Professor Alan Covich of Colorado State University puts it: "We have often ignored the high species richness associated with inland waters and have allowed many fresh water habitats to be dammed, channelized, drained, eroded, and polluted with nutrients, salts, silt, and chemicals. Biodiversity and ecosystem integrity are declining in a wide range of locations throughout the world ...."

AND THEN THERE WAS NONE

The Colorado River ranks among the most heavily plumbed water courses in the world. Controlled by 10 major dams, it now irrigates some 800,000 hectares (about 2 million acres) of farmland, serves the household needs of more than 21 million people, and generates nearly 12 billion kilowatt hours of energy annually. Its waters fill swimming pools and sprinkle green lawns some 400 kilometers away in Los Angeles, power neon lights in Las Vegas, and irrigate thirsty crops in the deserts of California, southern Arizona, and northern Mexico.

Ironically, it was in 1922, the same year Leopold experienced the wet, wild abundance of the Colorado River delta, that seven U.S. states started dividing up the river. They signed the Colorado River Compact, which gave 7.5 million acre-feet (about 9.25 billion cubic meters) to the upper basin states per year and an equal amount to the lower basin. Mexico finally got an assured supply in 1944, when the two countries signed a treaty committing the United States to send an average of at least 1.5 million acre-feet per year across the border.

Unfortunately, there were two major problems with these allocations. First, a total of 16.5 million acre-feet had been committed to the seven states and Mexico, but the long-term average flow of the Colorado produced only about 90 percent of that; more water had been promised than the river could reliably deliver. Second, none of the compacts and treaties dividing up the Colorado's water designated any flow for the river environment itself, including the delta and its abundant wildlife. As long as human demands remained well below the river's flow, this was not a problem. But except for unusually high flood years, virtually the entire flow of the river is now captured and used—and has been for some time (see figure, page 179). Indeed, flow readings at El Meritimo, the southernmost measuring station on the Colorado, were discontinued in 1968 because there was nothing to measure.

Only recently has much attention been given to the effects of these diminished flows on the river delta and estuary. The delta and upper Gulf of California comprise the largest and most critical desert wetland in the American Southwest, as well as one of the world's most diverse and productive sea ecosystems. Besides drying up wetlands and causing a severe deterioration in water quality, the reduction in freshwater flow has cut the flow of nutrients to the sea and reduced critical habitat for nursery grounds.

Catches from the upper Gulf shrimp fishery have dropped off steeply, and other fisheries are in decline as well. Although there is little hard data to correlate these declines with the drop in river flows, fishers believe that, along with overfishing, it is a major cause. Indeed, the "golden days" to con-

Flow of Colorado River Below All Major Dams and Diversions, 1905–1992

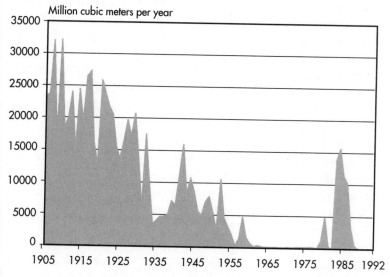

Million cubic meters per year

Sources: 1905–49, flow at Yuma, Arizona: U.S. Geological Survey; 1950–92, flow at southerly international boundary, International Boundary and Water Commission.

temporary fishers in the upper Gulf apparently refer to the mid-1980s, after the high flood year of 1983, when huge snowmelts in the upper Colorado basin caused the river to flow at rates not seen for several decades. And according to Alejandro Robles, executive director of Conservation International's Mexico program, many upper Gulf fishers believe that the rare flood flows of January 1993 temporarily brought back substantial numbers of fish species that had become scarce in the region.

But such rare events cannot reverse the long-term decline of the ecosystem or the economic, social, cultural, and ecological toll it is causing. A large number of species that depend on the lower Colorado-upper Gulf ecosystem are now threatened or endangered, including the green sea turtle, the Yuma Clapper Rail, the desert pupfish, the bonytail chub, and the razorback sucker. Much attention has focused on the vaquita, the world's smallest porpoise and most endangered sea mammal, whose population in the upper Gulf is believed to number just a few hundred. Also of special concern is the totoaba, a steel-blue fish that grows up to 2 meters in length and 135 kilograms in weight and that once supported a popular sports and commercial fishery. The totoaba used to breed in large numbers in the brackish waters of the Colorado estuary, while spending most of its adult life in the deeper waters of the nearby upper Gulf. Between habitat degradation and overfishing, the totoaba is now on the verge of extinction.

The Cocopa Indians, who have fished and farmed in the Colorado Delta for perhaps 2,000 years, are now a culture on the brink of extinction. For centuries they harvested a grain they called nipa, a unique salt-loving plant that tastes much like wild rice. They sometimes ate fish three times a day, and they hunted deer, wild boar, ducks, and geese. Known as "people of the river," the Cocopa had no formal calendar, but they keyed their lives to the Colorado's seasonal floods. No census exists to document their numbers, but historical accounts suggest that about 5,000 Cocopa were living in the

Delta 400 years ago.

Today, the Cocopa's millennia-old way of life hangs in the balance. Fishing and farming can no longer sustain them. They last harvested nipa in the early 1950s; by then, dams upstream had largely eliminated the annual floods that had naturally irrigated their staple grain. Now, just 40 to 50 families remain south of the border. With little means of subsistence or livelihood in the delta countryside, many of the tribal members have migrated to the cities. Anita Alvarez de Williams, a Mexicali-based expert on the Cocopa, worries that before long they "may no longer be river people at all."

Other communities of the upper Gulf—including El Golfo de Santa Clara, San Felipe, and Puerto Peñasco—were initially founded as fishing camps, and fishing remains the basis of their economic and cultural viability. According to researchers Marcela Vásquez León, Thomas McGuire, and Hernan Aubert, shipyards are closed, packing plants are operating well below capacity, local businesses are suffering, and households are struggling to survive. "The most direct way to revive the economies of the upper Gulf," they write, "is to revitalize the upper Gulf itself...."

EGYPT'S LIFELINE

All it takes is a single flight into Cairo in order to grasp what the ancient Greek historian Herodotus meant when he called Egypt "the gift of the Nile." A vast sea of desert sand surrounds a narrow green strip of life on either side of the river. This strip, along with fertile lands in the Nile delta near the Mediterranean Sea, have supported Egypt's civilization for millennia.

Like the Colorado, the Nile is a lifeline for this desert country that gets virtually no rain. It sustains 65 million people and irrigates some 3.5 million hectares of cropland. Moreover, with Egypt's population climbing by 1 million people every 9 months, and the need for drinking water and food rising proportionately, demands on the river are intensifying—even as upstream countries make plans to siphon off more Nile water for themselves.

Egypt has practiced irrigation perhaps longer than any other society, having drawn upon Nile waters for agriculture continuously for at least 5,000 years. For much of Egyptian history, the basic pattern of water use was that of "basin irrigation," in which a series of canals formed 5,000-to-10,000-hectare basins that stair-stepped slightly downstream. Nile water was diverted into the higher basins, flooding them and depositing nutrient-rich silt. The water then drained successively into each lower basin, until at the end of the sequence it re-entered the Nile to flow out into the Mediterranean. Egyptian geographer Gamal Hamdan described the ancient basin system as an ecologically sustainable adaptation to the natural environment—one that had a large enough water-to-land ratio to prevent a buildup of salt, and that let the bulk of Nile water run to the sea.

This system, however, limited crop production to just a third of the year. It was during the nineteenth century that Egypt converted to perennial irrigation with its extensive system of barrages (small dams) and canals. The culminating structure in the network was the High Dam at Aswan, which was constructed during the 1960s to provide virtually complete control over the Nile's waters and a crucial hedge against drought. Lake Nasser is able to store fully two years of the Nile's average annual flow.

Prior to construction of the Aswan High Dam, some 32 billion cubic meters of Nile water reached the sea each year, equal to 38 percent of the river's average flow. After the dam was built, flow to the sea dropped dramatically—to some 6 billion cubic meters—as flood waters were halted at Lake Nasser and diverted for crop production. With greater control over the river and continued expansion of irrigated lands, outflow to the sea sank to about 3 billion cubic meters in the mid-1980s. Today, the amount of freshwater from the Nile reaching the Mediterranean totals just 1.8 billion cubic meters per year, and all of it is released to the sea during the few winter months when crops need less irrigation. Moreover, in order to expand irrigated land further, the government hopes to be storing 80 percent of this remaining outflow in one of the northern coastal lakes by the end of the decade. That would leave less than 400 million cubic meters of fresh water flowing to the sea—scarcely one-half of one percent of the Nile's total annual runoff.

At this point, it should be noted that the patterns of diminution vary greatly from one river to another; and while very little of the Nile's fresh water reaches the sea, a fair quantity still reaches the delta. In contrast to the Colorado, which is virtually gone by the time it reaches its delta, the Nile still has a substantial amount of its water flowing far enough to irrigate its delta's rice, cotton, and other crops. From there, what is released to the sea each year is some 12 billion cubic meters of salty and polluted farm drainage. With the nation's water demand already bumping up against supply limits, the government plans to reuse as much of this drainage as possible.

Not surprisingly, the High Dam has greatly altered the river system, although with the Nile, as with the Colorado, cause-and-effect linkages are not altogether clear. Out of 47 commercial fish species thriving in the Nile prior to the dam's construction only 17 were still being harvested a decade after the dam's completion. And in the eastern Mediterranean, the annual sardine harvest dropped by 83 percent—a likely side-effect of the reduction in nutrient-rich silt entering that part of the sea.

Perhaps the most threatening long-term consequence of the Nile's diminished flow is that the delta, so essential to the country's economy, is slowly falling away into the sea. Most river deltas naturally subside from the weight of their own sediment, but under natural conditions this is usually countered by deposition of silt brought in by the river. The Nile transports an average of 110 million tons of silt each year, much of it fertile soil from the Ethiopian highlands. For thousands of years, 90 percent of this silt reached the coast to replenish the delta, while the remaining 10 percent was deposited on the Nile floodplain. The delta stopped growing about a century ago, after the first barrages were built by the British. But since completion of the High Dam, and the trapping of virtually all the silt in Lake Nasser, the delta has actually been in retreat. Borg-el-Borellos, a former delta village, is now 2 kilometers out to sea.

Global warming and the anticipated rise in sea level that higher temperatures will bring greatly increases this threat of inundation. Much of the northern delta lies only 3 to 4 meters above sea level. Researchers at the Woods Hole Oceanographic Institution in Massachusetts calculate that Egypt could lose 15 to 19 percent of its habitable land within about 60 years, displacing a similar portion of its population—which by then would likely total well over 100 million—and wiping out some 15 percent of its economic activity.

In the meantime, the paltry amount of Nile water reaching the sea is a harbinger of difficult times ahead for Egypt. Prospects for increasing Nile supplies have diminished since a joint project with Sudan to channelize part of southern Sudan's Sudd wetlands has been put on hold indefinitely because of the Sudanese civil war. Pumping more water from wells and recycling more of the drainage from farms will help somewhat, but these options are limited. And Egypt, last in line of the 10 countries in the Nile basin, also faces the prospect that its upstream neighbor Ethiopia—source of 85 percent of the Nile's water and now enjoying greater political stability—will soon begin capturing more of the river's flow for its own economic development.

SHRINKING SEAS

Some of the most dramatic consequences of river depletion are found where rivers empty into inland lakes. In the Sahel region of Africa, for example, the combined assaults of prolonged drought and diminished inflow—especially from the Logone and Chari rivers, which have been heavily diverted for irrigation—have shrunk Lake Chad by about three-fourths over the last 30 years. This lake and its tributaries harbor some of the richest fisheries in the world. The Grand Yaeres, an area of wetland twice the size of Luxembourg along the Logone River floodplain, is a crucial haven for fisheries, livestock, and recessional agriculture in the central Sahel. Diversions from the Logone River at Maga Dam, much of it to irrigate rice, are drying out these important wetlands and causing water tables to fall beneath some 150,000 hectares of the Logone floodplains.

The most publicized example of a lake dying for lack of river water is the great Aral Sea in central Asia. Once the world's fourth largest freshwater lake, the Aral has been shrinking steadily since 1960 because of the diversion of its two major sources of inflow—the Amu Dar'ya and Syr Dar'ya—for irrigation. Prior to 1960, these two rivers poured 55 billion cubic meters of water per year into the Aral, a little over half their average combined flow. Between 1981 and 1990, their combined discharge to the Aral dropped to an average of 7 billion cubic meters—just 6 percent of their total annual flow. Much of the time, these rivers now run virtually dry in their lower reaches.

The Aral Sea's demise may have been foreordained, after construction of the Karakum Canal in the late 1950s. Some 1,300 kilometers in length, the Karakum transports water from the Amu Dar'ya westward toward the Caspian Sea. Combined with a vast network of inefficient irrigation systems built to expand cotton production in the desert, this huge diversion of water began a process of slow desiccation that would eventually result in the bizarre sight of seagoing ships sitting on bone-dry land—the sea having literally evaporated from under them.

Under the direction of Moscow's central planners, irrigated agriculture in the basin expanded by half during the 1960s through the 1980s, reaching some 7.5 million hectares. As more and more river water has been siphoned off, the sea has continued to shrink steadily. In 1988, it actually split in two—into a larger lake in the south and a smaller one in the north. By the mid-1990s, the Aral's area had dropped by half and its volume by three-fourths.

This still-unfolding chain of ecological destruction and human suffering ranks the Aral Sea as one of the planet's greatest environmental tragedies. Some 20 of the 24 fish species in the Aral have disappeared, and the fish catch, which totaled 44,000 tons and supported some 60,000 jobs in the 1950s, has dropped to zero. Abandoned fishing villages dot the sea's former coastline. Each year, winds pick up anywhere from 40 to 150 million tons of a toxic dust-salt mixture from the dry sea bed and dump them on the surrounding farmland, harming or killing crops. The low river flows have concentrated salts and toxic chemicals, making water hazardous to drink. Coupled with poor sanitary conditions and heavy pesticide use, contaminated drinking water has contributed to rampant disease. The incidence of typhoid fever has risen nearly thirtyfold, and that of hepatitis, sevenfold. The rate of esophageal cancer in Muynak, an old fishing port, is 15 times the Soviet average.

Both river deltas have become severely degraded by the reduction in river flows. According to Philip Micklin of Western Michigan University, a leading U.S. authority on the Aral Sea basin, the tugay forests—assemblages of willow, poplar, tamarisk, and other water-loving trees and shrubs that were common in the delta regions—have been decimated, in turn destroying vital habitat for the region's animal life. Wetlands have shrunk by 85 percent. That, combined with high levels of agricultural chemical pollution, has greatly reduced waterfowl populations. In the Syr Dar'ya delta, for example the number of nesting bird species has fallen from an estimated 173 to 38.

Growing interest, support, and study have been directed

to the region by groups ranging from the United Nations Environment Programme, the World Bank, and European Union to Russian and Central Asian scientists and a variety of local and international NGOs. After the dissolution of the Soviet Union in 1991, responsibility for the Aral basin tragedy shifted from Moscow to the former Central Asian republics (Uzbekistan, Kyrgyzstan, Tajikistan, and Turkmenistan) and Kazakhstan, all now independent countries. They have formed the Interstate Council for the Aral Sea and several supporting institutions—key steps toward cooperation. Ameliorating the human suffering and stabilizing the Aral Sea environment is going to take an extraordinary level of commitment and funding by these young nations and international donors. And here, as in Egypt, high rates of population growth compound their water problems: the combined population of the five basin countries is projected to climb steeply during the coming decade.

DRY SEASON BLUES

Throughout Asia, where monsoon climates prevail, the management of rivers poses special challenges. Much of the region has substantial precipitation overall, but gets the bulk of it during a relatively short rainy season. India, for example, gets 80 percent of its rainfall during three to four months, with much of it coming in just a few monsoon storms.

This leaves many regions prone to both serious flooding and drought. Dams that capture and store runoff during the wet season have been a principal means of evening out the water flows—reducing flooding during the rains and assuring irrigation during drought. Even as population and food needs continue to expand, many Asian rivers are completely tapped out during the drier part of the year, when water supplies are so critical to irrigation. According to a 1993 World Bank study, "Many examples of basins exist throughout the Asia region where essentially no water is lost to the sea during much of the dry season."

Among the largest of these is the Ganges, which rises in the Himalaya mountains of Nepal and then flows through India and Bangladesh before emptying into the Bay of Bengal. In the early 1970s, India completed the Farakka Barrage with the aim of diverting Ganges water into the Hooghly River so as to improve navigation and increase water supplies for the port city of Calcutta. Newly independent Bangladesh was concerned that not enough Ganges water would cross into its territory during the dry season, and that its crop production would be reduced.

The two countries agreed in 1977 to a short term solution for sharing the Ganges' dry-season flow, and also guaranteed Bangladesh a minimum amount of water during extremely low-flow periods. That agreement expired in 1982, and a follow-up agreement lapsed six years later. In 1993, the dry-season flow into Bangladesh plummeted to the lowest level ever recorded, idling irrigation pumps and causing severe crop losses.

Finally, after many years of deepening tension, the two countries signed a water-sharing agreement in December 1996 that gives Bangladesh about three times more water than it had been receiving in recent years. While this agreement promises to relieve the long-standing dispute between the two countries, it will do little for the Ganges delta, which will continue to be deprived of river water during the dry months of the year. This lack of freshwater outflow to the Bay of Bengal has caused the rapid advance of a saline front across the western portion of the delta, resulting in serious and possibly irreversible damage. Rising salinity levels are damaging coastal mangrove forests, many species of which require fresh or brackish water. Mangroves are not only important sources of wood for cooking (rice can't be eaten without cooking), but also provide critical habitat and breeding grounds for many species of fish and shellfish. Unless more water is allowed to flow into the delta during the dry season, the damage to vegetation and loss of fisheries is likely to continue, along with a spreading disruption of the area's economy.

A similar problem is arising in the delta of Thailand's Chao Phraya basin. Water demands in the basin already exceed available supplies. Indeed, a team of World Bank water specialists has noted that "Inevitably, as nonagricultural demands increase, and if no additional water becomes available, supplies for dry season cropping will tend to decline.' Flows for navigation are consistently below optimum, and water supplies to the Bangkok area are not sufficient to alleviate the severe overpumping of groundwater there, which is causing portions of the land to subside. Yet unless water is allowed to flow into the delta during the, dry season, a saline front will advance through this delta, as well, threatening irreversible harm to the ecosystem.

In China, water projects that include major diversions for irrigation have dried up the lower reaches of many rivers during portions of the year. The Yellow River, known as "China's Sorrow" for its long history of flooding, is now frequently bone dry during the dry season. In 1995, its lower reaches were dry for a third of the year. Competition for water is particularly keen in the north China plain, where surface waters are nearly fully exploited and groundwater tables are falling at alarming rates. The drying up of surface streams signals mounting water scarcities in this country where some 100 cities and towns already suffer shortages.

CHANGING COURSE

An old Inca proverb says, "The frog does not drink up the pond in which it lives." It presages one of the looming challenges of our time—reconciling the growing water demands of expanding populations and economies with the need to protect water's fundamental ecological support functions.

The age-old notion that any runoff to the sea is "wasted" reflects a narrow view of what a river's work—or evolutionary purpose—really is. That purpose includes delivering nutrients to the seas, with their complex food webs; sustaining economically and culturally important fisheries; protecting wetlands, with their capacity to filter out pollutants; providing habitat for a rich diversity of aquatic life; safeguarding fertile deltas; protecting water quality; maintaining salt and sediment balances; and offering some of the most inspirational natural beauty on the planet.

Restoring and maintaining the integrity of river systems is going to take the deployment of new technologies, policies, and management strategies. It will take unprecedented cooperation both within and between countries. And, most fundamentally, it will take a new ethic of sharing water—not only with each other, but with nature as well.

A critical first step is for societies to recognize that there are limits to the amount of water that can be diverted from rivers. Exactly how much water needs to be left in-stream will vary with the time of year, the habitat requirements of riverine life, the system's sediment and salt balances, and other factors specific to each river basin. But setting even preliminary "minimum flows" for both average and low-flow periods would provide a needed degree of insurance for the health of river systems—even as scientists progress toward a better understanding of their complex ecological workings.

In regions where rivers are already overlapped, as in much of the western United States, meeting such minimum requirements will involve shifting some water away from farms and cities over to the environment. Even a decade ago, this might have seemed a radical notion. But thanks to a flurry of court decisions, legislative actions, administrative rulings, and citizen campaigns, the process has begun.

In late 1992, for example, the U.S. Congress passed legislation dedicating 800,000 acre-feet (987 million cubic meters) of water annually from the Central Valley Project in California, one of the largest federal irrigation projects, to maintaining fish and wildlife habitat and other ecosystem needs. Among other provisions, it set a goal of restoring the natural production of salmon and other anadromous fish (those that migrate from salt to fresh water to spawn) to twice their average levels over the past 25 years. Two years later, in December 1994, California and federal officials reached an agreement to work toward restoring the ecological health of the San Francisco Bay-Delta, a highly productive aquatic environment that is home to more than 120 species of fish, supplies a portion of the drinking water for 20 million people, and provides irrigation water for 45 percent of the nation's fruits and vegetables. The so-called CALFED program is working with all groups that have a stake in the outcome to arrive at a preferred alternative, which was expected to be identified by early 1998. It will almost certainly involve dedicating more water to the Bay-Delta ecosystem, which may mean shifting some water out of agriculture. But all Californians will likely gain in the long run, as economic activity comes into better balance with the water environment that supports it.

In yet another landmark shift in California, the courts have greatly broadened use of a legal doctrine called the "public trust," which asserts that governments hold certain rights in trust for the public and can take action to protect those rights from private interests. The California Supreme Court used this principle to require the city of Los Angeles to stop siphoning water from tributaries to Mono Lake on the eastern side of the Sierra, which had shrunk in volume by half—and dropped by 45 feet—because of decades of the city's water diversions. Since the city had legal rights to this water, which constituted some 15 percent of its supply, it fought the ruling for many years. Finally, however, in September 1994, Los Angeles reached an agreement with state and environmental officials that will allow Mono Lake's level to rise sufficiently to halt its ecological collapse. Since even existing water rights can be revoked to prevent a violation of the public trust, this doctrine offers a potentially powerful tool for restoring the aquatic environment.

While such site-specific cases are promising steps forward, broader government leadership will be needed to fully incorporate protection of the aquatic environment into water policies and river management. In the United States, for example, some impetus was provided by Daniel P. Beard, former Commissioner of the Bureau of Reclamation, which has been one of the world's predominant dam-building agencies during this century. In May 1994, Beard told an international gathering of water specialists that "the dam building era in the United States is now over," and went on to clarify a wholly new mission for his agency: "Every problem we must address has a common theme. That is: there isn't enough water in the river.... To solve these problems, we cannot build new reservoirs. Instead, we will have to encourage the movement of water from one use to another. We believe conservation, demand management, efficiency improvements and reuse offer our best opportunities for doing this."

A good candidate for such proactive effort is the lower Colorado River and delta. The Mexican government took a major step toward protecting this declining ecosystem and its threatened species in June 1993, when Mexican President Carlos Salinas de Gortari declared some 9,300 square kilometers of it a biosphere reserve and banned all fishing within a core area, noting that here, "ecology has priority over politics," and that "today, we are just realizing what we are at the point of losing." Underpinning his political statements are the potential economic benefits of restored fisheries, and possibly eco-tourism. Action by Mexico alone, however, will not be sufficient. Unless the United States joins its southern neighbor in restoring river flows to the delta ecosystem, the decline of this region will continue.

One possible source of "surplus" water could be the large quantities used for irrigation in the lower Colorado River basin. In the Wellton-Mohawk Irrigation District in southern Arizona, for example, the federal government heavily subsidizes three water-related operations—supplying water to the District, removing salty drainage from soils, and maintaining a desalting plant that was built (but never fully used) to make lower Colorado water fit to send across the border. Were the government to buy out these irrigators, it would not only save taxpayers money, but could free up some 370,000 acre-feet (about 450 million cubic meters) of water annually for restoring the lower Colorado ecosystem.

Saving water for nature will be far more difficult in developing countries, where demands for food and drinking water are rising apace with population growth. But in those countries as well, ensuring minimum water flows to satisfy ecological needs is critical to protecting fisheries, delta economies, and—as the tragedy in the Aral Sea basin underscores—the health of local people.

In all water-scarce river basins, cooperation among countries is essential not only to optimizing economic benefits from the river but to safeguarding its ecological functions. Unfortunately, while most water-sharing agreements have specified how much water each river basin country is allotted, they have allocated nothing for the river system itself. But if all countries in a basin agreed on a portion to be left instream to satisfy ecological needs, they could then divide up the remaining river water equitably among them.

For example, if scientists determined that at least 10 percent of the Ganges flow must reach the delta during the dry season in order to prevent the advance of a damaging saline front, this 10 percent would have to be agreed to and guaranteed by all three riparians—Nepal, India, and Bangladesh. Bangladesh's fair share of the Ganges dry season flow would then be added to this 10 percent to determine how much of the river must flow across the border into Bangladesh during the dry season. To be realistic, in the negotiations of such agreements, downstream countries such as Bangladesh would likely need to yield a slightly larger portion of their allocation to maintain minimum flows because they accrue the economic benefits of the delta ecosystems.

Unfortunately, most international rivers are not managed jointly by the countries that share them. Rarely do treaties allocate the water fairly among all the countries in a given river basin, much less establish shared responsibility for protecting the downstream environment. The countries of the Aral Sea basin have recognized the Aral Sea to be a legitimate water "user" deserving of its own allocation of river water, but this policy has not yet been translated into meaningful measures to free up water for the sea and surrounding delta ecosystems.

In rich and poor countries alike, meeting irrigation, industrial, and household water demands while also protecting the aquatic environment requires much greater incentive to use and allocate water more efficiently. In most developing countries and dry regions of wealthier countries, agriculture accounts for 75 to 90 percent of water use. In such areas, reducing irrigation needs by 5 to 10 percent can free up substantial quantities of water. Switching from sugar cane or rice to less water-intensive crops, investing in drip irrigation lines or low-pressure sprinklers to reduce evaporation losses, and scheduling irrigations to more closely match a crop's water needs are just a few of the ways farmers can save.

If farmers were required to pay prices for water that reflect its true cost, many would make these efficiency improvements. By heavily subsidizing water, governments give out the false message that this resource is abundant and can be affordably wasted—even as rivers are drying up, fisheries are collapsing, and species are going extinct. Yet virtually all governments do subsidize water use—typically by building large water projects and then charging farmers only a fraction of the water's true cost.

In some regions, the ability to sell river water can create incentives to use it more efficiently. Such water marketing implies clear property rights to the water, which do not currently exist everywhere in the world, and cannot replace governmental responsibility to ensure that ecosystems are protected. But where laws and infrastructure make marketing possible, as in the western United States, this approach can benefit the aquatic environment in two ways. First, rather than damming and diverting more river water, cities can purchase water from farmers who have saved it by improving their irrigation efficiency or have decided to fallow a portion of their cropland.

Second, the existence of markets allows private organizations and government agencies to purchase water rights and dedicate them to restoring river flows. For example, the Nature Conservancy, based in Arlington, Virginia, has returned water to rivers and wetlands by outright purchases of private instream water rights, as well as by working with state agencies to transfer existing water rights to instream uses. In Colorado, a coal-mining subsidiary of the Chevron Corporation donated $7.2 million worth of water rights on the Black Canyon of the Gunnison River to the Nature Conservancy, which then turned those rights over to the state Conservation Board for conversion to an instream water right. As a result, additional water will remain in this portion of the river to benefit the trout fishery, as well as three endangered fish species.

Such creative solutions mark an emerging era in water management. Pricing, marketing, regulations, and a brace of conservation technologies all have important roles to play in meeting human demands for water while at the same time restoring and protecting rivers. The tens of thousands of dams and vast lengths of diversion canals built over the last century stand as concrete testaments to impressive engineering skills and human control over nature. But in the years ahead, we may come to judge our success at water management quite differently—by our ability to share water equitably, to do more with less of it, and to restore life and integrity to the earth's rivers.

WHO WILL FEED CHINA?

By Lester R. Brown

When the article "Who Will Feed China?" was published in World Watch, *it precipitated a cascade of events, first in the international news media and then in the government of China.*

The waves began when the Associated Press and Reuters news services both came out with stories about the article—disseminating it to some 2,000 newspapers and 6,000 radio and TV broadcasts.

Among the readers, apparently, were officials of the government of China. Normally, China does not respond to articles in U.S.-based magazines, but our story hit a particularly sensitive nerve. After losing at least 30 million of their people to starvation during the Great Leap Forward a generation ago, the Chinese have become almost obsessed with the idea of self-sufficiency. Top officials found it intolerable to hear the world being told not only that their domestic production would soon be insufficient to feed their people, but that their need for imported grain would soon exceed the entire world's export capacity. The officials' irritation was no doubt exacerbated by a version of the article reprinted in The Washington Post, *under a somewhat more inflammatory headline than we would have chosen: "How China Could Starve the World."*

On August 29, in Beijing, the Chinese government called a press conference at which it sharply denounced the World Watch *report*. *The next day, newspaper stories appeared around the world under the AP headline "China Denies Environmentalist Report of Looming Food Crisis." As journalist Georgie Anne Geyer of Universal Press Syndicate recounted, "Deputy Agriculture Minister Wan Baorui huffed to reporters that not only would his enormous country of 1.2 billion people reach self-sufficiency by the year 2000 but that China's grain harvest would reach... 750 million tons by 2025. In place of such euphoric and ideologically-driven predictions of largess from China's very limited arable land mass, [Lester] Brown predicts instead that...China would be able to harvest 263 million tons."*

On the same day that the Chinese tried to dismiss Brown's analysis, however, the Wall Street Journal *elevated it further, under the headline "Possible Crisis in China Could Strain World's Grain Supplies, Expert Warns." The story noted, pointedly, "a number of Chinese academics share Mr. Brown's alarm, including Lin Zixin, the [former] director of The Institute of Scientific and Technical Information."*

Just two weeks later, the Chinese government was forced to admit there was *a huge problem—and that, in fact, the food shortages forecast by* World Watch *had already begun. The Agriculture Ministry had been unable to suppress statistics released by the State Statistical Bureau, revealing that grain prices had soared 60 percent higher in August than a year earlier, and meat prices 35 percent higher. Central authorities were reported to be releasing 20 million tons of food from stocks, with no assurance those stocks could be easily replenished. Other reports quickly followed, suggesting that the sleeping giant had awakened—however painfully—to the reality of its problem, and was assessing its options.*

After neglecting agriculture for several years during the country's breakneck effort to industrialize, official China is now beginning to focus on the long-term food prospect.

— The Editors

In April of 1994, the *Journal of Commerce* reported that grain prices in China's 35 major cities had shot up by 41 percent during the first two months of the year. In March, driven by panic-buying and hoarding, the rise had continued unabated. In response, the government released 2.5 million tons of grain from stocks to check the runaway rise in prices. This action calmed food markets—at least temporarily.

What happened last spring may be a precursor to the much larger disruptions that will occur as three extraordinary trends converge. China's population is growing by 14 million people a year. Incomes are climbing at a record rate, which means that even as the number of people increases, their consumption of meat is increasing even faster. And while the resulting surge in demand is occurring, the country's capacity to produce food is projected to shrink, due to the massive ongoing conversion of cropland to nonfarm uses.

In neighboring Japan, the soaring demand for grain driven by prosperity and the heavy loss of cropland to industrial development since mid-century have combined to push dependence on grain imports to 77 percent of total grain consumption in 1993. These same forces are now at work in China. It is one thing for a nation of 120 million people to turn to the world market for most of its grain, but if a nation of 1.2 billion moves in this direction, it could quickly overwhelm the export capacity of the United States and other exporting countries, driving food prices upward everywhere.

Rather suddenly, China is starting to lose the capacity to feed itself. The decline comes on the heels of four decades of impressive progress, particularly since the agricultural reforms of 1978, which transferred land from production teams to individual families. The energies unleashed by these reforms boosted the country's grain production by half, from 200 million tons in 1977 to more than 300 million tons in 1984. That put China ahead of the United States as the world's leading grain producer, and boosted annual output from the subsistence level of roughly 200 kilograms per person to nearly 300 kilograms.

Though growth in output has slowed since the mid-1980s, that gain was enough to effectively eliminate the traditional threat of famine. The issue now facing Beijing is not starvation, but the prospect of a gap between the market demand for food and its productions gap that will dwarf anything the world has ever seen.

This potential grain deficit is raising one of the most difficult questions world leaders have ever had to face: who will feed China? The only country to measure its population in billions rather than millions is moving into uncharted territory on the food front, and in an integrated world economy it will—one way or another—take the rest of the world with it.

While China's food production capacity is eroding, its demand is surging. The country is projected to add 490 million people over the four-decade span between 1990 and 2030, swelling its population to 1.6 billion—the equivalent of adding another Beijing every year for the next 40 years. Because its population is so large, even a slow rate of growth means huge absolute increases. Yet, those increases are only the beginning of the story.

MOVING UP THE FOOD CHAIN

Even as population expands, incomes are rising at an unprecedented rate. Economic growth of 13 percent in 1992 and again in 1993, plus an estimated growth of 10 percent in 1994, adds up to a phenomenal 40 percent expansion of the Chinese economy in three years. Never before have incomes of so many people risen so rapidly.

As their incomes rise, one of the first things that low-income people do with their money is to diversify their diets, shifting from a monotonous fare in which a starchy staple such as rice supplies 70 percent or more of the calories, to more meat, milk, and eggs. Last year, when asked by a *New York Times* reporter if living conditions were improving, a Chinese villager responded, "Overall, life has gotten much better. My family eats meat maybe four or five times a week now. Ten years ago, we never had meat."

Much of China is barren desert, and in a country where there is no vast grazing land like that of the U.S. Great Plains, the rising demand for livestock products translates directly into demand for additional grain. When the economic reforms were launched in 1978, only 7 percent of the grain was being used for animal feed, but by 1990 that share had risen to some 20 percent, most of it used to produce pork. Now, demand for beef and poultry is also climbing. More meat means more grain—2 kilograms of additional grain for each kilogram of poultry, 4 for pork, and 7 for each kilogram of beef added in the feedlot. As the Chinese get richer, they will eat more meat, milk, and eggs. But if the supply of grain does not expand apace with their appetites, food prices will soar.

To put this in perspective, consider the United States, where the use of grain to produce meat has reached its historic zenith. The United States is a leader in red meat consumption. The cowboy has been its mythic figure, the steak or hamburger its classic meal. Yet, the Chinese have eclipsed Americans in total red meat consumption almost entirely on the strength of their appetite for pork. At 21 kilograms per person in 1990, China's consumption of pork is approaching the 28 kilograms (62 pounds) consumed by the average American. Chinese consumption of beef, poultry, and milk is still minuscule compared to that of Americans. So, what happens if the Chinese start closing the gap in these other livestock products as they have with pork?

In fact, that is beginning to happen. Poultry was once a rare luxury in China, and the average person still eats only one-tenth as much as an American, but the appetite for chicken is growing fast. Ironically, that change has been spurred by a government policy that encourages production of chickens because they convert grain into meat more efficiently than pigs or cattle do. During the 1990s, poultry consumption has expanded from its small base at double-digit rates.

It is beginning to happen with eggs, too. The official goal for egg consumption has been set at 200 per person by the year 2000—double the quantity consumed in 1990 and close to the 235 consumed per year by the average American. With the population expected to reach 1.3 billion people by then, annual egg consumption will rise to 260 billion. If Chinese hens lay 200 eggs per year (U.S. hens averaged 252 last year), China will need a flock of 1.3 billion hens to satisfy this need. Yet, reaching this goal will take an additional 24 million tons of grain, an amount equal to the grain exports of Canada.

Clearly, China's expanding demand for animal protein could overwhelm the world's grain-producing capacity unless alternatives to livestock are found.

One precedent is that of Japan, which long ago adjusted to the limitations of its land by turning to the oceans for animal protein, giving rise to the now-traditional fish and rice diet. And, indeed, China's appetite for seafood too is rising—but with a key difference. In recent years, as fleets of other seafood-hungry countries have joined Japan in the aggressive pursuit of fish, oceanic fisheries have been pushed to their biological limits. According to the U.N.'s Food and Agriculture Organization (FAO), all 17 of the world's major fisheries are being fished at or beyond capacity. Nine are in a state of decline. The Japanese option has been eliminated for any major newcomers, which means that if China wants more fish, it will have to grow them in ponds. It is already doing so, at a rate of 6 million tons (mostly of carp) per year. But this, too, puts new demands on the country's shrinking grain-fields; close to 12 million tons of grain were used in 1993 in these marine feedlots.

And the good life for newly affluent Chinese doesn't stop with meat and fish. They are also acquiring a great enthusiasm for beer. To raise individual consumption for each adult by just one bottle takes another 370,000 tons of grain.

CROPLAND DISAPPEARING

As the demand for grain spirals upward, one might assume that at least a potential solution could be found in China's vast territory—in a commensurate planting of new cropland. But, in fact, much of that huge landmass is arid and unproductive, with the food-growing capacity concentrated in a relatively small area—a band of river valleys constituting about a third of the country along the southern and eastern coasts. This is also the area where the bulk of the population is concentrated. With the simultaneous growth of both the population and the industrial economy, there are competing demands on the land—for factories, housing, roads, and highways, as well as for crops. As a result, at a time when China most needs to expand the area of its cropland, that area is shrinking.

As this tug-of-war continues, the experience of three other countries that were densely populated before serious industrialization got underway—Japan, South Korea, and Taiwan—gives a sense of what to expect. Over the last few decades, the conversion of grainland to nonfarm uses (and, to a lesser degree, to production of the fruits and vegetables demanded by a more affluent populace) in these countries has cost Japan 52 percent of its grainland, South Korea 42 percent, and Taiwan 35 percent.

As the losses of cropland proceeded, they began to override the gains in land productivity, leading to steady declines in production. From their peaks, grain production levels have fallen by 33 percent in Japan, 31 percent in South Korea, and 19 percent in Taiwan. With the growth in population and affluence driving up the overall demand for grain, each of those countries has become heavily dependent on imports. By 1993, Japan was importing 77 percent of its grain, South

Korea 64 percent, and Taiwan 67 percent.

Now the same changes are commencing in China, and for the same reasons. The transformation of China from an agricultural to an industrial society is progressing at a breakneck pace. Shifting 100 million workers from the farm labor force to the industrial sector, broadly defined, and assuming 100 employees per industrial establishment (about par for China's private sector) means building one million factories, plus warehouses and access roads. Modernization of the Chinese economy, as in Japan, South Korea, and Taiwan before it, means sacrificing cropland.

The transportation sector, too, is claiming cropland as highways and railroads are built to replace dirt roads and trails. Increasing reliance on cars and trucks, sales of which totaled 1.2 million in 1992 and are expected to approach 3 million per year by the decade's end, will cover large amounts of cropland with roads and parking lots. New houses, larger than in the past, will spring up along these roads and will take still more of this land. In each of the last three years, the loss has mounted to nearly one million hectares, or 1 percent of China's cropland per year.

Along with the continuing disappearance of its farmland, China is facing the extensive diversion of irrigation water to nonfarm uses—an acute concern in a country where half the cropland is irrigated. Between 1950 and 1978, the irrigated area increased from 12 million to 45 million hectares, or nearly 1.2 million hectares per year. But since then, as water has become scarcer, irrigated area has expanded by only 190,000 hectares per year—not nearly enough to keep pace with the country's ballooning demand.

Early growth of irrigation came mostly from the construction of dams, some large and many small. But as the number of potential sites diminished, the growth shifted to wells. Today, roughly half of China's irrigated land is watered from dams and the other half from wells. It was the drilling of millions of wells for irrigation that is today lowering water tables in much of the country.

With large areas of North China now experiencing water deficits, existing demand is being satisfied partly by depleting aquifers—and the growing scarcity is slowing growth in food production. In late 1993, the Chinese Minister of Water Resources, Niu Mao Sheng, stated that "in rural areas, over 82 million people find it difficult to procure water. In urban areas, the shortages are even worse. More than 300 Chinese cities are short of water and 100 of them are very short." Even the capital itself is threatened; the aquifer under Beijing has dropped from five meters below the surface in 1950 to 50 meters below in 1993. In this respect, too, China's road to industrialization will be far more perilous than were those of Japan, South Korea, and Taiwan, where water is still relatively abundant. As the scarcity intensifies, both industrial and residential claimants are taking water from agriculture.

THE PRODUCTIVITY SLOWDOWN

With the cultivated area declining inexorably, China's ability to feed itself now rests entirely on raising the productivity of its cropland. In assessing the potential for raising yields, once again it is instructive to look at the case of Japan, which has led the world in raising rice yields for more than a century. Japan kept improving its yields until 1984, when it reached a plateau of just under five tons per hectare. Since then, even excluding the disastrous weather-reduced 1993 harvest, yields have actually fallen slightly.

Rice yields in China, which have been rising toward those in Japan, are starting to level off around four tons per hectare—suggesting that the potential for raising yields further is limited. Neither Japan nor any other country has been able to push the rice yield per hectare above five tons. In South Korea and Taiwan, too, the rise in yields slowed once they reached four tons per hectare—indicating that further dramatic boosts in China may not be possible without a major new technological breakthrough. But the prospect for that, so far, has not been encouraging. Agricultural economists Duane Chapman and Randy Barker of Cornell University point out that "The genetic yield potential of rice has not increased significantly since the release of the high-yielding varieties in 1966."

Farmers and policymakers have searched in vain for new breakthroughs, particularly from biotechnology, that could lift world food output quickly to a new level. But biotechnology has not produced any yield-raising technologies that will lead to large jumps in output, nor do many researchers expect it to. Donald Duvick, for many years the director of research at the Iowa-based Pioneer Hi-Bred Seed Company, one of the world's largest seed suppliers, offers a sobering appraisal: "No breakthroughs are in sight. Biotechnology, while essential to progress, will not produce sharp upward swings in yield potential except for isolated crops in certain situations."

With wheat, China's other food staple, the rise in yield is also slowing. In the early 1980s, China's wheat yield per hectare surged past that of the United States, and has remained well above it at roughly three tons per hectare. The big jump came immediately after the economic reforms of 1978, as yields climbed 83 percent from 1975–77 to 1984. During the following nine years, however, they rose only 16 percent.

Nor is there much prospect of any large gains from further use of fertilizer—which has been one of the keys to raising yields since the agricultural reforms. After climbing from 7 million tons in 1977 to nearly 29 million tons in 1993, fertilizer use appears to be leveling off, as it did in the United States a decade earlier. The reason for the leveling is not that there's any lack of fertilizer, but that farmers have encountered diminishing returns from further applications of it. Without the development of new cereal varieties that can respond to much heavier applications of nutrients, the rise in yields can be expected to slow dramatically—and could even come to a halt as it did in Japan.

ENVIRONMENTAL DEDUCTIONS

Food production trends in China will be shaped not only by the availability of cropland and water, but by several environmental trends—including soil erosion, waterlogging and salting of irrigation systems, air pollution, and global warming. On the half of China's cropland that is not irrigated, soil erosion is common. In fact, the Huang He or Yellow River that drains much of Northern China derives its common name from the 1.6 billion tons of ocher-colored topsoil that it annually transports to the ocean. So much of China's topsoil blows away that scientists at the Mauna Loa Observatory in Hawaii, the U.S. National Oceanic and Atmospheric Administration's official site for collecting air samples to measure changes in atmospheric CO_2 levels, can detect the dust within a matter of days after spring plowing starts in North China.

Waterlogging and salting are reducing productivity on an estimated 15 percent of China's irrigated land. When river water is diverted onto the land, part of it percolates downward, sometimes raising water tables. When the water table rises to within a few feet of the surface, deep-rooted crops suffer. When it gets within inches of the surface, water evaporates through the soil into the atmosphere, leaving a layer of salt on the soil surface. Unless an underground drainage system is installed to lower the water table, the accumulating salt eventually turns fertile land into waste land, as it did with the early Middle Eastern civilizations.

Air pollution and acid rain are intensifying too, largely as a result of increased burning of coal. The result is to lower crop yields and forest productivity not only in China, but as far away as Japan and South Korea. So far, there is no direct measure of how much this reduces yields. But one hint comes from the United States. If air pollution lowers the U.S. harvest by at least 5 percent, as U.S. Department of Agriculture figures indicate, then one has to wonder about the toll that even more severe air pollution will take on China's harvest.

Finally, there is the as-yet incalculable but potentially enormous toll of global warming. Even a modest loss of rainfall or increase in evaporation could disrupt China's finely tuned, highly productive agriculture. Climate research in the rice-growing south, for example, shows that a rise of 3 degrees Fahrenheit in average summer temperature would markedly reduce rice yields.

But among all these variables, the one that looms largest in the short run is that of shrinking cropland—the question of how much will be lost, and how fast. Rapid industrialization in recent years has already taken a large toll, as grain area has dropped from 90.8 million hectares in 1990 to an estimated 87.4 million in 1994. This annual drop of 850,000 hectares, or 1 percent—remarkably similar to the loss rates of China's three smaller Far Eastern neighbors in their industrialization heyday—is likely to endure for the foreseeable future if rapid industrialization continues.

That process will claim millions of parcels of farmland over the next four decades, not only for factories and warehouses, but for the housing of 490 million additional people. In 1994 alone, 10,000 miles of new highways are taking a toll as the construction crews pave their way across wheat and rice fields. As U.S. conservationist Rupert Cutler has noted, "Asphalt is the land's last crop."

Even if China were to launch a concerted national effort to preserve cropland, it is questionable whether it could be any more successful than Japan, which has long had some of the strongest agricultural land protection laws of any country. Even in the immediate vicinity of Tokyo, where land prices are among the world's highest, every tiny plot of rice land is fiercely protected from development. Some 13,000 families work farmland within Tokyo's city limits.

There is little prospect, then, that China can raise land productivity fast enough to offset the loss of cropland. None of the three newly industrialized countries that preceded it was able to do that—not even Japan, where the rice support price is six times the world market level. Given that Japan went to great lengths to protect its grainland, but still lost half of it over a four-decade span, it is difficult to see how China can avoid similarly heavy losses. With the plateauing production of recent years followed by a drop of 1 percent or more in 1994, the long-term decline may be starting.

THE COMING FALL

Taking all of these factors into account, and assuming that rapid industrial growth continues, it now appears likely that China's grain production will fall by at least one-fifth (or 0.5 percent a year) between 1990 and 2030. This compares with a 33 percent decline in Japan since its peak year of 1960 (a fall of roughly 1 percent a year), a 31 percent decline in South Korea since its peak in 1977 (1.9 percent a year), and a 19 percent decline in Taiwan, which also peaked in 1977 (1.2 percent a year). Seen against this backdrop, the estimated decline of one-fifth in China may, if anything, be conservative.

The resulting grain deficit will be huge, many times that of Japan—which is currently the world's largest grain importer. In 1990, China produced 329 million tons of grain and consumed 335 million tons, with the difference covered by net imports of just 6 million tons. Allowing only for the projected population increase with no rise in consumption per person, China's demand for grain would increase from 335 million tons in 1990 to 479 million tons in 2030. In other words, even if China's booming economy produced no gains in consumption of meat, eggs, and beer, a 20 percent drop in grain production to 263 million tons would leave a shortfall of 216 million tons, a level that exceeds the world's entire 1993 grain exports of 200 million tons.

But of course, China's newly affluent millions will not be content to forego further increases in consumption of livestock products. If per capita grain consumption climbs even modestly, from just under 300 kilograms at present to 350 kilograms in the year 2030, total demand will climb to 568 million tons of grain. By 2030, the deficit to be made up by imports will have risen to a staggering 305 million tons of grain. Imported grain as a share of consumption will climb to 56 percent, compared with 76 percent in the three smaller countries in 1993 (see Figures 1 and 2). In both of these scenarios, China's import deficit quickly surpasses the 28 million tons of grain imported in 1993 by Japan. If grain consumption per person were to rise to 400 kilograms, the current level in Taiwan, or one-half the U.S. level, total consumption would climb to a staggering 641 million tons and the import deficit would reach 378 million tons.

The Chinese themselves have apparently been making similar calculations. Professor Zhou Guangzhao, head of the Chinese Academy of Sciences, observes that if the nation continues to squander its farmland and water resources in a breakneck effort to industrialize, "then China will have to import 400 million tons of grain from the world market. And I am afraid, in that case, that all of the grain output of the United States could not meet China's needs."

Concern about food security runs deep in China. As a result of the 1959–61 famine following the Great Leap Forward, 30 million Chinese starved to death. Several times this number were close to death. The current generation of leaders, remembering all too clearly the Great Famine, are torn between the desire to remain largely self-sufficient in food and the desire to industrialize rapidly. But if the frenetic industrialization continues, imports of grain seem certain to escalate, reaching a level never seen before.

In confronting a deficit on the scale projected, two questions arise: will China have enough foreign exchange to import the grain it needs? And, will the grain be available? On the first count, if the premise underlying this demand is a continuation of the economic boom, there would likely be ample income from industrial exports to pay for the needed grain imports. Importing wheat or corn at 1994 prices averaging $150 a ton would require $15 billion to fill a 100-million-ton import deficit. In 1993, China's exports, growing by leaps and bounds, were close to $90 billion. In contrast to Africa, which cannot afford to import much grain, China's trade surplus with the United States in 1993 totaled $23 billion, more than enough to buy all U.S. grain exports.

Given the likely continuing growth in China's non-agricultural exports, importing 200 or even 300 million tons of grain at current prices would be within economic range if the country's leaders were willing to use a modest share of their export earnings for this purpose. Of course, this would mean cutting back on capital goods imports, which in turn would diminish the inflow of technology needed to sustain rapid economic growth.

The more difficult question is, who could supply grain on this scale? The answer: no one. Since 1980, annual world

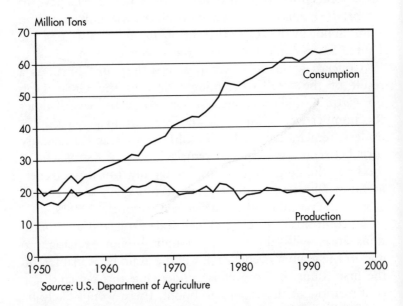

Source: U.S. Department of Agriculture

Figure 1: Grain Production and Consumption in Japan, South Korea, and Taiwan, Combined, 1950–94

grain exports have averaged roughly 200 million tons, of which close to half comes from the United States. But the United States is also faced with losses of cropland and irrigation water to nonfarm uses. And, given the projected addition of 95 million Americans over the next four decades, including both natural increase and immigration, the U.S. exportable surplus may not increase much, if at all. With more than 100 countries already importing U.S. grain, and with their import needs projected to climb, this exportable surplus is largely spoken for. For example, between 1990 and 2030, Egypt's grain imports are projected to rise from 8 to 21 million tons and Mexico's from 6 to 19 million tons.

Among the few countries that are now grain exporters, Argentina could substantially boost its output and perhaps double its annual grain exports of 11 million tons if it adopts appropriate farm price policies. But that would do little to

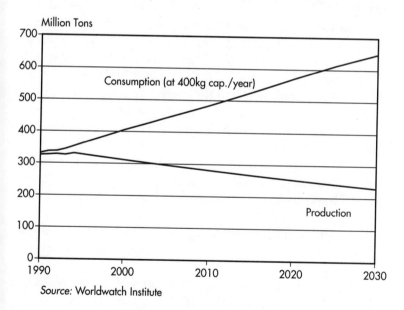

Source: Worldwatch Institute

Figure 2: Projected Grain Production and Consumption in China, 1990–2030

help China. Europe, with a remarkably stable demand and supply of grain, is likely to maintain exports at close to the current level even with the GATT-required reductions in farm subsidies. The reality is that no country, or combination of countries, has the additional export potential to fill more than a small fraction of the potential food deficit forming in China.

At the same time, huge deficits are projected for other parts of the world. Africa, notably, is expected to need 250 million tons of grain by 2030—ten times current imports. The Indian subcontinent is expected to rack up a deficit several times larger than its present one. Scores of countries with rapid population growth—among them Iran, Ethiopia, and Nigeria—will find themselves facing huge food deficits in the years ahead. In these circumstances, the vast deficit projected for China will set up a fierce competition for limited exportable supplies, driving world grain prices far above familiar levels.

China may succeed in importing much more grain than it now does, but to some degree that success would have to come at the expense of other, less affluent societies that lack the foreign exchange needed to compete in the world market. And, as U.S. consumers find themselves competing with their Chinese counterparts for U.S.-produced grain, the political fallout could lead to pressure for export restrictions or even outright embargoes.

Exactly when this competition among importing countries will develop, no one knows. But if recent trends continue, the buyer's market of recent decades could become a seller's market overnight. The government of China may not be able to withstand the spreading public protests if there is a resumption of runaway food prices such as those experienced in 1994.

At issue is how to bridge the projected gap between China's import needs and the inability of the rest of the world to supply those needs. If the chasm develops as projected, rising food prices will forcibly curb demand for food worldwide, reducing consumption among rich and poor alike. For the former, it will mean less fat-rich livestock products and less cardiovascular disease, much as happened in the early 1940s in the United Kingdom, when U-boats cut off grain shipments. But for the hundreds of millions of rural landless and urban poor who remain on the lower rungs of the global economic ladder, food consumption could well drop below the survival level.

In the face of unprecedented social stress, some national governments may attempt to ration food supplies, as some industrial countries did during World War II. Whether the government in Beijing is strong enough to reinstate a national foodrationing program is not certain. Alternatively, governments could ask those living near the top of the food chain to voluntarily move down, thus lessening the amount of grain used to produce livestock products. At least one senior official in Beijing has suggested that China should move back toward a more vegetarian diet.

Economic growth could also slow or come to a halt, dropping incomes and food purchasing power throughout the world. In an article on the fragility of the Chinese economy's environmental underpinnings, *New York Times* correspondent Patrick Tyler wonders "How long can China's economic engine roar?" Acute food scarcity could bring the Chinese economic miracle to a premature end.

On the supply side of the equation, higher prices will doubtless stimulate greater investment in production, but unfortunately some once-promising avenues are closed. When world grain prices doubled in the early 1970s, farmers expanded the cultivated area, only to eventually pull back as the mostly marginal land eroded and as profits fell. With water tables already falling in so many farming areas, drilling more irrigation wells will only hasten aquifer depletion. Unless new, more fertilizer-responsive grain varieties can be developed, applying more fertilizer will have limited effect. Investing more in agricultural research can help, but there are no new technologies in prospect that will lead to a quantum jump in output.

The bottom line is that when China turns to world markets on an ongoing basis, its food scarcity will become the world's scarcity; its shortages of cropland and water will become the world's shortages. Its failure to check population growth much more aggressively will affect the entire world.

Whether or not we are ready to accept it, the economic future of the world outside of China and that of China's 1.2 billion people are now inextricably linked. This prospective deficit in China will force other governments—however reluctantly—to painstakingly reassess their countries' population carrying capacity and the closely related questions of population and consumption policies.

It will probably not be in the devastation of poverty-stricken Somalia or Haiti, but in the booming economy of China, that we will see the inevitable collision between expanding human demand for food and the limits of some of the earth's most basic natural systems—including the capacity of oceanic fisheries to produce seafood, of the hydrological cycle to supply fresh water, and of crops to effectively use more fertilizer. The shock waves from this collision will reverberate throughout the world economy with consequences that we can now only begin to foresee.

FACING FOOD SCARCITY

By Lester R. Brown

At 1:30 a.m. on Tuesday, September 12, 1995, a small group of high-ranking agricultural economists, meteorologists, and remote-sensing satellite experts entered a corridor on the fifth floor of the U.S. Department of Agriculture's massive "South Building" in Washington, DC. Behind them, an armed guard closed a heavy steel door, which was then locked. Inside, the blinds were drawn down on all windows, the stairwells and elevators were locked, and the telephones switched off.

Through the night, the group pored over the data they had brought—information on grain crop supply and demand that had been compiled from more than 100 agricultural countries and confirmed by a sophisticated array of satellite observations and weather analyses. At 5 a.m., the group—known as the World Agricultural Outlook Board—assembled around a table in a conference room inside the locked area, and began a final review of their findings.

Around dawn, a score of international wire service reporters—all with security clearances—began converging on the building, and at 7 o'clock they were admitted to a guarded room inside the locked area. Under heavy surveillance, they were given computer discs and secured phone lines, and permitted to begin looking at what the Board had found. At exactly 8:30, the "lockup" ended: the reporters' phone lines were switched on, the blinds were raised to the morning sun, and the steel door was opened. Simultaneously, the Board's report went out over the Internet.

At first glance, what the various tables that had been compiled through the night revealed was that the world's stocks of rice, wheat, corn, and other grains had fallen to their lowest level in two decades. But a mile away at the Worldwatch Institute, we aggregated the crop totals and linked them to global population data, with an even more disturbing result. Measured in days of global consumption, the world's estimated carryover stocks of grain for 1996 had fallen to 52 days—the lowest level ever.

The Outlook Board's report, which is released each month, is little known to the public but of incalculable value to commodities traders and agribusinesses—some of whom stand to gain or lose fortunes on the information it contains. But on this occasion, the data had even more meaning: in a world of rapidly expanding human population, carryover grain stocks are the key indicator of the world's capacity to meet that population's growing demand for food. Grain is the planet's largest source not only of food for direct consumption, but of feed for livestock and poultry products, and farm-raised fish—of the major protein sources on which humans depend.

The Outlook Board reported that crop-withering heat waves had lowered grain harvests in the northern tier of industrial countries, including the United States, Canada, parts of Europe, and Russia. In many farming regions, the summer of 1995 was the hottest ever recorded. Thus, many of the world's farmers found themselves contending not only with the usual vagaries of weather but with temperatures higher than they have ever known—much as global climate models had projected would result from the planet's rising levels of atmospheric carbon dioxide. As that trend continues, shrunken harvests could become the price of our addiction to fossil fuels.

The scarcity implicit in the reported trends and the higher food prices that would result was bad news for the world's low-income consumers. Already spending nearly all their meager incomes on food just to survive, many will not make it to the next harvest. In the global race between food and people, they would be among the early losers.

For decades, grain stocks have remained more or less adequate; as population has surged, so has food production. Boosted by new crop varieties, fertilizer, and irrigation, yields improved dramatically. But in recent years, farmers have faltered, and much of the optimism engendered by those ever-rising yields is evaporating. Since the bumper crop of 1990, there has been little growth in global grain production—while population has grown by some 420 million people, or the equivalent of 40 New York Cities.

In 1995, a small amount of cropland was held out of production under commodity set-aside programs, including some 7.5 percent of U.S. cornland and 12 percent of the grainland in Europe. But even if all this land had been in production, the additional 34 million tons or so of grain that it would have produced would not be enough to offset the year's 49-million-ton drop in global stocks. In fact, world stocks have now been drawn down for three consecutive years, helping to cushion the lack of growth in world production. But now that they are down to 52 days (little more than pipeline supplies), the cushion is nearly gone.

In effect, the world's food economy may be shifting from a long-accustomed period of overall abundance to one of scarcity. Of course, the abundance of the past half-century hasn't eliminated hunger, as the episodes of starvation in Ethiopia and Somalia attest—not to mention the less publicized deprivation of many of the world's billion "absolute poor." But that deprivation has been largely a result of poverty, not of overall supply. In the coming era, the supply itself will be limited, and the effects of shortages will be felt everywhere. Already, the 80 million being added to the global population each year are being fed only by reducing the consumption of those already here.

If the September World Outlook report came as coveted business intelligence for shrewd commodities traders, it did not come as any great surprise to those who have been studying the earth's carrying capacity. Environmentalists and scientists have long argued that the environmental trends of the past few decades could not continue. We could be heading for unimaginable trouble, they said, if we continue to strip the planet of its forest cover, to erode its cropland, overgraze its rangelands, overpump its aquifers, deplete its oceans, pollute its air, pump excessive amounts of carbon dioxide into the atmosphere, and destroy the habitats of our fellow creatures.

Some thought the crisis might come in the form of an epidemic of pollution-induced illnesses and rising death rates. Others thought the effects might first show up in the collapse of local ecosystems. Indeed, such perturbations have become increasingly visible at the regional level—in the surging death rates of Russians, or the desertification of once productive land in Africa. But globally, it is food scarcity that may soon become the principal manifestation of continuing population growth and environmental mismanagement. If so, the first economic indicator of environmental stress will be rising food prices.

THE SHRINKING LAND

One reason the world's opinion-makers find it hard to believe there will be any problem with food is that they have lived in a period of unbroken abundance, with much of that abundance concentrated in the same regions where the most influential news media are concentrated. Tragedies like the starvations in Ethiopia and Somalia are thus seen as isolated aberrations. But perhaps the most compelling reason for thinking there's no problem is the assumption that if it really comes to the crunch, farmers can always bring more land into cultivation. After all, on every continent, there are vast areas of unpopulated, uncultivated territory.

That assumption is unwarranted. Food cannot be grown just anywhere; it can't be grown in places where the land is too cold, too dry, too steep, or too barren. It also can't be grown where there is no water or where the soil has been degraded by erosion. Of the land that is still free of all these constraints, nearly all is already in cultivation. Moreover, some of the most erodible land is slowly losing its productivity.

All over the world, farmers have begun pulling back, abandoning much of the marginal land they first plowed in the mid-1970s. That land had been pressed into service after the Soviet Union's surprise decision, in 1972, to import massive quantities of wheat after a poor harvest. The decision had caused world grain prices to double, and gave farmers a strong incentive to raise output. But today, with much of that land being depleted still further by erosion, it is no longer

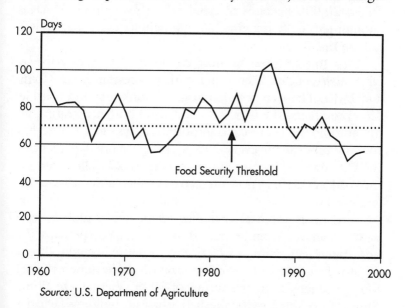

Source: U.S. Department of Agriculture

Figure 1: World Grain Carryover Stocks as Days of Consumption, 1963–98

worth tilling. In the former Soviet Union, the harvested grain area has shrunk from its peak of 123 million hectares in 1977 to 94 million in 1994. In the United States, the Conservation Reserve Program established in 1985 retired much of the highly erodible land that was plowed in the late 1970s, paying farmers to return it to grass before it became wasteland.

While the United States, Russia, and Ukraine are abandoning or retiring marginal grainland, some of the more densely populated countries are losing prime cropland to nonfarm uses. As Asia industrializes, the construction of thousands of factories, roads, parking lots, and new cities is wiping once-productive crop land off the map. Japan, South Korea, and Taiwan, the Asian countries that industrialized first and can serve as models of what may happen elsewhere, have collectively lost about 40 percent of the grain harvested area they had in 1960. Each year, Indonesia is losing an estimated 20,000 hectares of cropland on Java alone, which is enough to supply rice for 360,000 people, even as it adds 3 million people per year.

Even so, the losses in those countries may be dwarfed by what now appears likely—and perhaps inevitable—in China and India. The two population giants rank first and third as food producers (the U.S. is second), and both are gearing up for automobile-centered transportation systems. China has roughly one car for every 200 people—a mere 1 percent of the U.S. ownership rate. But an increase to 22 million cars on the road by 2010, as now projected, would cause heavy cropland losses.

Yet, shortsighted as that may seem, it is a global trend with enormous momentum. It is epitomized, perhaps, by how quickly Vietnam, now a rice exporter, managed to break its own vow not to let industrialization undermine essential food production. In the spring of 1995, Vietnamese Prime Minister Vo Van Kiet established a ban on building factories in rice paddies. Just four months later, he changed his mind— in order to allow Ford Motor Company and other firms to build on 6,310 hectares of farmland near Hanoi.

While development encroaches on farmland, most farmers have nowhere else that they can retreat to in turn—and in fact, many are giving up farming and moving to the cities. In most countries, the agricultural frontiers have disappeared, and nowhere is there any large area of highly productive cropland waiting to be plowed. In a few places, such as the *cerrado* (a dry plain) in Eastern Brazil, there is marginally productive land that can be used if grain prices rise high enough. But that will do little more than help to satisfy local demand. Brazil, now the largest grain importer in the western hemisphere, is facing a population increase of nearly 100 million people over the next half-century. If it can feed its own people, it will be doing well; it is unlikely to do much for China or Bangladesh.

THE DEHYDRATION OF THE LAND

The human body consists largely of water, as does the food that sustains it. But the water in an ear of corn or a quarter-pound of beef is a mere drop in the bucket compared to the water needed to produce it. A pound of wheat takes about 1,000 pounds of water to grow. A pound of beef takes much more. A large part of the world's food production therefore depends on supplementing rainfall with irrigation—either from underground aquifers or from rivers. Yet, both groundwater and surface water are becoming scarce. While the quantity of water on the planet remains unchanged, the proportion of it diverted to uses other than agriculture—to residential and industrial needs—is climbing hand-in-hand with population and industrialization. At the same time, pressures are growing in many watersheds to limit both agricultural and other human uses of water in order to protect threatened ecosystems.

Water tables are now falling in major food-producing regions. In the U.S. Great Plains, farmers from South Dakota through Nebraska, Kansas, eastern Colorado, parts of Oklahoma, and the Texas panhandle were able to greatly expand their irrigation from mid century through 1980, by pumping from the great Ogallala Aquifer. But the Ogallala is mostly a fossil aquifer—meaning that most of it is not recharged by rainfall. Reliance on it, therefore, is ultimately unsustainable. And, in its more shallow southern reaches, it is already largely depleted. As a result, since 1982 irrigated area in Texas has shrunk 11 percent, forcing farmers to return to traditional—and less productive—dryland farming. Irrigated area is also shrinking in Oklahoma, Kansas, and Colorado. An estimated 21 percent of U.S. irrigated cropland is watered by the unsustainable practice of drawing down underground aquifers.

In India, water tables are falling in several states including the Punjab—the country's breadbasket. In the Punjab, the double-cropping of winter wheat and rice has dramatically boosted the overall grain harvest in recent years, but it has also pushed water use beyond the sustainable yield of the underlying aquifers. In such areas, the rate of pumping for irrigation will eventually be reduced to the rate of recharge. If water is being pumped out twice as fast as rainfall is recharging it, for example, the supply of irrigation water will one day have to be cut by half. In an area like the Punjab, this may mean that the double-cropping of wheat and rice will have to be modified by substituting a lower yielding dryland crop, such as sorghum or millet, for the rice. For India, which is adding 18 million people each year, that is not a pleasant prospect.

In China, which is trying to feed 1.2 billion increasingly affluent consumers, much of the northern part of the country is a water-deficit region. Around Beijing, for example, the water table has dropped from 15 feet below ground level in 1950 to more than 150 feet below today. In the northern provinces of Shanxi, Hebei, Henan, and Shandong, the amount of water available for irrigation has fallen to a fraction of that needed to maximize yields. And Vaclav Smil, a China scholar at the University of Vancouver in Canada, observes that the growing water needs of China's cities and industrial areas "will tend to lower even those modest irrigation rates."

If that is the case—if groundwater is falling not just in China, but all over the world—it becomes a question of some urgency whether the difference can then be made up from surface water. The planet's great rivers, after all, are perpetually renewing. Yet here, too, there are signs of trouble. In more populated regions, rivers have been tapped, diverted and dammed until often there is little water left to continue on its way. In fact, many rivers now run dry before they reach the ocean.

Several months before the World Agricultural Outlook Board issued its September report, for example, China's great Yellow River completely disappeared some 620 kilometers from its mouth on the Yellow Sea. At the same time, on the opposite side of the globe, the Colorado River was disappearing into the Arizona desert; since 1993, it has rarely reached the Gulf of California. In central Asia, the Amu Darya is drained dry by Turkmen and Uzbek cotton farmers well before it reaches the Aral Sea, thus contributing not only to the sea's gradual disappearance but also to that of the huge fishery it once supported.

Draining rivers dry may be rationalized as essential to human food production, but the benefits that draining confers on one front have to be weighed against the heavy toll it takes on another. Dried-up or diminished outflows threaten the survival of those fish that spawn in them. Estuaries that have served as breeding grounds for oceanic species are destroyed.

Accordingly, some governments are moving to restore river flow to protect these fisheries—even though it means reducing irrigated area. In California, for example, officials have decided to restore nearly a million acre-feet of water to the annual flow of the Sacramento River in an effort to maintain the health of the San Francisco Bay estuary. Thus the irrigated area in California is declining even as the demand for food is climbing. Worldwide, with some two-thirds of all the water that is diverted from rivers or pumped from underground now used for irrigation, any cutbacks in water supply affect the food prospect. In regions where all available water is now being used, the competition between farmers and cities is intensifying.

The dilemma is that as population grows, the resulting increases in urban and industrial demand can be satisfied only by diverting water from the very irrigation needed to supply that population's food. In Colorado, the small town of Thornton, which lies northwest of Denver, has purchased water rights from farmers and ranchers in Weld County on Colorado's northern border. It plans to build a 100-kilometer pipeline to transport the water as its needs begin to exceed local supplies in the years ahead.

Similarly, in 1995, the city of Fukuoka in southern Japan bought irrigation water from some 700 rice growers to avoid a water shortage. In China, officials decided in early 1994 to ban farmers from the reservoirs around Beijing, so the water could be used to meet the city's soaring residential and industrial demands. Those demands are further heightened by the population's growing affluence, which increases per-capita water use as more people get indoor plumbing, replete with flush toilets. These diversions of irrigation water to nonfarm uses are but three isolated examples of a practice that is fast becoming commonplace.

COULD MORE FERTILIZER HELP?

If the cropland area is no longer expanding, then the prospects for producing food from land come down to raising the output from the existing cropland. That was the global strategy for four decades, and it worked. A glance at the figure on page 225 shows how: as long as farmers kept increasing the amount of fertilizer they used, the amount of crop-

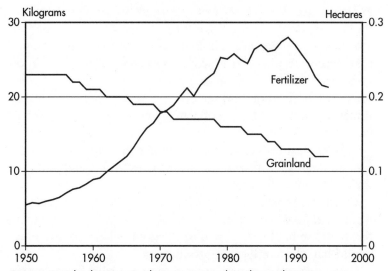

Sources: Grainland: USDA; Fertilizer: International Fertilizer Industry Association.

Figure 2: World Fertilizer and Grainland Per Person, 1950–94

land per person could continue to shrink, as it did, without noticeably disrupting the food supply. In effect, more fertilizer made up for having less land. But of course, adding more and more fertilizer to the land can't go on forever. It's like a baker adding more and more yeast to the dough.

Historically, of course, abundant increases in output have been achieved by this strategy. Between 1950 and 1989, fertilizer use expanded ten-fold—from 14 million tons to 146 million tons, helping to nearly triple the world's grain harvest. But now it appears that the limits have been reached, and in some regions exceeded. In country after country, farmers have discovered that they are already using the maximum amount of fertilizer that existing crop varieties can effectively use. Over the past six years, global fertilizer use has actually fallen, to 122 million tons.

The principal reason for the drop can be traced to an

excessive use of fertilizer in the former Soviet Union before the agricultural economic reforms that were launched in 1988. During the preceding decades, Moscow had hoped that heavy fertilizer use would eliminate dependence on imported grain. When the farmers were faced with real-world prices for both grain and fertilizer, however, their use of fertilizer became far less profligate—falling some 60 percent between 1988 and 1995.

Other countries have also re-trenched on this front. In the United States, fertilizer use peaked around 1980 and has dropped some 10 percent since then as new soil fertility tests have enabled farmers to more precisely determine fertilizer needs and avoid overuse. In both western Europe and Japan, fertilizer use has been refined to the point where adding more would have little effect on production.

The substitution of fertilizer for land, the formula that worked so well for farmers for nearly half a century, is now failing them. Unless plant breeders can develop new varieties that can effectively use still larger quantities of fertilizer, the world's farmers will have trouble reestablishing steady growth in food output. The challenge to agricultural scientists, to find a new formula to expand world food output as needed, has thus far gone unanswered.

THE LIMITS OF FISHERIES

Jules Verne long ago suggested that when we reached the limits of food production on the land, we could turn to the oceans. Unfortunately many countries have been doing just that over the past several decades. Between 1950 and 1989, the fish catch expanded more than four fold, climbing from 22 million tons to 90 million tons. During the six years since then, the catch has leveled off. United Nations marine biologists count 17 major oceanic fisheries, and report that all are now being fished at or beyond capacity; thirteen are in a state of decline. Contrary to the prognosis of Jules Verne, we reached the limits of the oceans first.

Between 1950 and 1989, the seafood catch per person went from 8 kilograms to 17 kilograms. Since 1989, it has declined 8 percent. Predictably, seafood prices are rising. As a result of our failure to stabilize population before reaching the limits of oceanic fisheries, we now face a declining seafood catch per person—and rising seafood prices for as far as we can see into the future.

Cessation of growth in the world fish catch is putting additional pressure on land-based food sources. If the annual growth in the world's animal protein supply—the 2 million more tons we were once able to haul from the sea—is now replaced with fish reared in ponds by fish farmers, it will require roughly 4 million tons of grain, approximately the amount of grain consumed each year in Belgium.

THE DEMAND SIDE

While there has been no growth in the last five years in either ocean- or land-based food production, the demand for food has continued to expand, driven by population growth and rising affluence. Although the rate of world population growth has declined from the historical high of 2 percent in 1970 to 1.5 percent in 1995, the annual addition of some 80 million is now greater than at any time in history. Feeding that many more people each year requires that the world's farmers annually expand their production capacity by 26 million tons of grain per year, or 71,000 tons per day.

Even as population grows at a record pace, those with low incomes, who account for most of humanity and who typically depend on a starchy staple, such as rice, for 70 percent or more of their calories, want to diversify their diets by consuming more livestock products. This desire to move up the food chain appears to be universal. In every society where incomes have risen, so has consumption of livestock products. Our long existence over evolutionary time as hunter-gatherers may have created an innate taste for meat and eggs, while the taste for milk and milk products, such as butter, cheese and yogurt, followed the development of agriculture.

As incomes have risen since 1950, world meat consumption has leaped four-fold, from 44 million tons to 184 million tons. Consumption per person has nearly doubled—from 17 kilograms in 1950 to 33 kilograms in 1994.

Within two years, rising meat consumption transformed China from a net grain exporter of 8 million tons to a net importer of 16 million tons. Its overnight emergence as a leading importer of grain, second only to Japan, is helping drive up world grain prices. Over the next few decades, as China's population adds some 300 million people, and as rapid industrialization continues to drive up incomes and the demand for grain even as it paves over cropland, the country's import deficit will continue its dramatic expansion.

It is only a matter of time until China's grain import needs overwhelm the export capacity of the United States and other exporting countries. But before that happens, the shortage will spread, because even as China is bidding for a growing share of the world's exportable supplies, so are scores of other countries. The grain import needs of countries such as Indonesia, Iran, Pakistan, Egypt, Ethiopia, Nigeria, Mexico, Bangladesh, and India could easily triple by 2030. In the competition for high-priced exportable supplies, the weaker economies will lose out. In more human terms, so will many of the world's poor.

Even among the affluent, however, spending money on food is not unaffected by the growing shadow of global limits. As people shift toward more meat-based diets, the pattern of meat consumption itself is changing. The production of beef and mutton has leveled off in recent years, largely because the number of cattle, sheep, and goats being raised has pushed the limits of rangeland carrying capacity much as the quantity of fish being taken has reached the sustainable yield limits of the oceans. Most future gains in beef production will have to come from the feedlot, which puts beef in competition with pork and poultry for available grain supplies.

CARRYING CAPACITY

As both fishermen and farmers fall behind the growth in world population, that growth raises a fundamental question about how many people the earth can support. The answer depends on a second question: At what level of consumption?

Grain use per person measures both the amount of grain consumed directly, which accounts for half of human caloric intake, and the amount consumed indirectly in the form of livestock products, which accounts for a large share of the remainder. Grain use varies from a high of roughly 800 kilograms per person in the more affluent societies, such as the United States, to a low of 200 kilograms per person in low-income societies, such as India. If the current world grain harvest, averaging 1.75 billion tons thus far during the 1990s, were boosted by roughly 15 percent to 2 billion tons, that harvest—if equitably distributed—could support 2.5 billion people at the American level of consumption, 5 billion at the Italian level, or 10 billion at the Indian level.

These numbers point to a looming gap between the projected growth of world population to 8 to 11 billion, and the strains on both oceanic- and land-based food production imposed by the current population of 5.7 billion—most of whom would like to move up the food chain. This gap underscores the need for governments to assess their *national* carrying capacities so that they and the people they serve can understand the difficult choices that lie ahead.

Now that the global fish catch has levelled off, we have a good sense of just how much food the oceans can sustainably provide. We are also beginning to develop a clearer sense of what can reasonably be expected from the land. Barring any new technologies that could lead to quantum jumps in food production, the way the discovery of fertilizer did, there is no possibility that the entire world can adopt the American diet. Indeed, for the first time in history, humanity is facing the prospect of a steady decline in both seafood and grain consumption per person for as far as we can see into the future.

THE POLITICS OF SCARCITY

The fall in world grain carryover stocks in each of the last three years may mark the early stage of a transition from a buyer's market to a seller's market, one in which long-term grain prices are more likely to be rising than falling, and in which the politics of surplus, which have dominated the period since World War II, will be replaced by a politics of scarcity. Instead of a few exporting countries competing for markets that were never quite large enough, more than a hundred importing countries will compete for supplies that never seem adequate. Already, 1995 has witnessed the steepest rise in prices of wheat, rice, and corn seen in many years.

Experience with world food scarcity in the last half century has been limited to a few years in the mid-1970s, after the Soviet Union secretly cornered the wheat market in 1972 and drove grain prices abruptly upward. The U.S. government, in an effort to keep domestic food prices from rising in response to the scarcity, imposed an export embargo on soybeans, a crop that supplies much of the world's cooking oil and a large share of the protein meal fed to livestock. Since the United States was supplying over half the world's soybean exports, the economic shock waves from this decision reverberated throughout the world.

It was during this time of relative grain scarcity that the use of food for political purposes became an international issue. The U.S. State Department was accused of maintaining a blacklist of countries that voted against U.S. interests in the United Nations, and of putting blacklisted countries at the end of the line awaiting scarce food aid.

In the integrated economy of the 1990s, the effects of food scarcity sweep even more quickly across international borders than they did two decades ago; as USDA statistician Fred Vogel observed on the morning of the Outlook Board report, once the news was released at 8:30, it was "around the world in seconds."

Governments of exporting countries, sensitive to the speed with which the vagaries of a global market can generate food scarcities and inflation at home, are often tempted to impose export embargoes. In May of 1995, Vietnam imposed a partial embargo on rice. Because grain prices in neighboring China had risen well above the world market level, large amounts of rice from Vietnam were crossing into China. But with rice prices climbing by up to 70 percent in northern Vietnam, making it difficult to control inflation, the government restricted exports while waiting for the new harvest to come in. Since Vietnam is the third largest rice exporter, after Thailand and the United States, this raised the world rice price. Meanwhile, in China, some provinces have even banned grain shipments to other provinces within the country in an effort to stop price rises.

The prospect of chronic world food scarcity raises new questions about the morality of restricting or banning food exports. One question is whether a grain-exporting country can be justified in restricting exports in order to quell domestic food price rises, even though it will lead to even more rapid price rises—with potentially tragic effects—in the rest of the world. Another question concerns the role of the international community in protecting national versus international interests. The General Agreement on Tariffs and Trade, or GATT, is not well equipped for this task; it has been designed mainly to ensure access to markets. The challenge now is to devise a set of trade institutions and rules that will assure access to supplies.

In the world of the late 1990s, many more countries will be seeking food supplies—some of them desperately—than will be in the market to sell. Even now, only a handful of countries consistently export grain on a meaningful scale: Argentina, Australia, Canada, France, Thailand, and the United States. Current world grain exports add up to roughly 200 million tons per year, of which the United States accounts for close to one-half. That puts great power in the hands of one government; and the possibility that food could be used for political purposes may be of growing concern to a majority of countries.

The politics of commodity control gained worldwide in 1972, when the Organization of Petroleum Exporting Countries successfully engineered a tripling in the world price of oil. Of course, there are differences between grain and oil. First, people can survive without oil, but not without food. Oil can be replaced with other energy sources, but there's no replacement for grain. And second, the United States controls a larger share of grain exports than Saudi Arabia does of oil.

With seafood, the politics of scarcity is raising its head in the increasingly frequent clashes among countries over access to fisheries. Although only a few of these disputes actually make international news, they are now an almost daily occurrence. Their pervasiveness is evident in a Greenpeace statement released at the U.N.-sponsored conference on regulating fishing on the high seas in July 1995: "Tuna wars in the northeast Atlantic, crab wars in the North Pacific, squid wars in the southwest Atlantic, salmon wars in the North Pacific, and pollock wars in the Sea of Okhotsk are all warning signs that fish stocks are in serious trouble."

No other economic indicator is more politically sensitive than rising food prices. If the grain scarcity that will now continue at least until the 1996 harvest should continue indefinitely, millions of low income breadwinners could find that soaring food prices threaten the survival of their families. Food scarcity could bring into question the legitimacy of numerous national governments that have failed to address the growing imbalance between human reproduction and food production. Food prices rising out of control could trigger not only economic instability, but widespread political upheaval.

As of 1995, many aid donor countries, including the United States, were cutting food assistance budgets. These cuts, combined with higher procurement prices for grain, have reduced food aid from the historical high in fiscal 1993 of 15.2 million tons to an estimated 7.6 million tons in 1996.

The world is moving into a new era, one in which the problems we face will be vastly different from those with which most governments and news organizations are now preoccupied. With the world fish catch no longer expanding, if some people raise their consumption of seafood (as seems virtually certain), it will now be at the expense of others. Given the reality of rising prices, and of the wide disparities in income worldwide, the same may soon be said of food in general. In the past, as long as the pie was expanding, political leaders could always urge patience, arguing that everyone's lot would soon improve. But when the pie stops expanding, not because of a temporary lag of technology or planning, but because our collective consumption has finally overtaken some of the planet's productive limits, the political dynamic changes. The question of how the pie is sliced takes on a new prominence.

OUR GREATEST CHALLENGE

For the first time during the half century since population growth accelerated after World War II, the world's farmers do not have the technologies needed to match the growth in population. If farmers cannot rely on the steadily expanding use of fertilizer to boost their grain harvests, and if agricultural scientists cannot quickly come up with a new technology that will lead to a quantum jump in world food output, then the world will need a new strategy for balancing human numbers and food supplies. With neither fishermen nor farmers able to keep up with population growth, most of the responsibility for achieving a humane balance between food and people rests with family planners. Beyond that, every effort will be needed to exploit each technological potential, however small its contribution, to expand food output.

As the difficulty in feeding 80 million more people each year becomes apparent, food security may replace military security as the principal preoccupation of governments. For many countries, security now depends more on protecting their territory from soil erosion than it does on protecting it from military invasion. As the food balance becomes more fragile, national security may depend more on stabilizing population than on developing new weapon systems.

In scores of developing countries, the population-driven growth in demand for food is now overrunning the capacity of local agricultural support systems, generating potentially huge import deficits. Given the overpopulation of so much of the world today, it may now be time to ask whether couples anywhere can morally justify having more than two children, the number needed to replace themselves.

The challenge is to quickly make the transition to smaller families everywhere. Historically, two countries have man-

IN A NUTSHELL:
Why even with the advances of modern agricultural technology, we are falling behind

Years needed for the human population to reach . . .

Its	1st billion	2,000,000
	2nd billion	105
	3rd billion	30
	4th billion	15
	5th billion	12
	6th billion	11

One billion people is equal to 100 cities the size of Cairo or Los Angeles.

aged to reduce their population growth rates by half in a matter of years, and what was learned from those experiences is both painful and instructive. Japan did this during the seven years from 1949 to 1956, after it had to adjust to surviving without the overseas territories lost as a result of its defeat in World War II. China did the same thing between 1970 and 1976, when it first introduced family planning and adopted the two-child family as a goal.

The urgency of implementing the U.N. World Plan of Action adopted in Cairo in September, 1994, which calls for linking a global population strategy to more equitable development for poor nations and for women, increases as food scarcity spreads. One of the key components of the Plan is to fill the family planning gap as soon as possible. There are an estimated 120 million women in the world, mostly in developing countries, who want to limit the size of their families but lack access to the family planning services needed to do so.

The Plan also emphasizes the importance of educating females. There is no social indicator that correlates more closely with the shift to smaller families than the level of female education, and this is a correlation that holds across all cultures. Few investments by the international development community can yield a higher return—in economic productivity, human well-being, and ultimately in political stability—than these.

If national governments undertake carrying capacity assessments, some may find that they cannot provide even for the projected growth in their populations, much less the aspirations of these populations for more varied diets. Under these circumstances, any hope the world's poor have of improving their diets depends on stabilizing world population long before it reaches the 8 to 11 billion now projected. Those countries that wait too long to address the population threat, as China did, may find themselves choosing between the reproductive rights of the current generation and the survival rights of the next.

There are a number of steps that can be taken to expand food production and buy additional time to stabilize population. These include:

• Discontinuing the use of grain to produce ethanol in the United States. Releasing the 10 million tons of corn now used for this purpose would support world population growth for an additional four months.

• Converting the land used to produce tobacco into the production of food. If the 5 million hectares of cropland now used to grow tobacco were turned over to growing grain, it would not only provide enough grain to support world population for six months, but it would also reduce mortality rates and sharply lower health care costs.

• Investing more in agricultural research, specifically in developing more fertilizer-responsive varieties or an alternative formula that will replace the use of fertilizer in expanding world food production. This effort demands an all-out effort using both conventional plant breeding techniques and those of biotechnology.

• Raising the efficiency of water use by shifting from free distribution of water to water marketing, a step that would permit more land to be irrigated.

• Designing a world action plan to stabilize soils, recognizing that every ton of topsoil lost to erosion today diminishes the food supply for the next generation.

• Devising national programs to protect cropland, particularly the most productive land, from being converted to nonfarm uses. This could be done either through zoning or through the adoption of a cropland conversion tax, one that would be large enough to reflect the land's long-term contribution to food security.

• Encouraging home gardening, particularly in affluent societies where land is available, much like the U.S. "victory gardens" of World War II.

There are also opportunities for reducing per-capita consumption, which in some societies is conspicuously excessive. In affluent societies, overeating today is regarded as unattractive; in the future it may be unconscionable. There are several ways of lowering per capita grain consumption to alleviate the effects of scarcity.

- One is to let the market do it. When grain prices doubled in the 1970s, Americans lowered their consumption of meat, milk and eggs enough to reduce grain feeding by 46 million tons, which would cover 20 months of world population growth. The disadvantage of this approach is that prices that are high enough to move the affluent down the food chain can inflict severe suffering on the poor.
- A second way is to educate people about the health risks associated with excessive consumption of fat-rich livestock products. The healthiest people in the world are not those living at the top of the food chain or those at the bottom, but those in the middle. Italians who use about 400 kilograms of grain per year, for example, live longer than Americans who consume twice that, even though the Italians spend much less on health care. The growing popularity of semi-vegetarian diets in the United States in the early 1990s, when grain and meat prices were relatively low, demonstrates the possibility.
- A third technique, one widely used by industrial countries during World War II, is the rationing of the consumption of livestock products. The disadvantage of this approach is that it requires a nationwide bureaucracy to administer the program and to enforce compliance.
- Fourth, and perhaps the most effective and efficient technique, is a tax on livestock products, one not unlike that applied by most governments to alcoholic beverages, another grain-based product. Although a tax on livestock products might not be politically popular among the affluent, it does moderate grain price rises, and in a time of acute scarcity it could be the price of political stability.

Reducing the consumption of fat-rich livestock products, through whatever means, could help buy some additional time to stabilize population size. If the world's affluent could reduce their consumption of grain fed livestock products by 10 percent, they could free up 64 million tons of grain for direct human consumption. This would cover world population growth for another 26 months. A 20 percent reduction would buy more than four years.

One of the sustaining forces of modern civilization has been the expectation of a better life in the future. If the food situation continues to deteriorate, with no prospect of reversal, people in those societies least able to compete for these supplies will begin to lose hope. With the loss of hope comes the risk of social disintegration.

The economically integrated world of the late nineties is moving into uncharted territory, facing a set of problems on a scale and of a nature quite different from those faced in the past. If we are unable to reverse the trends of recent years, food scarcity may well become the defining issue as we exit this century and enter the next. History judges political leaders by whether or not they respond to the great issues of their time. For today's leaders, the challenge is to achieve a humane balance between food and people on a crowded planet.

5

Better Use of Materials

THE CHANGING
WORLD VIEW

By Alan Thein Durning

This article appeared in 1997, as a followup to an earlier article describing the six waves of "extractive" industry that swept through the Pacific Northwest region of North America over the past two centuries. The Northwest's history, we noted, has been a microcosm of the world's. Those industries brought great short-term wealth to the region's human populations, but the cost of that wealth was a dangerous drawing-down of the region's natural capital. The fur trade brought profits to colonial traders and luxury to European aristocrats, but it decimated populations of mammals in the Columbia River basin. Similar patterns followed with the industries of high-volume salmon fishing, irrigation-intensive farming, industrial logging, hydroelectric power, and mining.

Those industries aren't inherently destructive, of course; but the enormous scale on which they are practiced couldn't be sustained without courting calamity. When the Chinook Indians extracted small quantities of fish, furs, or wood for the sustenance of small, stable communities, natural balances were sustained. But when the human population surged along with the quantity of resources consumed by each person, the demand for products grew exponentially and the natural balances crashed. It is these two forces—population growth and consumption—that are the "horses pulling the Northwest economy off the track of sustainability," says Durning.

How to rein in these horses? While stabilizing population growth is essential and has become an overriding concern in most regions, Durning argues that the goal of cutting excess consumption is equally essential. In the following sequel to his account of the Six Waves, Durning offers a strategy for achieving that goal. This strategy requires two key changes: first, to reform the prices of natural resources and the products made from them (prices that are now fundamentally dishonest because they avoid covering many of the real costs of production); and second, to reform the dominant "world view" that drives modern economies—a view that subordinates the natures and needs of local communities to abstract "national" and "global" economic demands such as the demand for incessant economic growth. The two changes are connected, of course, since that demand for unfettered growth is one of the reasons prices have become so dishonest in the first place; it's easier to show profits when a lot of the true costs are not paid.

In his discussion of prices, Durning begins by relating a conversation he had with Carolyn Alkire, a resource economist for the Wilderness Society, who came to the Yakima Basin of the Cascade Mountains to assess the condition of one of the region's chief natural assets—its salmon.

—The Editors

"Wild salmon are natural capital," says Carolyn, sitting on a rock beside Lake Keechelus.

"They're just like financial capital or physical capital. The fish that aren't harvested or killed go off and reproduce and produce new wild salmon in the same way that if you have stocks, you get dividends. In the case of wild salmon, however, we have dipped into our capital; we have harvested and killed many more fish than we should have to maintain a constant stock.

"A wild chinook salmon in the Columbia basin is natural capital worth $2,148. A wild coho is worth $488. But on the market, they go for $49 and $10 respectively.

"As natural capital, you are looking at each fish as what the potential earning value is," she explains: how much income a fish's offspring would provide over the next century if people allowed the fish to spawn rather than killing it with cattle grazing, clear cuts, fishing nets, hydroelectric dams, irrigation diversions, and water pollution. Her assessment is conservative, Carolyn notes, because it ignores nonmonetary values.

The value of chinook is so high because many Columbia basin chinook populations are endangered. They should not be killed or caught at all. Yet nobody behaves as if each of the Columbia basin's remaining wild chinook salmon were a share of stock worth $2,148. The money economy, and government cost-benefit analyses, have long treated salmon as cheap, abundant, and indestructible. This largely explains their near eradication in the Yakima and in many of the region's other rivers.

Similar discrepancies between cost and price are woven through the fabric of the Northwest economy. Prices—the money economy's main tool for conveying information—do not tell the truth. They therefore fail to do their job of regulating consumption so as to maximize good and minimize bad. Prices are blind to most ecological and many social costs.

In commodity after commodity critical to the long-term viability of life in the Northwest, market prices are a fraction of true costs. The gasoline burned by the automobile that brought Carolyn over the Cascades from the airport in Seattle was priced at $1.29 a gallon. The full cost of that gallon of gasoline, including such side effects as air pollution damage to human lungs and farm crops, was perhaps $6. The price of using the highway to get here, paid through fuel taxes, was less than one cent a mile, but the cost of using the highway—if you add in tax subsidies from nondrivers and damage to air, water, and wildlife habitat—was closer to a dime a mile. The map that guided Carolyn to the lake sold for $2.50, but its cost—counting the pollution released in making and transporting its paper and ink—may have been three times that.

The list goes on and on. The clothes Carolyn wears, the water that runs past her feet and into irrigation canals or hydroelectric turbines, the airplane ticket she bought to get here, and just about everything else that uses natural resources intensively is also underpriced.

Meanwhile, things that use labor intensively, including health care and most other services, are overpriced. So too are things where the peculiar nature of the market results in hoarding, speculation, artificial scarcity, and underinvestment.

If the Northwest economy is to endure, Northwesterners will have to make prices tell the truth. While laws, regulations, and individual efforts to live ethically are crucial in moving toward sustainability, only prices are powerful enough to fundamentally redirect consumption and production patterns. Look at the record. Study the trends for energy consumption in the Northwest—the best single indicator of the environmental responsibility of the region's economy. Over the decades, the lines have soared upwards in great, uninterrupted sweeps, rising even through most recessions.

On the graphs of energy consumption, there is no evidence of the great events of environmental consciousness raising. There is no sign of the publication in 1962 of Rachel Carson's *Silent Spring*, regarded by many as the birth announcement of the modern environmental movement. There is no sign of Earth Day 1970, when environmental awareness burst onto the public scene. There is no sign of milestone environmental regulations passing legislative bodies. There is no sign of Earth Day 1990, history's largest teach-in. The lines for production and consumption of energy just keep rising. Environmental education, moral exhortation, and government regulation do not visibly alter the curve.

Where there are significant decreases, they are the consequences of rising energy prices. For petroleum, the line dips twice: once after the Arab oil embargo jacked up prices in 1973 and again after the Iranian revolution did so in 1979. For electricity, the line goes flat after the region's disastrous venture into nuclear power elevated most Northwest electric rates in the early 1980s.

Each of these price increases caused inflation and contributed to recessions. They did so, however, because they were sudden, unanticipated, and siphoned money from the Pacific Northwest to oil exporters and utility bond holders in faraway places. If prices of energy—and of labor, salmon, water, housing, parking spaces, and everything else—were gradually and predictably aligned, upwards or downwards, to match true costs, and if the money stayed at home, the economy would benefit enormously. Jobs would proliferate even as the environment improved.

This contention may seem exaggerated. Most people believe that they must choose between a vibrant economy and a healthy environment. But listen to thinkers such as Carolyn Alkire. Their message is so simple and so revolutionary: To thrive—even just to survive—the Northwest must teach prices to tell the ecological truth.

You cannot wave a wand and change the prices of hundreds of goods and services. But there is a way to do it: by partially replacing existing taxes with taxes on the pollution, depletion, and disruption of nature. Prices, realigned through a shift of taxes, are the reins for consumption.

How would a tax shift work? It would revise the existing tax structure from top to bottom, because that structure has no reason to it. It has an explanation: it is an accident of history, or a history of accidents. It was cobbled together by a century and a half of political compromises, half-baked theories, and special pleading. But it has no reason, no consistent rationale, no underlying principle or unifying form. The local, state, and national taxes affecting the region exist solely to draw money for governments. They succeed at that: they claimed about thirty percent of the region's gross domestic product in 1994, a total of $89 billion in government revenues that was spent in pursuit of various public goals.

Yet the taxes' side effects work at cross purposes with those public aims. Taxes in the Northwest penalize work, enterprise, and investment, aggravate inequality, and accelerate environmental decline. They give the wrong incentives to almost everyone. They are, to borrow a phrase from energy analyst Amory Lovins, "spherically senseless"—no matter how you look at them, they are nonsense.

By custom, economists speak of land, labor, and capital as the three "factors of production." Whatever a business wants to sell, it needs some combination of land, labor, and capital. In this abstract but useful framework, labor refers to people. Capital refers to physical objects created by people, such as buildings, tools, and machinery. And land refers, somewhat opaquely, to all the gifts of nature—everything that is not created by people. Land includes not only tracts of earth and natural resource commodities but also basic ecosystem functions, such as the cycles of water, nutrients, and energy. These goods are provided by nonhuman forces, free of charge. The mispricing and consequent misuse of these gifts constitutes much environmental harm.

Taxes on the gifts of nature raise the price of using them,

which tells people to conserve these gifts. Taxes on labor and capital tell businesses and households to scrimp on workers and tools—in other words, to practice unemployment and underinvestment. A reasonable tax policy would tax the gifts of nature first and only tax labor and capital as a last resort.

Yet most existing taxes affecting the Pacific Northwest stand reason on its head; they fall overwhelmingly on labor and capital. The Northwest can stand reason on its feet again by shifting the tax burden. Over the space of one to three decades, Northwest jurisdictions could eliminate many existing taxes—most of them levies on income, sales, and property—and replace them with taxes on the gifts of nature.

A tax shift alone will not solve the Northwest's problems. The region will always need a strong framework of laws and regulations against crimes, whether social, economic, or environmental. Taxes are no substitute for prohibition of inadmissible actions. The Northwest will also need to eliminate counterproductive subsidies, such as below-cost and below-market sales of public timber, parking space, and water. It will need to rewrite perverse regulations like those affecting auto insurance. And it will need to make public investments in the human services that meet vital social needs and reduce unintended pregnancy.

Yet a tax shift, more than any other large-scale policy change, would help align prices with costs, putting the power of the marketplace behind the reconciliation of people and nature.

AFTER THE DELUGE: THE CASE FOR A NEW WORLD VIEW

There is a yawning chasm between what is politically possible and what is achingly necessary. Ecological pricing, population stabilization, and other requisites of sustainability are, politically speaking, preposterous idealism. The short-term prospects of any government in the region shifting from income, sales, or property taxes to resource and land-value taxes are nil. Nor is there hope of swift progress against the anti-ecological subsidies that riddle tax and spending codes, such as fire-sale prices on publicly owned timber and grass, deeply discounted hydropower rates for aluminum smelters and irrigators, and the billion-dollar giveaways under U.S. hardrock mining law.

This is true because advocates for the long-term future are up against something devilishly difficult to fight: they are up against a worldview.

Everyone operates from a worldview. It is a set of simplifying assumptions, an informal theory, a picture of how the world works. Worldviews are rarely brought out into the light of day. So people are not usually aware of them. They sit down deep in human consciousness somewhere, quietly shaping reactions to new ideas and information, guiding decisions, and ordering expectations for the future. Worldviews are not necessarily internally consistent. Often, they are not; in fact, they usually contain parts that are demonstrably false. Still, their historical and psychological roots are long enough to prevent easy uprooting.

In the Pacific Northwest, as elsewhere in North America, the commonly held worldview is an old one from the frontier. It comes from the rear-view mirror, reflecting times when the world was big and people were few. Through this lens, the world looks empty and indestructible. The environment and human community appear subordinate to the economy, as things worth protecting if you can afford to after paying the bills. In this worldview, production looks like the creation of tangible objects that meet basic human needs. Resource industries—logging, farming, mining, energy production— seem to be the locomotive that drags the entire economy along. This view is familiar and comforting, and demonstrably false.

The emerging worldview, held as yet by a minority of citizens, is grounded in the reality of the present: a time when the world is small and people are many. Through this lens, the world looks full and fragile. The economy and human community are subsets of the broader ecosystem. Production is the provision of desired amenities, services, and qualities, physical and nonphysical, to people enmeshed in communities. The pursuit of quality of life—through the application of human ingenuity—is the locomotive of the economy. This set of assumptions is new, unfamiliar, and accurate. Because few people yet see the world in its terms, the majority of citizens misconstrue their interests. They do not see their interests as tied up with those of forested watersheds or as threatened by climate change.

Worldviews are parts of culture and change over time. They are influenced by what parents teach their children, by what young people learn in school, by what adults learn from peers, books, and social institutions such as churches. They are also influenced by mass media. The politics of sustainability, therefore, is about changing not only laws and habits, but also—even primarily—worldviews. The challenge is to change them quickly enough.

Drawing on its tradition of turning outlandish dreams into practical reality, the Northwest may be the place that demonstrates how to trade the old worldview for the new and, in the process, exchange sprawl and malls for compact, vibrant cities; clearcuts and monoculture for enduring farms, forests, and fisheries; throwaways, overpackaging, and rapid obsolescence for durability, reuse, and repair; volume for value; and consumerism for community.

The Northwest could model a way of life—of less stuff and more time, of fewer toys and more fun. Above all, it could become a place whose civility, culture, and humanity are as stunning as its scenery.

The politics of place is a politics of hope. It is sustained by a faith—somewhat mystical perhaps—in place itself. Whether they are descendants of Asian hunters who crossed the Bering land bridge during the Ice Age or mongrels with New

England puritan-Irish-Polish-Jewish blood, all people who put down roots are shaped by their home ground. Over time, it seeps into them, and they become natives. In the Northwest this means that they look up at twilight and draw strength from the mountains. They seek renewal at the rivers and the shores. They taste communion in the pink flesh of the salmon. The rains cease to annoy.

Here is the hope: that this generation becomes the next wave of natives, first in this place on Earth and then in others. That newfound permanence allows the quiet murmur of localities to become audible again. And that not long thereafter, perhaps very soon, the places of this Earth will be healed and whole again.

THE SUDDEN NEW
STRENGTH OF RECYCLING

By John Young

Of all the things we can do to help protect our threatened environment on a day-to-day basis, probably no activity is more widely recognized than recycling. Throughout the United States, Europe, and Asia, systematically collecting used glass, paper, plastic, and aluminum—and sending it off for reprocessing—has become routine.

Yet, recycling still has a long way to go, to gain full acceptance. In the 1950s and 1960s, when most of today's senior business executives and political leaders were growing up, the concept of household recycling was virtually unheard-of. In those decades, the word "new" was a favorite adjective of advertisers, and the idea that "used" materials can have as much value as virgin ones is still regarded with skepticism by some of the older generation. A few years ago, the Wall Street Journal *published an article entitled "Recycling is Garbage," in which the author seemed to take the view that recycling is a "fringe" activity and thus not to be taken seriously as a part of the mainstream economy.*

But that article missed a key point: that the recycling of basic materials is fundamental to the way our planet sustains life. All of the soil from which our food or wood is grown, for example, contains essential organic matter that as been recycled from decomposed plants and animals. All of the matter in our bodies has done duty before—many times—in other organisms. The water we drink has been drunk before. By reusing oxygen, carbon, nitrogen, and so on over and over, nature is able to make a finite supply of materials last indefinitely.

What we accomplish by systematically recycling our bottles, cans, newspapers, and building materials, is to model our economic activities more closely on the natural ones—helping to convert our economy to one that will last, rather than exhaust or contaminate its limited resources. And limited resources are not just those that can run out. In a finite environment, even resources that are renewable can be limited. Trees, for example, can be renewed. But in an ecologically stable environment (a natural forest), they can't be grown fast enough to meet the world's surging demand for lumber and paper. So, even though new trees can be grown, the forest ecosystems of which they are a part can be used up—and that can destabilize the processes by which other essential materials (such as topsoil or fresh water) are supplied.

Recycling also reduces the amount of toxic substances dumped in water, soil, or air, because making products from recycled materials generally produces less pollution than making them from raw trees, ores, or petroleum. It also results in less waste after the product is used, because it diverts discarded products from landfills or dumps (or casual trashing of the environment) back into useful production.

When new industries are just getting started, their production costs are often higher than will be the case a few years later, after they have worked out the bugs and learned how to operate at larger, more cost-effective capacities. In the mid 1990s, as the volume of municipal recycling grew, many communities in the United States began to find that recycling household waste could have major economic, as well as environmental, benefits. The following article appeared in 1995, and it marked an important milestone for recycling.

—The Editors

Recycling, one of the key strategies for alleviating the pressures of the human presence on natural systems, has finally—and dramatically—arrived as a mainstream industrial activity in North America.

It's ironic that the breakthrough took so long. North America—or at least the U.S. and Canadian part of it—is where materials consumption is most profligate, and where the impacts of that consumption (in pollution from landfills and incinerators, energy production for manufacturing, and the spreading damage left by extractive industries) are therefore most troublesome. Yet, for a quarter-century after the first Earth Day, recycling advocates were forced to spend much of their energy trying to make their case to skeptical decisionmakers.

In the 1980s, recycling was still seen largely as a "do-good" activity. It was of little interest to fast-track business investors, who in those days were too busy pursuing "high-tech" ventures. The idea of founding a profitable business on old newspapers and empty bottles did not fit well with the ascendant lifestyles of the era. Local governments, many of which had to cope with rising landfill costs, were a bit more responsive, but still tended to regard their new recycling programs as burdens.

But now, suddenly, what was seen as a burden has become a major asset, and those communities that had the foresight to set up solid recycling programs a few years ago are beginning to reap real rewards. Since early 1994, prices for nearly all commonly collected recyclables have skyrocketed. In San Francisco, for example, recycling director Sharon Maves reports that the used paper, plastic, and metals the city picks up from curbs is bringing in "unprecedented revenue"—allowing the city to actually reduce household assessments for waste collection and recycling.

The story is the same across the continent. New York City,

which in the early 1990s was paying $6 million per year to get rid of its newsprint, now expects to earn $20–25 million per year from selling the same material, says recycling chief Bob Lange. Early in 1994, Madison, Wisconsin was paying $13 per ton to the processors who took its recyclables; by the end of the year it was receiving nearly $23 per ton. Madison recycling coordinator George Dreckman calls his city's program a "cash cow" that yielded the city $240,000 in net revenue (after processing costs, but not including collection costs) in the first four months of 1994.

Such numbers are making recycling increasingly attractive to many city waste administrators. While every city's economics are different, and some still have cheap municipal landfills with years of remaining capacity, many well-run programs are collecting and marketing materials at costs well below those of landfilling or burning waste. Madison now saves $40 for every ton of material it keeps out of its landfill by recycling. In Seattle, the city's total cost of collecting and processing recyclables fell from an average of $89 per ton in 1993 to $28 per ton by 1995—about $77 per ton less than what the city pays for disposal of what it can't recycle. In Canada, a number of communities in the province of Ontario are now earning profits of Cdn $50 per ton or more on recycling, including collection, processing, and capital costs, according to Atul Nanda, a senior official in Metro Toronto's recycling program.

Where recycling is not succeeding, a close look often reveals poor management. In Washington, DC, for example, where city officials moved in 1995 to halt residential collection of recyclables, municipal administrators did not take into account the costs of landfilling and incineration that the city avoided by recycling. They tied funding for the recycling program to revenue from dumping by commercial waste haulers at the city landfill, which meant that the more trash was recycled, the less funding it received. And finally, they failed to renegotiate materials marketing contracts to take advantage of rising prices.

Even some communities with a history of successful recycling, such as Metro Toronto, have not been in a position to benefit from improved markets, because they locked themselves into long-term, fixed-rate contracts before materials prices soared. William Ferretti, director of the New York state Office of Recycling Market Development, says municipal officials and waste haulers alike need to "stop acting like garbagemen" and realize that they are now in the business of selling commodities.

As recently as 1993, North American markets for many recovered materials were unreliable, prices were low, and many communities were unsure about their long-term ability to sell the materials they collected. Now some cities are moving to expand their collection programs to take advantage of high prices for recyclables. San Francisco, for instance, is doing extensive public outreach in an attempt to more recover more recyclables, and is expanding its program to cover previously uncollected materials. The high demand for recycled materials is allowing the city to market even lower-grade materials that in previous years might have been hard to sell.

THE BIG TURNAROUND

The most dramatic growth has occurred in prices for used paper products. Between January 1994 and March 1995, the average U.S. price of old newsprint—which had hovered near or below zero since mid-1991—rose 22-fold, according to *Recycling Times*. The price of old corrugated cardboard—used cardboard boxes—jumped five-fold. In early May 1995, a ton of baled corrugated cardboard that sold for $45 to $50 in 1991 or 1992 was commanding $230 to $250 (see figure, page 256). Other grades of paper saw smaller, but still substantial, price increases.

Over the same period, used aluminum beverage can prices doubled, and recycled glass prices rose 80 percent. Prices of

HDPE and PET—the two plastics most commonly collected for recycling—went up by 260 percent and 160 percent, respectively.

What happened to cause these jumps? To some degree, they are a result of international economic developments. Simultaneous economic upturns in Japan, North America, and Western Europe have driven up demand and prices for many commodities, both primary and recycled. Increased aluminum prices, for example, are largely the result of a January 1994 international agreement between the major aluminum-producing nations to reduce their production. Prices for both primary and recycled aluminum had been depressed since 1991, when Russian smelters—which former-ly sold nearly all of their output within the Soviet bloc—began selling large amounts of the metal on already-slack Western markets. Higher prices for some plastics are related

Prices for Two Grades of Scrap Paper, 1992–95

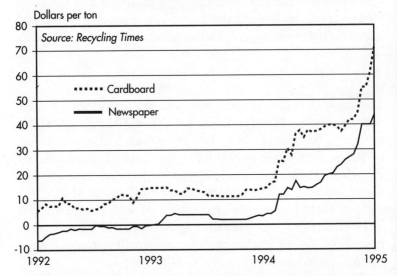

Note: Prices shown are national averages paid by processors for various grades of material. Prices paid by end users were substantially higher.

to poor crops of cotton in several major growing regions which have driven prices for the natural fiber to all-time highs and sent clothing manufacturers hunting for substitutes. China has been importing used plastic soft-drink bottles and turning the polymer they contain into new synthetic fibers for jackets and other garments.

But other factors are more basic and likely to last. Demand for products with recycled content has increased substantially with the rise of government prices and private procurement programs that give them preference, and experience with recycled-content products has removed much consumer apprehension about their suitability for a variety of uses. Most important, large capital investments have resulted in a dramatic expansion of industrial capacity for recycling. North American industry is "buying in" to recycling.

Structural Change

The paper industry is at the leading edge of this change. Paper accounts for a larger share (38 percent) of U.S. municipal solid waste than any other material, and has received more market-development attention from governments than other materials. Such efforts are now bearing fruit. The Environmental Protection Agency estimates that the amount of paper recovered from U.S. municipal waste grew from 13 million tons in 1985 to 26 million tons in 1993. During much of this period, wastepaper prices lagged, as the amount collected grew faster than the overall capacity of paper recycling plants. In 1994, however, the tables turned dramatically. Recovered paper consumption began growing more than twice as fast as total fiber consumption, and mills were scrambling for used paper supplies.

Behind this situation, say many in the paper industry, is a major change in the industry's structure. Heavy investment by papermakers in building new recycled-paper mills and retooling old plants to take in recycled fiber has created a much more mature, stable market for used paper. While prices will eventually decline again—as is to be expected to some degree with any commodity in response to normal business fluctuations—observers believe that the tremendous paper price crashes seen in previous years are unlikely to recur. Dan Cotter, of Pacific Forest, a major broker of both used paper and new paper products, argues that recycled fiber has become a "primary" input for many paper manufacturers, rather than a last-resort substitute for virgin pulp. As a result, recycled fiber should experience future price swings no worse than those experienced in virgin pulp markets, whereas until recently, recycled-paper markets were far more volatile.

Recycling is revolutionizing the paper industry. The industry is actively moving to site its plants in areas with untapped reserves of wastepaper, and new paper mills are now being built in and near cities rather than in more remote areas near large forests. Weyerhaeuser, for example, is a major partner in a large mill in Iowa—a state better-known for corn than for forests—to take advantage of the substantial amounts of wastepaper available from Midwestern cities. The industry is also moving to recycle not just relatively low grades of paper—such as newsprint and old corrugated cardboard—but also office and coated papers, and is also making higher-grade products from recycled fiber.

The North American paper industry is pouring money into a resource it once resisted stubbornly. The American Forest & Paper Association (AFPA), its main trade group, estimates that its members will invest a total of $10 billion in recycling by the end of the 1990s. They have set a goal of recycling or reusing half of all U.S. paper production by the year 2000. AFPA estimates that the United States recycled 40.5 percent of the paper it used in 1994. More than 80 percent of this was paper recovered from the post-consumer waste stream, while the remainder was scrap from paper mills and printing plants.

So much new paper recycling capacity has come on-line

that existing collection programs are barely providing enough fiber to meet the demand. And new plants have added several million tons of paper-recycling capacity. As a result, recycled-papermakers are becoming vocal supporters of paper collection programs. One paper broker describes the industry as "panicked" about future supplies of recycled fiber for the mills they have spent billions to build. Weyerhaeuser—a Fortune 500 company best-known for its timber production—has invested so much in recycling capacity that it is now offering cities 20-year, guaranteed market-rate contracts to purchase all the wastepaper they can collect. The company took in about 3 million tons in 1995.

The paper-recycling situation has completely reversed in just a few years. Before, paper companies were reluctant to invest in recycling because they saw limited markets for recycled paper, and because they feared that large-scale municipal paper collection programs would not survive. Now, some industry officials are voicing caution about further investment in recycling capacity for the opposite reason—because markets have grown so fast that they are worried about obtaining adequate supplies of secondary fiber. Ironically, governments now need to reassure the companies not about the survival of the collection programs, but about their commitment to expand those programs over the long term.

THE GLUT THAT WAS

The reason that many governments embarked on market-development programs for recycled materials is that for much of the late 1980s and early 1990s, collection of recyclables grew far faster than industrial capacity to absorb them. Thousands of recycling collection programs were initiated in North American communities in the last decade. According to *BioCycle* magazine's annual waste management survey, the number of U.S. curbside pickup programs for recyclables grew from 1,042 in 1988 to 6,678 in 1993. This growth, and similar growth in drop-off and commercial-waste recycling programs, led to an extraordinary increase in the overall tonnage of recycled materials collected, from some 16 million tons in the United States in 1985 to 45 million tons in 1993.

Not surprisingly, such rapid growth created a glut of materials. The hundreds of communities all starting up recycling programs at the same time created a structural problem in the recycling economy. Collection programs can be implemented almost as quickly as trucks can be purchased. The capacity to turn the materials collected into new products, however, can take years—and billions of dollars in capital investment—to build. Few communities devoted the same energy to developing recycling industries that they applied to their collection programs. But the market-development efforts of a few influential cities and states—and more recent actions by the U.S. federal government—set the stage for 1994's market turnaround.

The most obvious way to develop markets is to ensure that a guaranteed minimum quantity of goods with recycled content will be purchased. Governments are among the largest buyers of many goods, and among the first prominent market-development efforts were state laws requiring or encouraging government procurement of products with recycled content. Nearly all states now have such laws, with widely varying degrees of stringency. In 1993, the U.S. federal government joined in with an executive order requiring that the paper it purchases have 20 percent recycled content by 1995 and 25 percent by 2000. The action immediately guaranteed a huge market for recycled paper, since the federal government, at 300,000 tons per year, is the world's largest buyer of paper.

States have also moved to ensure that large private buyers of some commodities buy a minimum of recycled material. The newsprint market has been most notably affected by such measures. Thirteen states now have standards for minimum recycled content of newsprint; 15 more have negotiated voluntary agreements with newspaper publishers to increase their purchasing of recycled content. According to New York's William Ferretti, the recycled-content standards for newsprint some states enacted in the late 1980s—and the threat of standards in other states—were the primary factors in the newsprint market's shift toward secondary fiber. Then, as publishers got accustomed to using recycled newsprint, they found that it could perform as well as virgin paper, and resistance to its use fell away.

FROM ENVIRONMENTAL PROTECTION TO ECONOMIC DEVELOPMENT

As municipal solid waste officials have realized that recycling can be a cheaper disposal method than landfilling or incineration, collection programs have taken off. Faced with market problems, procurement and recycled-content requirements have been governments' first answer. But a few states are now beginning to make a crucial transition from viewing recycling simply as an environmental measure—a waste-disposal strategy—to seeing it simultaneously as an economic development opportunity. The most notable successes have come when economic development offices begin to promote recycling.

New York state took the lead in this area in 1988 when it created the Office of Recycling Market Development within its Department of Economic Development. The office offers financing, technical assistance, and market information—and a helping hand through the regulatory thickets—to companies that use recycled materials. Similar efforts are now underway in at least 18 other states, according to a 1994 *BioCycle* survey.

Bringing in state, regional, and local economic development officials to help promote recycling helps such businesses get access to a wide variety of proven tools: Industrial Development Bonds and other financing mechanisms, special property-tax treatment, siting assistance, and expedited regulatory action on permits, zoning, and related matters. Twenty-seven states now offer some form of tax incentive for recycling. The Environmental Protection Agency has supported these efforts by establishing a "Jobs Through Recycling" project, which offers grants for hiring Recycling Economic Development Advocates in state economic development offices, and has also helped establish Recycling Business Assistance Centers in four states.

California has become the laboratory for what is probably the most extensive effort in North America to develop recycling industries. The state has created 40 Recycling Market Development Zones, which are, in effect, enterprise zones specifically targeted toward recycling-based businesses. The state's Integrated Waste Management Board offers technical assistance with financing and marketing, and local governments also offer strong incentive packages designed to meet their communities' needs. The Board has approved some $12 million in loans for such enterprises, and is currently considering $3 million more. Board officials—who see the state financing as a bridge to much greater amounts of commercial capital—estimate that the zones have created 1,000 new jobs since the program was established in 1989.

During the long market slump—when cities were offering a few dollars per ton to anyone who would haul away their newsprint—extraordinarily cheap secondary materials helped lure entrepreneurs into recycling-related businesses. In the long run, however, businesses don't need cheap raw materials so much as they need predictable prices for what they buy and what they sell. In an effort to alleviate the uncertainty and unpredictability of recycled-materials markets, the Recycling Advisory Council (a program of the National Recycling Coalition) has been working with the Chicago Board of Trade, one of the world's premier commodities markets, to develop a formal trading system for recycled materials.

Among the project's elements are the development of product specifications that materials will have to meet to be traded, the design of an electronic trading system, development of dispute-resolution procedures, and an effort to inform and involve potential participants. The system initially will be only a cash market, but the feasibility of futures markets will be investigated. Trading in glass and plastic began in the summer of 1995.

DOING GOOD ... AND MAKING MONEY

While recycling is worth doing for environmental reasons, its success will eventually be measured in dollars as well. Recycling is a business. Whether that business thrives will eventually determine the success or failure of community recycling programs.

The broad environmental benefits of recycling—especially, savings in natural resources and energy—will only be realized if manufacturers substitute used materials for a major share of the virgin wood, metals, and plastics they now consume. For this to happen, there must be a large, vigorous industrial sector devoted to taking used materials, processing them, and turning them into salable commodities. In North America, that sector is clearly now developing on a large scale, at least for some materials—and the environmental benefits, though hidden, are substantial. The United States and Canada are now substituting generally less-polluting recycling facilities for virgin materials industries that are often among the greatest offenders in air and water pollution, energy use, and damage to ecosystems. The United States alone is now saving about 1 exajoule of energy—about 1 percent of total U.S. energy use—each year by recycling municipal solid waste.

With recycling beginning to fall into place, it is time for the next step. Within the limited universe of municipal solid waste (which is only a fraction of total U.S. waste production), growth in recycling appears to be stabilizing the amount of garbage going to landfills and incinerators, which had been growing for decades. Yet, U.S. waste generation is still increasing. In the long run, market mechanisms need to be developed not just to increase recycling, but to reduce the quantity of waste that we generate in the first place. Only then will a truly sustainable materials economy—one that consumes a minimum of virgin products and recycles most of what it takes in—be achieved.

6

Social Instabilities

CHIAPAS: THE FRUITS OF DESPAIR

By Michael Renner

On New Year's Day 1994, a group of towns in Chiapas, Mexico's southernmost state, was seized by a ragtag peasant army composed mainly of indigenous Mayan people. Two weeks and at least 145 deaths later, the government had forced the Zapatista National Liberation Army (Ejército Zapatista de Liberación Nacional, or EZLN) to retreat to its jungle strongholds in the eastern portion of the state. That New Year's Day also marked the coming into force of the North American Free Trade Agreement or NAFTA, the treaty intended to integrate Mexico, the United States, and Canada into a unified trading bloc.

In a sense, NAFTA and the EZLN are the forces that define modern Mexico. Resolving the tensions of that troubled society will require a view broad enough to embrace both the rarefied world of international finance, and dirt-poor towns where most people don't even have access to proper latrines. Dealing with the tensions in places like Chiapas is a matter of prime international importance: the poverty, environmental degradation, and social inequities that underlie Mexico's troubles can be found throughout the developing world.

Worldwide, about 1.3 billion people, or 23 percent of the global population, live in poverty, according to the United Nations. At least 600 million of these people live in "absolute poverty"—a condition only several hundred calories a day away from the slide into starvation. Some 1.2 billion people are landless or do not have access to enough land to feed themselves. At least 400 million people live in ecologically fragile areas—areas where drought, deforestation, pollution, and other forms of environmental degradation are putting increasing numbers of livelihoods at risk. Some 120 million people are unemployed, while another 700 million are working long hours for next to nothing. Today, the richest 20 percent of the world's people have 150 times the income of the poorest 20 percent—a disparity that, to varying degrees, can be found in virtually every country.

The Zapatistas present a genuine challenge to the Mexican version of this predicament—but the challenge is really political, not military. They take their name and their basic ideology from Emiliano Zapata, the leader of a peasant army during the Mexican Revolution of 1911 to 1917. After his assassination in 1919, Zapata became a figure of mythic proportions and a source of inspiration for Mexican campesinos, as small-scale farmers and farm laborers are called. The Zapatistas' ideals can perhaps best be summed up in a slogan they adopted from that earlier peasant army: "the land belongs to those who work it." But despite their rhetoric, the Zapatistas are not revolutionary in the usual sense of the term. In contrast to most Latin American guerrilla movements, the EZLN has insisted from its inception that it has no interest in overthrowing the government. It sees itself as involved in a desperate struggle for democracy—and its leaders have a clear record of practicing what they preach. At every turn of events they have taken pains to consult with their supporters. In its talks with the government, for instance, the EZLN has made a point of having proposed agreements ratified by its constituency.

Even in Mexico, few people had heard of the EZLN before January 1994, but the movement dates back to at least 1983. In the poor communities of eastern Chiapas, people have long been keenly aware that the deck is stacked against them. Enormous economic inequalities, a political system that is almost completely unaccountable to its poorer constituents, desperate poverty, and the degradation of the land: these are facts of life in Chiapas, and to growing numbers of the poor, they made a strong case for the EZLN. By the early 1990s, the EZLN's ranks were expanding rapidly. By early 1993, when the Mexican military had its first brush with the EZLN, Zapatista supporters probably numbered at least 70,000.

At that time, the authorities had little to say about the Zapatistas; official Mexico was eager to project the image of a stable country in order to guarantee passage of NAFTA and encourage the growing ranks of foreign investors. But it was impossible to cover up the January 1994 uprising. Zapatista demands for land and election reform found wide resonance throughout the country. The Zapatistas succeeded in galvanizing national discussion of these issues—as well as some local action. Sympathizers throughout southern Mexico seized dozens of town halls to protest the string of fraudulent elections that had allowed Mexico's ruling party, the Partido Revolucionario Institucional or PRI, to maintain its decades-old grip on power. Land-hungry peasants invaded private ranches; some landowners fled, while others counterattacked with hired gunmen. Domestic and international interest intensified and by the end of February, then-President Carlos Salinas de Gortari had begun peace talks with the EZLN.

A Dumping Ground for the Marginalized

Chiapas has long been known as "a rich land, a poor people." The state accounts for only 3 percent of Mexico's population, but has 5 percent of its oil production and 12 percent of its natural gas production. Chiapas grows 13 percent of Mexico's corn, the country's staple food crop, and 46 percent of its coffee—a major export crop. It also produces half of the country's hydroelectric power, yet only one in three Chiapanecan households is hooked up to the electrical grid. Fewer than half of the state's people regularly eat meat, even though Chiapas is a leading beef producer. In 1990, only 58 percent of Chiapanecan households had running water—well below the national average of 79 percent. Literacy stood at 70 percent, 17 points below the national rate. In comparison to the country as a whole, Chiapas also lags behind in terms of household income and education, and has above average rates of infant mortality.

Within Chiapas, the same inequities repeat themselves on a finer scale. The western part of the state is relatively prosperous, thanks to the large-scale commercial farms in the Grijalva River valley and the coffee plantations along the Pacific coast. The central highlands are poorer, and the eastern lowlands, inhabited primarily by people of Mayan descent, are deeply impoverished. These people, whose forebears built one of the greatest pre-Columbian civilizations, now live in a kind of de facto statelessness. They have virtually nothing in the way of government services, political power, or economic opportunity. Eastern Chiapas, in the words of George Collier, a social anthropologist at Stanford University, "is a kind of dumping ground for the marginalized." By every conventional indicator of social and economic well-being, the people of eastern Chiapas score far lower than the national average—and lower even than the average for Mexico's indigenous population. Profound discrimination is the lot of indigenous people all over Mexico, but Chiapas excels in this respect. Tom Barry, founder of the Interhemispheric Resource Center, a research institute in Albuquerque, New Mexico, puts it bluntly: "nowhere else in Mexico is racism so pronounced."

Despite the huge number of problems, the Zapatista core issue is clearly farm land—or the lack of it. In part, the land troubles are a function of population growth: the number of Chiapanecans doubled between 1970 and 1990, to 3.2 million. In absolute terms, the state's cropland area is actually still expanding, although this is being accomplished largely through the clearing of rainforests and the cultivation of other areas of marginal agricultural value. But per capita cropland area has been declining since 1975.

The population pressure is exacerbated enormously by a highly inequitable land tenure system, which has bedeviled the area since the days of Spanish colonialism. A tiny farming and ranching elite controls much of the state's best land and dominates its political system. Among coffee growers, for instance, the richest 0.15 percent—those with more than 100 hectares in production—own 12 percent of coffee-growing land; 91 percent of coffee growers have less than 5 hectares each. Cattle ranching, too, is dominated by a handful of wealthy ladino (nonindigenous) families. The number of cattle in the state grew from under 1 million in 1960 to almost 4 million in 1980 before declining to its current level of about 3 million. Today, an estimated 45 percent of Chiapanecan territory is used as cattle pastureland. And in Chiapas, as in other parts of southern Mexico, the ranches have displaced many campesinos. Often, says Barry, the campesinos were "pushed off their lands by cattlemen protected by the army and their own paramilitary bands."

The growth of ranching over the past few decades has been a national phenomenon. To serve an expanding urban demand for meat, large swaths of land have been converted to cattle pasture all over the country. The ecological costs have been huge: ranching accounts for some 60 percent of tropical forest loss in Mexico. The social costs have been substantial as well. There is a paradox in the country's obsession with cattle—an equity issue defined by Philip Howard and Thomas Homer-Dixon, who direct the University of Toronto's Project on Environment, Population, and Security: "Sixty percent of the productive territory in Mexico is pastureland, producing meat for a population 50 percent of whom never eat meat." To support the cattle industry, a growing number of farmers have switched from foodgrains to feedgrains. During the late 1970s, this trend cost Mexico its self-sufficiency in food production. In 1996, Mexico import-ed a full third of its food, primarily from the United States.

LAND REFORM: A PROMISE DENIED

In large measure, it was the promise of land reform that brought the PRI to power in 1929, and built the party's pop-ular base. During the presidency of Lázaro Cárdenas, from 1934 to 1940, a tenth of Mexico's land was redistributed to peasants and indigenous communities. The proportion of landless laborers in the rural work force dropped from 69 to 36 percent (before the revolution, 92 percent of Mexico's population was landless). It seemed as if Cárdenas was on his way to achieving real land reform—a basic aim of the Mexican Constitution, which was enacted in 1917, in the wake of the revolution. In Chiapas, the PRI won widespread approval among the poor, and despite all of the subsequent disap-pointments, Chiapanecan peasants were until recently among the party's most reliable supporters. (In fact, some have remained strongly loyal to the PRI, engaging in skirmishes and mutual expulsions with villagers that support the EZLN.)

But in the years following the Cárdenas presidency, the pace of redistribution slowed dramatically, and the little land that was offered to peasants was generally of inferior quality. By the late 1950s, peasants throughout Mexico had begun to demand more and better land. In the southern states espe-cially, people backed up their demands by physically occupy-ing large estates, where they found themselves at odds with state and federal authorities, and in some cases with the pri-vate armies of big landowners as well. By 1967, a peasant guerrilla force called the Party of the Poor had been organized in the southern state of Guerrero. All across southern Mexico, the number of occupations exploded in the early 1970s, and land skirmishes became a chronic feature of rural society.

The skirmishes themselves never seriously threatened the Mexican military and by 1974, the Party of the Poor had been crushed. But it was obvious that military force offered no hope of a lasting solution. To defuse the situation, President Luis Echeverria (1970–76) returned to a cautious policy of land reform. He also encouraged the colonization of Mexico's remaining frontier lands, including eastern Chiapas, which at the time was still largely intact rain forest. The colonization continues, but successor governments gradually abandoned even Echeverria's luke-warm commitment to agrarian reform.

More than in other Mexican states, the large landowners of Chiapas have managed to delay or halt land transfers—often with the help of their own paramilitary bands, and with the collusion of police and military officials. Their own farms often surpass the legal limit on individual farm size, which in Chiapas is 8,000 hectares—3,000 hectares higher than elsewhere in Mexico. The land that is designated for redistribution is usually the least productive and is often promised to more than one campesino community. Land claims can languish in a tangle of state bureaucracies for years. In 1992, unresolved land claims in Chiapas accounted for almost 30 percent of the total land reform backlog in all of Mexico. More than 100,000 hectares of idled land remain to be distributed in the state.

Whether that land will ever be redistributed is now an open question. In 1992, President Salinas formally ended the promise of land reform by amending Article 27 of the Mexican Constitution. That action was presented as a step towards greater agricultural efficiency—especially for the production of export crops of the sort envisioned under NAFTA. But whatever its merits for agribusiness, its social implications could hardly have been more grave. Although he invoked the memory of Zapata, Salinas had formally repudiated one of the founding ideals of the Mexican republic. And by withdrawing the single most important promise that the state had made to the campesinos, he effectively disenfranchised some 25 million Mexican citizens. Salinas, as Stanford's Collier puts it, "robbed many peasants not just of the possibility of gaining a piece of land, but, quite simply, of hope." Tom Barry quotes a young indigenous campesino from Chiapas: "The land is all we have, all we know. Without the land ... we will be begging on the streets of Mexico City or working as peones like our grandfathers did." The amendment was a crucial catalyst in the Zapatista rebellion.

The amendment opened the door to another important change in the land tenure system. The government legalized the private sale of land from the ejidos—the plots that make up the communal farming system established after the revolution. Previously, a campesino could have a permanent right to farm a parcel of ejido land, but he could not own the land outright. The change gave farmers direct ownership of the land they worked. That approach might seem to be in keeping with the Zapatista creed, but critics charge that given the general lawlessness of rural Mexico, the legal possibility of transferring title is a virtual guarantee that the best ejido land will eventually end up in the hands of the wealthy, leaving the poor in even worse shape than they were before. The ejido system includes 70 percent of all Mexican farmers and accounts for 49 percent of the country's total land area. The system contains much more than farmland: some 70 percent of Mexico's remaining forests are located within the ejidos and other agrarian communes. Increased privatization is therefore likely also to mean increased deforestation.

Some ejido land is used for commercial farming, but much of it supports subsistence agriculture. One-fifth of ejido holdings are not arable at all, and 64 percent of ejido farmers work parcels of less than 5 hectares. Since most of the land is very arid, that's often not enough to support a family. And millions of Mexicans have no land at all. In total, between 4.5 and 5.6 million people are classed as landless or land poor. Many campesinos, in the words of Tom Barry, are "rural proletarians who depend on seasonal planting, weeding and harvesting work on estates that are sometimes far away from their villages."

The ejido system was already under considerable strain, as was apparent from occasional bloody clashes between neighboring ejidos, and an increasing number of illegal sales. But dismantling the system without providing an alternative greatly deepened the political discontent. It also increased migration into urban slums and illegal immigration into the United States. Campesino farming has suffered from the privatizing of other parts of the agricultural system as well, beginning in the mid-1980s. The government has ended most production subsidies, and has abandoned its traditional role in agricultural marketing and distribution. Meanwhile, the removal of agricultural tariffs under NAFTA has boosted imports of cheap food from the United States. This development benefited Mexico's 8-million strong middle class (who make up less than 10 percent of the population), but it portends a bleak future for millions of small-scale farmers, who can neither compete with the foreign producers nor afford the imported food. According to the National Union of Regional Autonomous Peasant Organizations, a Mexican campesino umbrella group, up to 80 percent of rural Mexican producers are caught in this bind.

A Harvest of Ruined Land

A corrupt land tenure system and inexorable demographic pressure are only part of the story. Various forms of environmental degradation have also contributed to the desperation that resulted in the Zapatista uprising. Roughly 85 percent of Mexico's land area is arid or semi-arid, and drought is a frequent hardship. The Mexican north, for instance, has been in the throes of a multi-year drought, making it the worst in a quarter century. Large numbers of destitute farmers have been forced to move to urban areas or to cross into the

United States; many of those who remain face the prospect of foreclosure because they cannot repay their bank loans. At least 29 percent of the country's territory is desertified, and 70 percent of its cropland is seriously affected by soil erosion. The depletion of arable soils, the food needs of a growing population, and the inroads of cattle ranching are increasingly undermining the traditional milpa system, which relied on fallow periods to allow the land to recuperate.

In addition to bringing more land into continuous cultivation, these pressures are forcing more and more people into areas where farming is bound to cause serious degradation, such as forests or steep hillsides. Agriculturally marginal areas now account for one-fifth of the country's cropland. More than half of all Mexican farmers, for example, are eking out a living on highly erodible slopes.

In eastern Chiapas, this trend can be observed in the Lacandón rain forest. Originally covering some 1.5 million hectares and virtually uninhabited until the mid-20th century, the forest has since attracted several waves of colonists. Some of the initial settlers had been forcibly relocated to allow for dam construction in the Grijalva River basin. Others were fleeing land scarcity—a form of migration that the Echeverria administration encouraged during the first half of the 1970s, when migration to places like eastern Chiapas became a kind of social "safety valve" for intense land pressures elsewhere. Still other settlers arrived for different reasons. During the late 1960s and 1970s, people from all over Mexico fled to the Lacandón to escape various episodes of political persecution, such as the 1968 crackdown on the student movement. During the 1980s, refugees from the civil war in Guatemala arrived in the area. And all of these people are locked in competition not only with each other, but with loggers, ranchers, and oil and gas prospectors. All told, population in the Lacandón has grown 25-fold since 1960, from 12,000 to 300,000.

The settlers have reduced tree cover in the Lacandón from

90 percent in 1960 to 30 percent today. Most of the migrants came from the intensively cultivated highlands of central Chiapas, but the farming techniques that worked well in their homeland proved poorly adapted to the forest soils. The productivity of their plots tended to drop rapidly, driving them ever farther into the forest. Meanwhile, ranchers were converting both the forest itself and the exhausted farm plots into grazing land. During the 1980s, they more than doubled the amount of pastureland within the Lacandón. The rate of deforestation in eastern Chiapas has far outpaced even that of the Brazilian Amazon. Large swaths of the area are now so deforested that the border between Chiapas and neighboring Guatemala is clearly visible from space.

Official attempts to stop the deforestation have been undercut by the same kind of self-defeating corruption that pushed people into the forest to begin with. The government created the 325,000-hectare Montes Azules Biosphere Reserve within the Lacandón in 1978, in what is now the single largest remaining tract of tropical forest in Mexico. During the 1980s, the number of colonists in the reserve grew substantially, but official attempts at relocation were met with resistance, and opposition parties picked up support. When the Salinas administration came into office in 1988, it attempted to shore up its power base in the area by recognizing the land claims of reserve settlers allied with the PRI, and rejecting the claims of those who were not. Predictably, this favoritism sharpened antagonisms in the area and increased popular distrust of the government.

In the Shadow of the Debt

The Zapatista uprising cannot be understood without taking into account Mexico's tumultuous economic development over the past few decades—a course of events that has greatly widened the gap between the country's rich and poor. During the 1970s and 1980s, Mexico went through an oil boom-bust cycle and a severe debt crisis. Subsequent efforts to accelerate the country's integration into the world market threw Mexico into its worst economic crisis in 70 years.

During the 1970s, rising oil revenues allowed the government to kick off ambitious development projects, such as the Grijalva River dams in Chiapas. Such projects basically bought the support of those sectors of the public who stood to benefit from them. But Mexico was also borrowing heavily to finance its oil development, and when oil prices plummeted in the early 1980s, the country found itself unable to service its mammoth foreign debt. International lenders forced the country to implement a "structural adjustment" program that cut social expenditures, slashed wages, phased out price controls, and removed subsidies important for the poor.

The results were documented by Carlos Heredia and Mary Purcell, economists at Equipo Pueblo, a Mexico City think tank. Social services spending fell sharply between 1982 and 1988 and despite a subsequent increase, 1993 spending was still below the 1980 level. Total public spending on education declined by 20 percent from 1982 to 1990. The health care budget was cut so severely that in 1990 even the World Bank—generally a strong advocate of structural adjustment—argued that Mexico "may be under-spending on health care."

The cut-backs in social programs did not affect all agricultural sectors equally. Most of the remaining farm credit went to cattle ranchers; small commercial and subsistence farmers were the biggest losers, and many were compelled to abandon their land. By 1990, 87 percent of agricultural producers in Chiapas had no access at all to government credit. Falling world market prices for coffee worsened the agricultural picture and Salinas exacerbated the effects of that problem by dismantling INMECAFE, the Mexican Coffee Institute, which had guaranteed markets for small Chiapanecan coffee growers.

The oil boom-bust cycle hit the labor market as well. In Chiapas and elsewhere, many people left their farms to take higher paying jobs during the boom of the 1970s. When the contraction hit, the agrarian economy could not reabsorb them, and they joined the ranks of the unemployed. The numbers of the poor grew, and so did the depth of their poverty.

Yet another corrosive force within Chiapanecan communities was the replacement of in-kind exchanges with cash transactions. This broke down many traditional relationships of mutual dependency that had once helped poorer citizens and generated a sense of solidarity. Increasingly, only pesos— and a substantial number of them—could buy food, clothing, and other necessities. A day's labor no longer had much trading value. This shift coincided with the cuts in social services; the result, as Collier describes it, was that "the impoverished have had no place to turn and little to lose by joining the Zapatista rebellion."

On the international scene, the bust had by the early 1980s made Mexico a symbol of the Third World debt crisis. Although that image has faded away, the effects linger on. Over the past 15 years, Mexico has transferred more than $150 billion to its public-sector creditors, but remains trapped in the debt treadmill. Between 1982 and 1994, the country's outstanding foreign debt rose from $86 billion to $140 billion. Interest and principal repayments on the debt cost Mexico an estimated $27.7 billion, or 10 percent of its GNP, during 1996 alone.

Nevertheless, during the NAFTA negotiations, the Salinas administration was touting Mexico as a country rapidly shedding its Third World status, and ready to join the United States and Canada as an equal partner on the world trading scene. Salinas achieved his ambitions for NAFTA but the PR effort fell apart soon thereafter. Towards the end of 1994, foreign investors began to pull out of short-term, speculative portfolio investments that the government had encouraged in order to cover its deepening current accounts deficit. The pull-out quickly became a run and by the time it was over, in

December, $5 billion had been withdrawn from the country. The overvalued peso collapsed and Mexico entered a severe economic depression.

Fred Rosen, editor of the NACLA Report on the Americas, a U.S. magazine that covers social issues in Latin America, summed up the consequences: "The country's internal market collapsed, credit for small- and medium-sized businesses virtually disappeared, formal employment dramatically contracted, and poverty grew at an alarming rate." During 1995, Mexico's GDP fell by almost 7 percent and at least 1 million Mexicans lost their jobs. Because inflation has far outpaced wages, the purchasing power of Mexican wages has fallen 43 percent over the past 9 years. Two-thirds of the country's economically active population of 34 million are now earning incomes below the poverty line. The number of Mexicans living in extreme poverty, according to official figures, rose from 14 million in 1988 to 22 million today.

One effect of the economic crisis has been to amplify the disparities between the rich and the poor. Tens of thousands of Mexican companies went bankrupt during 1995, but the 500 largest businesses weathered the storm by laying off workers and by increasing their export sales to offset collapsing domestic demand. Jorge Castañeda, a political scientist at the National Autonomous University of Mexico, reports that the share of national income going to the poorest half of the population dropped from 21 to 16 percent from 1984 to 1994, while the richest 10 percent of Mexicans saw their share rise from 33 to 41 percent over the same period. The very wealthy have done best of all: between 1988 and 1993, the number of Mexican billionaires rose from 2 to 24.

The effects of the economic crisis on Mexicans' wellbeing are plain. Malnutrition now afflicts anywhere from 40 to 65 percent of the population, and is especially prevalent in indigenous communities. Heredia and Purcell report that infant deaths due to nutritional deficiencies almost tripled over the period 1980-1992. And the UNDP Human

Development Report noted in 1991 that the 53-year life expectancy of the poorest Mexicans was 20 years less than that of their richest compatriots.

IN THE SHADOW OF THE PRI

Ever since coming to power, the PRI had taken considerable care to give all sectors of society, including the poor, a sense that they had a voice and a stake in the political system. The system was obviously autocratic, and designed to maintain the PRI's political monopoly. But it was also durable: it remained stable for more than half a century. During the 1980s, however, this social pact was broken by the shift toward privatization and structural adjustment—policies known collectively in Mexico as "neoliberal."

The austerity of the 1980s eroded the PRI's ability to maintain its elaborate system of patronage. At the same time, the party's legitimacy was being called into question from many quarters, because of its resistance to democratization, rampant corruption, and a growing sense that the PRI was less and less able to reconcile the diverging interests of "modern" and "backward" Mexico. The 1988 presidential election was closely contested, and Salinas was widely considered to owe his victory to massive electoral fraud.

To shore up its patronage system and provide some relief to the poor, the Salinas administration launched a development initiative called the National Solidarity Program (PRONASOL) in 1989. By 1994, a total of $15 billion had been channeled into PRONASOL anti-poverty programs. Chiapas received more of these funds than any other state: its share rose from $30 million in 1989 to almost $150 million in both 1992 and 1993. Yet PRONASOL has never won popular support in Chiapas, and the reason is not hard to grasp: PRONASOL funds are channeled to PRI supporters, but denied to the party's opponents.

As it became increasingly clear that PRONASOL would

not ensure campesino loyalty in the poorer regions of the country, federal and state officials, along with the increasingly despised "caciques" (local PRI bosses) reacted with more coercive measures. They denied government services to people whose political allegiance was in question; they evicted them from communally held land; and increasing numbers of dissidents were threatened or simply turned up dead. In Chiapas, governor Patrocinio González Garrido, a former army general, pushed through a penal code in the early 1990s that defined collective efforts of self-defense on the part of campesinos as criminal acts. He also spent a large share of social welfare funding on prison construction. For the Chiapanecan elite, Garrido's policies produced a reassuring illusion that campesino unrest had been eliminated, according to Antonio Garcia de Léon, a historian at the National University of Mexico. But Garrido was only adding to the desperation that would become the Zapatista uprising.

Talking and Killing

The peace talks between the Zapatistas and the government, begun on February 21, 1994, made little headway over the ensuing year. By the next February, some foreign investors and domestic businesses had managed to convince Mexico's current president, Ernesto Zedillo, that the Zapatistas were a threat to their interests. Zedillo broke off negotiations and sent in the troops. Some EZLN jungle strongholds were recaptured in the fighting, but the Zapatistas remained a potent political force. Shortly thereafter, Zedillo changed course again and resumed negotiations. One year later, the parties had reached an agreement promising limited autonomy to indigenous communities throughout Mexico. But this agreement is only the first of six planned sets of negotiations, and it does not address some of the toughest issues, such as land reform and democratization. In any case, the government has given little sign that it is prepared to carry out even this limited accord.

Since then, the negotiations have slipped back into dead-lock, and the level of violence in Chiapas is growing. The years 1996 and 1997 were marked by frequent reports of harassment of political dissidents, killings by pro-PRI gun-men, and arrests of alleged Zapatista sympathizers. In late 1997, Chiapas made the headlines again after 45 villagers were murdered by pro-PRI gunmen. In August 1996, the EZLN suspended talks, charging that the government was no longer engaging in meaningful dialogue. And the military presence in Chiapas remains heavy. Some observers fear that the government may once again be tempted by the mirage of a military resolution. Mexico's military, incidentally, has done well even during the recent hard times: since the late 1980s, military spending has doubled, to about $2 billion a year.

Despite the impasse in the negotiations, the Zapatistas have managed to catalyze a great deal of grass roots activity. In July 1994, they helped set up a "State Assembly of the Chiapanecan People"—a loose coalition of citizen groups, campesino organizations, independent unions, and other NGOs. And a growing number of Chiapanecan communities are establishing autonomous municipal organizations as an alternative to the official bodies. Many communities are prac-ticing a kind of collective civil resistance by refusing to pay for the meager public services they receive. And in 1995, several indigenous groups came together to form the "Plural Indigenous National Assembly for Autonomy," as a means of pressing for the right to self government.

Part of the Zapatista strategy is to transform what began as a local insurgency into a nationwide grassroots movement. By mid-1996, more than 400 Zapatista committees had sprung up all over Mexico, and the EZLN had formed an alliance with another dissident organization known as El Barzón ("the harness"). El Barzón started in 1993 as a group of deeply indebted farmers in the western state of Jalisco; it has since become a militant, though peaceful, national orga-nization of both rural and urban debtors. El Barzón may greatly extend the clout of the country's political dissidents, since its membership includes not just poor campesinos but debt-ridden and disaffected farmers from the middle class. The Zapatistas have also taken their message beyond Mexico's borders, by organizing conferences attended by delegations from all over the world. In July 1996, they held a "Special Forum on Reform of the State." A month later, they held the "First Intercontinental Forum for Humanity and Against Neoliberalism."

A NEW GUERRILLA FORCE

"Tinder boxes awaiting a spark" is how Andrew Reding, a senior fellow at the World Policy Institute, describes many of Mexico's southern states. Growing poverty, electoral fraud, and the violent repression of dissent are ever more common facts of life throughout the region. Like Chiapas, the states of Guerrero, Tabasco, and Oaxaca have become increasingly militarized. In Guerrero, Tabasco, Puebla, and in the more northern state of San Luis Potosi, local indigenous rebellions have broken out.

In early 1996, Tabasco was the scene of widespread unrest in response to election fraud and environmental damage caused by the state oil company, Pemex. Thousands of campesinos blocked access to dozens of oil wells to protest the oil spills, toxic waste dumps, and other forms of environmental damage that are injuring the health and livelihoods of the mostly indigenous local people. Nacajuca, one of the state's most blighted municipalities, has suffered a substantial drop in its corn, bean, coconut, and banana harvests. Rivers and lagoons are so polluted that once abundant fisheries are all but gone. But authorities have showed little interest in discussing these problems; the blockades were broken up by force.

Most opposition activity in Mexico is peaceful, but the summer of 1996 marked the appearance of a new guerrilla force, calling itself the Popular Revolutionary Army (or EPR, its initials in Spanish). The EPR first appeared en masse that June, when about 100 heavily armed fighters participated in a memorial service for 17 campesinos killed by the police a year earlier, at a place called Aguas Blancas in the state of Guerrero. The killings were part of a campaign of intimidation against campesino groups opposed to increased corporate logging in the Costa Grande region of the state. An unusual legal proceeding later revealed that the victims had been ambushed, and that weapons were afterwards placed in their hands, to make the murders look like the results of a fight. But at the time they occurred, the Aguas Blancas killings were nothing special—hundreds of activists have been murdered in Guerrero over the past several years. What made this case different was that the international news media happened to notice it; the event made news worldwide, and the authorities were seriously embarrassed. An investigation by the Mexican Supreme Court implicated the state leadership, and Ruben Figueroa, the governor of Guerrero, was forced to resign last March. But nobody was ever prosecuted for the murders. At the memorial service, the EPR fighters disappeared before police could intervene. Two months later, the EPR staged a series of attacks on military and government facilities in seven southern states; 15 people were killed.

Many observers agree that conditions in Guerrero in particular—its mix of grinding poverty and repression on one hand and its luxury tourist resorts like Acapulco on the other—made the state ripe for an armed uprising. But it remains unclear how much of a social base the EPR has, although it claimed 23,000 followers all across Mexico. It is clear that this new force does not share the Zapatista enthusiasm for democratic change: the EPR has stated flatly that it is fighting to overthrow the government. Even the EZLN's spokesman, Sub-Commandante Marcos, has joked about the differences between his forces and the EPR fighters: "They are well armed, well uniformed. Those are clear signs that they are not Zapatistas."

FROM THE MARGINS TO THE CENTER

In a recent article in the World Policy Journal, Andrew Reding dismissed the Zapatistas and other southern Mexican guerrilla groups as marginal: "they are based in peripheral communities in peripheral states. Their revolt is a last-ditch attempt to preserve a vanishing way of life."

There are many such struggles in the world today. A campesino from southern Mexico would probably have little trouble understanding the plight of such people as the Ogoni, who live in Nigeria's Niger River delta and are being persecuted for opposing the ruin of their land and water by oil development. Perhaps the Ogoni would remind him of what is happening around Nacajuca. And perhaps he would think of the logging in Costa Grande if he heard the story of the Lubicon Cree, who live in Alberta, Canada and whose traditional lands are being clearcut to feed pulp mills.

There's no question that Reding's assessment is on target in the most obvious sense. Places like Chiapas or Ogoniland or northern Alberta are not going to dictate the future of the states that contain them. Certainly, in a Mexican context, the very idea is absurd. As Jorge Castañeda explains, roughly one-fifth to one-quarter of the country's population is basically living in an extension of the U.S. economy, which absorbs three quarters of Mexico's exports and produces three quarters of its imports. This group includes the Mexican elites and urban professionals, along with various industries—tourism, the export sector, the border maquiladoras, some migrant workers, and so on. Most of these people are well off at least by Mexican standards, and some are very wealthy indeed. They control most of the country's resources; they are largely immune to the political and economic convulsions that periodically rack the rest of Mexican society. And in Castañeda's view, they are largely indifferent to the fate of Mexican society in general.

But there is a larger point at stake as well. The main issue is not so much the fate of a peripheral community. It is the wounds within the society as a whole; and as the agony of Chiapas shows, those wounds cannot be healed simply by trying to suppress trouble on the periphery. After all, the people in Chiapas and the places like it are not going to go away. The environmental degradation in such places will not heal of its own accord, and the corrosive forces unleashed in these agonies on the margins will inevitably poison the other parts of a society.

What happens when entire communities, classes, and regions are left behind or written off? What happens when an economy distributes its profits and losses in a fashion as spectacularly uneven as in Mexico? The fact that such questions can never be answered with precision doesn't make them any less pressing. Chiapas cannot tell us what will happen in similar circumstances elsewhere, but it demonstrates clearly that extreme inequity is an appalling social risk.

In a sense, then, these "peripheral" areas are really central. Over much of the globe, they may embody the basic predicament of the modern state. Almost all the violent conflicts in the world today are taking place within, rather than between countries, and over and over again, the basic ingredients of these conflicts are the same environmental and political pressures that are torturing Chiapas. Such places, therefore, present a challenge to conventional statecraft. As leaders struggle to evaluate international trading agreements like NAFTA, or the effects of structural adjustments, they would do well to ask themselves what such policies would mean for places like Chiapas. In the 21st century, sound policy may need to come increasingly from the places we now regard as marginal.

THE RESURGENCE OF
INFECTIOUS DISEASES

By Anne Platt McGinn

In May 1993, a physically fit 20-year old Navajo Indian—a cross-country and track star—began gasping for air while driving to his wife's funeral near Gallup, New Mexico. For several hours, the man suffered from what seemed to be a severe but otherwise unremarkable case of the flu. Then, abruptly, his condition worsened. Blood filled his lungs. He was taken to an emergency room, where he died—drowning in his own serum. Reports confirm that around the same time, three other healthy Navajos in the Four Corners area (where New Mexico, Arizona, Colorado, and Utah meet) died from cases of flu or pneumonia gone suddenly awry. Clearly, something horrific was on the loose—but what?

Medical authorities from the state of New Mexico, the Indian Health Department, and the U.S. Centers for Disease Control and Prevention questioned families, relatives and friends, pored over medical records, and investigated possible links among the victims. They collected blood samples to analyze for viruses. Newspaper headlines warned cryptically of "Navajo flu," and "the mystery illness." As the death toll mounted, people in the affected region panicked, and some began to avoid anyone who was sick, for fear of contamination.

Investigation found that ground zero was a mouse—a rural deermouse, *Peromyscus maniculatus*, which is a native of

288

most of North America, including the American southwest. Apparently, the deer mouse harbored a strain of the Hanta virus (named after the Hanta River in Korea where it was originally discovered), which causes severe damage to the pulmonary tract and lungs. It was not clear, however, why this normally reclusive animal had suddenly begun to appear—and leave its droppings—in people's kitchens and playgrounds.

The press treated the Hanta virus of 1993 as an anomaly, a disturbing but isolated incident. In fact, however, it was part of a larger pattern that involves a growing list of illnesses—and growing risks to hundreds of millions of people. At the end of the century in which infectious diseases were thought to be well controlled, disease-causing (pathogenic) microorganisms are breaking out all over the world. Some of these pathogens, such as the *Escherichia coli* O157:H7, Hepatitis C, and Rift Valley Fever are new and unfamiliar. Others are old ones we thought had been beaten, such as the microbes that cause tuberculosis, malaria, the plague and measles.

AN EPIDEMIC OF EPIDEMICS

Despite the fact that most such afflictions are curable—and despite the major advances that have been made in sanitation, medical care and increased public awareness of diseases and health in this century—infectious diseases still kill more people than cancer, or car accidents, or war. They killed more than 17.3 million people in 1995, and global incidence is on the rise.

Worldwide, 3.1 million are killed by tuberculosis each year, while another 2.7 million people die from malaria, predominantly in tropical regions. And for every person who dies, more than one hundred are infected. One-third of the world's people—some 1.8 billion—now carry the tubercle bacillus, the bacterium that causes tuberculosis. More than 500 million people are infected with tropical diseases such as malaria, sleeping sickness, river blindness and schistosomiasis.

As the 20th century approaches its end, changes of unprecedented magnitude and speed are taking place in the planet's physical and social environment, with the cumulative effect of allowing infections to spread far faster than anyone has been able to spread the means of preventing and treating them. The killing of forests, contamination of water, destabilization of climate, and explosion of urban population have all contributed to the weakening of public health protections. As a result, transmissions of infectious diseases through all media—air, water, food, insects, rats, and the human body itself—are on the rise.

Haunting these changes is an omnipresent biological pattern. As evolutionary biologists E. O. Wilson and others have observed, rapid disruption inevitably seems to favor some life forms over others.

This is a pattern seen at all levels, from microbes to mammals and from algae to trees. When a forest is burned, opportunistic, short-lived species spring up ahead of stable, long-term ones. When a building is bulldozed to an empty lot, weeds spring up before the return (if ever) of whatever species were there before. When coastal wetlands are filled in to make room for resort hotels and golf courses, algal blooms spread over the fragmented wetlands and choke them.

Among microbes, as among larger life forms, there are opportunistic varieties: bacteria or viruses that invade human blood or cells. Just as weeds exploit disturbance more quickly than slower-growing trees of a stable forest ecosystem, or insect pests exploit the reduced biodiversity of a crop, infectious agents can adapt fast enough to overwhelm societies whose "natural" environments are disturbed.

An undisturbed ecosystem imposes a set of checks on the growth of microbes, but during severe disruptions, the balance may be skewed in their favor. The more disruption there is in the human habitat, the bigger the biological risks are for people.

BIOLOGICAL MIXING

The environment in which the human species evolved and developed its basic defenses against disease was one that remained—despite natural disturbances—basically stable for thousands of years. In the past 100 years, it has changed radically—in forest cover, air and water quality, land use patterns, human behavior and diet, and most recently in patterns of weather. The changes have boosted the spread of microbes and made the planet more accommodating to disease carrying microorganisms, thereby increasing human vulnerability to infection.

The planet has become not only more vulnerable, but also—in effect—smaller and easier for small organisms to move around on. Surging growth in global tourism, migration, and trade has done the trick; distances that were once rarely covered within the life-span of a microbe are now covered routinely and easily, not just thanks to increased air travel but thanks to new roads cutting through wilderness areas. Microbes, which can hitch rides on anything from the boots of travelers to the wheel wells of planes, are extending their reach and coming into contact with more people.

One result is that pathogens which previously remained hidden in remote rainforests suddenly have access to people. Rapid encroachment and settlement into the Amazon, for example, contributed to the spread of malaria-carrying mosquitos. The paving of the Kinshasa Highway across central Africa gave a fateful boost to the outbreak of HIV/AIDS. And the sheer volume of traffic between different ecosystems has brought about a process of planet-wide biological mixing.

This mixing goes in both directions: mobility brings microbes to human populations, but human expansion also carries diseases into new areas. The bestselling book *The Hot Zone*, by Richard Preston, recounts how the deadly Ebola viruses were released from a remote African rainforest, as though the rainforest were a kind of Pandora's Box.

According to Princeton University ecologist Andrew Dobson, however, what more often happens is that humans bring new vectors into the rainforest.

One reason the spread has been hard to stem is that these microbes are invisible stowaways, carried unwittingly by their hosts—and we have no way of knowing where the next outbreak will occur. Some changes in the environment may reduce the risk of disease transmission, while other factors will increase it. Changing agricultural practices can create new jobs and increase crop output, for example, but the changes may also invite new species to colonize. In any alteration of the landscape, there is potential for unforeseen consequences. After the Indira Gandhi Canal was built in Rajansthan, to irrigate desert-like areas of western India, farmers switched from cultivating traditional crops of jowar and bajra to more commercially profitable wheat and cotton, which require large amounts of water. Large numbers of people came to the area in search of work. Then the monsoons came.

As it turned out, the main canal—445 kilometers long, from Masitanwali to Ramgarh—served as an ideal breeding site for mosquitos. Instead of high crop productivity and prosperity, the heavy rains brought the farmers tragedy and death in the form of cerebral malaria, caused by a parasite in *Anopheles* mosquitos. Excess rain, combined with water logging behind the canal and inadequate drainage in the fields, created an epidemic of malaria that quickly spread through extensive canal areas. Malaria and water-borne diseases are common during monsoon season, but the canals carried the malaria epidemic to a much larger area, exposing workers and farmers who then transmitted the disease to friends and families.

A different project in the region, India's Sardar Sarovar dam along the Narmada River, also triggered an epidemic of malaria. "The ignition wire of construction-related stagnant water, and the gunpowder of immigrant labor, [created] an explosion of malaria," reads the World Bank-commissioned independent review of the project.

The dangers of irrigation projects are no worse than those of hydroelectric projects, road-building, logging, mining, agriculture, and even urbanization. By displacing wild populations and habitats, development activities such as logging often deprive microbes of their usual hosts—in effect forcing them to find new ones. Essentially, this is what happened in 1975 with the Borrelia bacteria that causes a relapsing fever known as Lyme disease. The bacteria lives in four different tick species which spread it in their saliva—usually to deer and raccoons. But suburban development in Old Lyme, Connecticut, tended to substitute people for these other mammals in the disease cycle. Borrelia bacteria has since spread throughout the United States, and Lyme disease is rampant in New England and the upper midwest states of Wisconsin and Minnesota.

Along with the 100-to-200 microbes known to be dangerous, another 1,000 or more may be "out there," according to Paul Ewald, a biologist at Amherst College, Amherst, Massachusetts. "It's a lottery" as to whether or not a pathogen will be introduced into the population. Understanding all the various links between environmental disruption, microbial outbreaks, and health may be nearly impossible, but identifying the conditions conducive to an outbreak and recognizing some general patterns will allow for better prediction and disease prevention. Four syndromes—water contamination, climate change, human actions that magnify natural disasters, and increasing social disruption—have been associated with such "unpredictable" occurrences as the Hanta and Gandhi canal incidents.

BAD WATER

Many of the outbreaks have been linked to the degradation of natural systems, particularly of water. Infectious illnesses are widespread in areas with overburdened sanitation facilities and unsafe drinking water. Even in regions where water quality is considered fairly good, that impression is belied by the high levels of human waste and sewage carried in prominent rivers—the Danube, the Ganges and the Mekong, among them—from which disease-carrying bacteria and viruses make their way into drinking supplies.

Waterborne diseases—including diarrheal diseases caused by *E. coli*, salmonella, vibrio cholera, and viral diseases such as hepatitis A and dysentery—cause hundreds of times more illness worldwide than chemical contamination of drinking water does. Eighty percent of all disease in developing countries is spread by unsafe water. Globally, about 250 million new cases of waterborne infection are reported each year. In Russia, the very rivers that people depend on for life—the Volga, the Dvina, the Ob—are now hazardous to public health. The rivers harbor strains of cholera, typhoid, dysentery and viral hepatitis that spread through water systems and contaminate drinking supplies.

"Epidemic diarrheal diseases are both preventable and curable," says Dr. Ronald Waldman, coordinator of WHO's Global Task Force on Cholera Control. "With a rapid and effective response, case-fatality rates from cholera, for example, can be kept to less than one per cent. As health care professionals, we cannot allow a lack of preparedness to be responsible for an unnecessary loss of lives."

One method for predicting cholera may be detecting and monitoring plankton blooms. Dr. Rita Colwell, University of Maryland biologist and former President of the American Association for the Advancement of Science and Dr. Paul Epstein, of the Harvard School of Public Health, have studied the bacteria and viruses that catch a ride with plankton, and (with others) have shown that where there are blooms, there are corresponding outbreaks of diseases in humans, marine mammals and fish. In the late 1980s, toxic algal blooms and morbillivirus were associated with dolphin die-offs in the Mediterranean Sea.

Cholera, which comes from the Latin word for diarrhea,

erupts seasonally, when the temperature, sunlight, nutrient levels, and acidity are right. (At other times of year, the bacteria become dormant and hibernate with their plankton hosts.) During blooms, and in areas that have a history of waterborne illnesses, medical providers can curtail outbreaks by teaching residents how to diagnose cholera and how to avoid infection—by boiling drinking water and washing food thoroughly.

In 1905, a new type of cholera was identified in the corpses of Moslem pilgrims who died at the El Tor quarantine camp en route to Mecca. The El Tor strain was more virulent than the classic strain of cholera because it proved to be a hardy survivor outside the human body, and the infection lasted longer in victims. By 1982, El Tor was the dominant strain in Bangladesh.

Even where there is a well-trained medical community, however, a seemingly minor event can sometimes trigger an epidemic. In 1991, for example, bilge water from a Chinese freighter was responsible for releasing this Asian strain of cholera into Peruvian waters. Once the bacterium of *Vibrio cholerae O1*, biotype El Tor, was released, it quickly spread through the marine environment and into drinking water supplies where it infected people. The bacterium also infected fish, mollusks and crustaceans—which heightened the public health threat, because *ceviche*, raw fish and lemon juice, is an important local food. By 1993, there were more than 500,000 cases of cholera throughout Latin America, with 200,000 in Peru alone. Since then, efforts to improve water sanitation, sewage treatment, food safety, and public education have helped control the epidemic, but chronic water quality problems continue to plague poorer communities in rapidly-growing urban areas like Caracas and São Paulo, posing an ever-looming danger of illness and death.

In the late 1980s, scientists in North Carolina uncovered a particularly stealth form of algae that progresses through 24 different life stages and defies containment by dispelling poison directly into the environment to paralyze prey, rather than retaining the substance internally. This new type of plankton, *Pfiesteria piscicida*, was identified after a series of fish mysteriously died from bleeding lesions and open wounds. More recently, Pfiesteria has triggered fish kills in the Chesapeake Bay.

Given worldwide population growth and increasing pressures on scarce water supplies in many areas, the incidence of waterborne infections can be expected to keep rising, unless water quality protection is made a top priority in the planning and management of all water-using activities—from irrigation and hydropower to the disposal of sewage.

BAD WEATHER

Second, many outbreaks seem to be related to ongoing and incipient changes in climate. Warmer weather can expand the range of vectors: in July 1994, for example, 24 cases of malaria were reported in Houston, Texas, where warm weather had attracted malaria-infected mosquitos from Latin America.

Such conditions are likely to worsen before they improve. The Netherlands-based institute, Research for Man and the Environment (RIVM), reported in 1994 that a global mean temperature increase of three degrees Celsius in the year 2100 increases the epidemic potential of mosquito population in tropical regions two-fold and in temperate regions more than ten-fold. Mathematical models estimate an increase in malaria cases of several millions in the year 2100. And RIVM calculates that more than 1 million people could die each year as a result of "the impact of a human-induced climate change on malaria transmission" during the next 60 years—as many people as were killed in both World Wars. Yet, that would be the toll of just one disease among many. Viral encephalitis, leishmaniasis, Lyme disease, dengue fever, and cholera might all extend to wider geographical areas due to warmer temperatures, ecological changes, and temporal variations in vector and parasite breeding and feeding behavior.

To address these threats, governments need to track the broad connections between their energy and transportation policies. Because these policies affect the rate of climate change, they can profoundly affect the long-term risks to public health. Combining short-term weather forecasting and longer-term climate trend models with remote sensing and satellite imagery that map out animal and vector habitats, human settlements, and bodies of water will enable scientists and health officials to better anticipate health effects of climate change and target interventions.

HUMAN AMPLIFICATION

Third, infectious outbreaks appear to follow on the heels of human activity that in some way magnifies the effects of natural disturbances—whether of floods, storms, or earthquakes. For example, some experts believe the outbreak of plague in Surat, India, in September 1994 was connected to the flooding of the Tapti River during that summer, and an earthquake a year earlier. The quake had left the landscape devastated by ruin, and thousands of people homeless. Emergency aid and medical supplies were flown in for the survivors of the earthquake, but the effort was so successful that excess food had to be stored in warehouses, where rodents crawled in and feasted. The rodents reproduced quickly, allowing the pneumonic plague bacterium—harbored in the fleas that infest the rodents' fur—to greatly extend its range.

During the summer, the monsoon flooded the Tapti River and inundated the poorest districts of Surat with three meters of water. Again, people were forced to leave their homes. The rodents, too, were forced to seek shelter on drier land. Rats and people crowded together on the same high ground, increasing people's exposure to the plague bacterium. Although India was medically prepared to deal with waterborne diseases such as gastroenteritis, cholera and dengue fever, it had no plans for plague. The disease had not been seen in more than 40 years.

When the first cases were reported, more than one-third of the Surat's private physicians left town. Panic erupted as plague cases proliferated, overwhelming the medical system with fearful patients. Video footage showed victims being carted off in wheelbarrows, while families packed onto trains and roads to flee. All over the world, news reports warned travelers to stay away from India.

At Surat, a combination of weather patterns and earthquake and flood damage was exacerbated by social factors: shantytowns, squalid living conditions, warehoused food, inadequate health care, and panic fanned into hysteria by media coverage that focused on the disaster without explaining its causes. What could have been prevented or controlled at an early stage became a financial as well as social disaster, as international airline flights to and from India were canceled and trade came temporarily to a halt.

SOCIAL DISRUPTION

Finally, the vulnerabilities brought about by increasing environmental disruption and exposure are, in many ways, further amplified by the world's growing problem of internecine social disruption. With about 30 civil wars taking place in the world each year, the systems needed for prevention and treatment of disease have been repeatedly shattered—often opening the way for infections to spread unchecked.

In Russia, health conditions are worsening because of the combination of unstable political conditions, deteriorating infrastructure, and the transitional economy. According to the head of the Russian Academy of Medical Sciences, as quoted in the 1992 *Russian State Report on the State of Health of the Population of the Russian Federation*, "we (Russia) have already doomed ourselves for the next 25 years."

Poor hygiene and diet, compounded by inadequate food

supplies and high levels of pollution have brought an onslaught of ecological and human health problems to this part of the world. In the early months of 1994, Russians were hit by 22 percent more cases of tuberculosis than in the same months of 1993. Measles rose by 260 percent and mumps by 10 percent during the same period. In 1976, diphtheria had all but disappeared from the former Soviet Union thanks to childhood immunizations. But it surged back in the 1990s, rising from 1,200 cases in 1990 to 15,210 in 1993. The disease had come back everywhere, including Moscow and St. Petersburg. After 3-year nationwide immunization program that reached more than 97 million people, the rise in diphtheria began to reverse in 1996. But for mumps, measles, and a host of gastrointestinal infections including abdominal typhoid, incomplete vaccination coverage, especially among children, continues to spark outbreaks throughout the country.

Although it is a half-day's plane ride from Moscow, Russia's Pacific coast of Khabarovsk is not immune to the wave of infectious diseases that have swept across Russia since the collapse of the Soviet Union. People travelling to this mountainous coastal region have brought diphtheria with them. Meanwhile the mass exodus of refugees from southern regions of Russia has made it nearly impossible to stop the transmission of diseases that move directly from person to person.

In summer 1994, after recording nearly 1,000 cases of cholera, health officials in Dagestan, approximately 120 kilometers west of the Caspian Sea, imposed a quarantine to stop people from leaving the area. The quarantine was not successful at controlling the epidemic, since by then most people in the area were harboring the cholera bacterium whether they showed signs of it or not. In nearby Chechnya, all attempts at public health control have failed because of the war.

What has befallen Russia is echoed, in varying degrees, in India, in Latin America, and in the Four Corners area of the American Southwest. The paradigm is relentless: disrupted environments increase biological stresses on humans every-

where; mobility and population expansion increase their exposure to opportunistic microbes; and political or economic disruption prevent the application of known preventions or cures.

WRITING THE PRESCRIPTION

How this cycle can be broken is not something that can be
determined by medical research alone. Enough research has
already been done to yield the knowledge needed to control
many of the epidemics spreading around the world: tuberculosis and malaria, for example. The problem is that the knowledge is not not being widely applied, and the diseases continue to spread.

Stopping the world's growing "epidemic of epidemics"
may not be possible, in fact, until considerations of human
health are integrated into all major human activities—including the planning of irrigation and dam projects, road building and transportation systems, agricultural practices, and
extractive industries such as mining and logging.

In the future, along with keeping ecosystems intact, min-
imizing habitat alterations, and maintaining the natural
checks and balances, communities should require planners
to prepare for all the unanticipated consequences of development. And they would do well to provide ongoing health
education for their populations, especially in areas that are
particularly vulnerable to environmental disruption. While
it is crucial to address the underlying causes of infectious
disease, the nuts-and-bolts of public health can do much
to reduce the numbers of people suffering and dying. Of
equal importance is to use the tools we have more effectively: to expand access to clean water and health services, and
to improve distribution of medicines, vaccines and educa-
tional materials.

Since infections do not stop at the borders of communities and countries, neither should control efforts. Individual
nations need to coordinate with the World Health

Organization and with each other to establish a reliable global surveillance system which would provide early warning, monitor incidence, and help coordinate the response. Adequate medical supplies and complete treatment therapies can then be targeted to at-risk populations. Individual communities will need to adapt these programs to local conditions. In China, for example, the government set up a program to control schistosomiasis 40 years ago. At the national level, public health, water resources, agriculture, planning, and finance officials draft laws, plan programs and monitor progress. But it is up to leaders at the county and city levels—who know the local weather and terrain—to find and exterminate snails, educate their people, and treat the afflicted. The program is working.

When we begin to routinely take health impacts of our industries and societies into account, the outbreaks of disease that now shock us won't seem so puzzling. When the Hanta virus broke out in Arizona, for example, it was not as mystifying to some of the Navajo medicine men, whose traditions had taught them to see the interconnectedness of all living things, as it was to the medical specialists and the media.

The scientists, alerted that deer mice were carrying the problem, tested the mice and were able to identify the exact culprit. But they failed to notice that it was the environment that was changing, not the pathogens.

The Navajo medicine men meanwhile observed that prior to the outbreak, snow melt cascading down to the valley desert below, combined with a spring of heavy rains, had reminded some of their elders of the years 1918 and 1933, when there had been similarly unpredictable weather. In each of those years, there had been a disease. In each of those years, piñon trees produced an abundance of pine nuts. Mice had descended on the extraordinary harvest and reproduced ten-fold in one season. The rains had then forced the mice out of their flooded burrows to scurry about above ground, looking for food and shelter and increasing exposure to humans. Disease was what happened when the balance of life was upset.

"When there is disharmony in the world, death follows," said one of the medicine men. He understood that when strange symptoms appear, they are not anomalies.

7

Paying for Change

FOREIGN INVESTMENT IN THE DEVELOPING WORLD: THE ENVIRONMENTAL CONSEQUENCES

By Hilary F. French

L ast winter, at an informal summit of the world's political and business elite, a *New York Times* correspondent found a general preoccupation with just one issue. At the World Economic Forum, an annual policy get-together at Davos, Switzerland, "The Globalization Question reigned in the way that the German Question once dominated European politics." The "Globalization Question," as the *Times* put it, is not whether the world economy is growing ever more integrated—there is no serious doubt about that. The question is what it will mean.

This fascination with globalization comes in the wake of a dramatic increase in the amount of private capital flowing into the developing world. North-South transfers of private money have increased more than five-fold over the last several years, rising from $44 billion in 1990 to $244 billion in 1996, according to preliminary estimates by the World Bank. A number of factors seem to lie behind this trend, including surging economic growth rates in the "emerging market" countries of Asia and Latin America, and a wave of privatization that is sweeping over much of the developing world. Electric utilities and telecommunications networks, for example, are moving from state to private sector control in many developing countries. At the same time, many of the coun-

tries supplying the private capital—principally Japan, the
United States, and western Europe—have seen a deregulation
of their capital markets. And this new legal latitude is
matched by a growing technical prowess: computerized
financial networks now allow investors to shift vast sums of
money from one part of the globe to another, as quickly as
electricity can move through a cable.

Yet while private money has been flowing into the developing world at a record rate, public money has been drying
up, as developed countries attempt to trim budget deficits by
paring down their foreign aid programs. Overall levels of
development aid declined by nearly a quarter between 1995
and 1996 alone. As a result of these two trends, private
finance now dominates the development ledger. At the beginning of this decade, less than half the international capital
moving into the developing world was from private sources,
but by 1996 the private share had risen to 86 percent (see
figure, page 307).

Few economists or policy analysts would deny that the
private investor is now a leading figure on the world stage.
But there is bitter disagreement about what the social and
environmental consequences are likely to be. Private investment enthusiasts point out that the growing inflows have
reversed the "negative net transfers" of the 1980s, when
developing countries were paying out more money, in the
form of loan interest and returns on foreign investment, than
they were receiving in new private and public finance. In
1988, these "negative net transfers" amounted to $1.5 bil-
lion; by 1996, the net flow in the opposite direction—from
North to South—amounted to $176 billion. In some parts of
the developing world, particularly in Asia, these funds have
helped fuel a record-breaking economic boom that is often
credited with bringing down national poverty rates.

Yet critics of large-scale private investment argue that
macro financial flows are exacerbating the huge gap between
rich and poor that already plagues so many developing soci-

eties. In many countries, the market boom does not reach large segments of the population—and in some cases it may actually be injuring them. In China, for instance, the crushing poverty of the inland countryside continues largely unabated, despite the prosperity of the coastal cities. In Mexico, the Zapatista rebellion of 1994 was in part a revolt against policies intended to attract foreign investors—policies like legalizing the private sale of communal land. (See Michael Renner, "Chiapas: An Uprising Born of Despair" in Chapter 6.) These critics cite a long list of horror stories— about dangerous working conditions, child labor, and the violent repression of dissent—which they see as flowing from

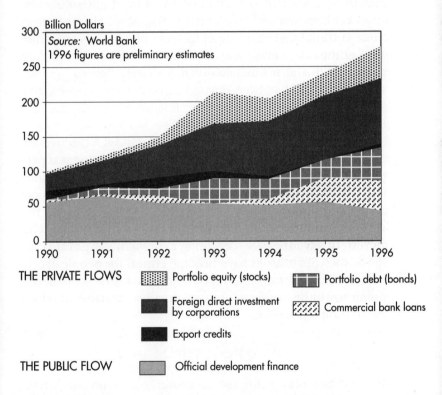

Capital Flows to Developing Countries, 1990–96

the growing power of poorly regulated private companies.

The environmental implications of growing private capital movements have received less attention than the social ones, but they too are likely to be enormous and somewhat contradictory. In the most general terms, economic globalization is exporting Western consumerism. Given the unsustainable patterns of consumption in the developed countries—which account for only 21 percent of the world's population, yet use nearly 80 percent of its paper, for example, and almost 70 percent of its energy—this spread of the consumer culture is ominous. The new-found mobility of international capital also allows it to seek out the most hospitable home—which may well be a place with weak or unenforced environmental laws. Yet international investment is also now helping to promote cutting-edge environmental technologies, as companies all over the world make use of foreign capital to upgrade their plants. And a growing array of deliberately "green" investment strategies has been devised in recent years—programs aimed specifically at using private finance to restore the natural capital of the developing world.

For nongovernmental organizations (NGOs) active on environmental issues, the growth of private investment is perplexing, to say the least. "With yesterday's centralized funding, NGOs could lobby particular organizations and stage demonstrations outside meetings," notes a report by the environmental group, Friends of the Earth. But it is difficult to "effectively influence something as nebulous as private capital flows." Such issues have become critical for people everywhere. The question is: Can private capital flows to the developing world be redirected in support of sustainable development? And if so, how?

FOLLOWING THE MONEY

Perhaps one reason for the controversy over private investment is the difficulty involved in tracking this kind of money.

With official development assistance such as that provided by the World Bank, detailed reports spell out what the money is being spent on—whether it is dams, highways, and other infrastructure projects, social services such as health care and education, or "environmental" projects, such as reforestation and pollution control. But private capital flows are something of a black box. We know they are growing fast, but the available statistics tell us little about what, exactly, is being financed.

We can, however, construct a general picture of private flows. During the 1970s, most private flows came in the form of loans from commercial banks, as these institutions extended more and more credit to developing country governments. That trend paved the way for the debt crisis of the 1980s and the consequent stagnation in lending. The last few years have seen a resurgence of commercial bank loans, but this time the recipients are more likely to be private enterprises than governments. In 1996, commercial bank lending accounted for 14 percent of total private flows, or $34 billion.

The other traditional route for private capital moving into the developing world is as "foreign direct investment" (FDI) of corporations setting up local plants. In recent years, FDI has expanded rapidly, as multinational corporations build a stronger presence all over the developing world, often through joint ventures with local companies. FDI has climbed from $25 billion in 1990 to $110 billion in 1996, or 45 percent of total private flows.

Nearly all of the remaining private flows—just under 40 percent of the total—are moving through a category that barely existed less than a decade ago. This is "portfolio" investments, in which developing country stocks and bonds are purchased abroad—both by individual investors and by institutional ones, such as pension plans or mutual funds. Anyone who has followed the workings of a stock market will know why these portfolio investments are the most volatile ingredient in the mix of private flows. Stock or "equity" investors may withdraw their funds quickly if they lose confidence in a country's economic prospects, as happened in Mexico, when the value of the peso plummeted in 1994, and in Southeast Asia in 1997. Stephan Schmidheiny and Federico Zorraquín, who chair a task force on green international finance for the World Business Council for Sustainable Development, and who have co-authored a book on the subject, explain the risks simply: "Whereas equity investors focusing on the United States may switch companies, emerging-market investors are more likely to switch countries instead."

Stock investments rose from just 7 percent of total private flows in 1990 to 29 percent in 1993. The Mexican peso crisis triggered a sharp decline over the next two years, but by 1996 portfolio equity had bounced back. By the end of the year, it had reached an all-time high of $46 billion, or 19 percent of total private flows. Preliminary estimates suggest that they reached another new high in 1997, despite projected declines in flows into the battered Southeast Asia markets. Bond issues, in which private investors make long-term loans to governments or businesses at fixed interest rates, largely mirror this trend. Bonds increased from 5 percent of private flows in 1990, to 23 percent in 1993. After a two-year decline, they rebounded to $46 billion in 1996, and were expected to increase in 1997 yet again.

In terms of absolute value, private flows are concentrated in a small group of countries, and most of these are rapidly rising from the ranks of the "developing" world. Just 10 countries account for some three-quarters of all private flows to the developing world. For FDI specifically, inflows are similarly concentrated: the top 12 FDI recipients take in nearly 80 percent of the total. But when measured as a percentage of economic activity, private flows broaden out considerably. Indeed, FDI has increased as a share of GNP for all regions of the developing world since 1990.

Private capital is no longer moving solely from North to South. In recent years, several developing countries have become significant sources of capital as well as recipients of it. The economies of Brazil, Chile, China, Hong Kong, Kuwait, Malaysia, Singapore, South Korea, Taiwan, and Thailand are all investing abroad, increasingly as far afield as Africa, Europe, and North and South America. Outflows of direct investment from the developing world as a whole have risen rapidly in recent years. According to estimates by the U.N. Commission on Trade and Development, they reached $51 billion in 1996—15 percent of total world outflows. This trend adds another layer complexity to the investment picture. It could mean, for example, that a U.S. mutual fund is buying stock in a Korean conglomerate, which is in turn investing in a lumber project in Latin America. Imagine hundreds of similar transactions, then suppose that Friends of the Earth decided to lobby investors against the lumber project: where would it intervene?

Even at the broad level of economic sectors, a comprehensive picture of private flows is difficult to obtain, as the data are sketchy and conditions vary greatly by country and region. For instance, many African countries remain highly dependent on natural resource extraction—logging, mining, and drilling for oil. Consequently, most of their foreign investment is focused on this primary, raw commodity sector, which is the traditional mainstay of international investment. In Tunisia, for example, the primary sector receives some 80 percent of incoming FDI, much of which goes to the oil and gas industry.

Yet many other countries, particularly the "emerging markets" of Asia and Latin America, are diversifying their economies into manufacturing and services, a move that is changing the complexion of international financial flows. In Indonesia, for example, some 53 percent of incoming FDI went to manufacturing in 1996, 35 percent to services, and the remaining 13 percent to the primary sector. In these more robust countries, private investment has helped fueled a boom in infrastructure construction. Private companies are building power plants, telecommunications networks, water treatment plants, dams—even toll roads. According to the World Bank, the amount of foreign money flowing into new private infrastructure projects in developing countries climbed from $2.6 billion at the beginning of the 1990s to $22.3 billion by 1995.

SHORT-TERM PROFITS, PERMANENT LOSSES

Wherever it is going, foreign investment is all too often an accomplice to environmental degradation on a massive scale. Today's economy is threatening the world's climate through increased fossil-fuel emissions and devastating global forests through unsustainable wood and paper production. It is building dams that destroy the ecology of entire watersheds and underwriting mining operations that are poisoning the homelands of the earth's remaining indigenous peoples. Private investment is not inherently destructive, of course, but in its present form it has a hand in all these types of environmental damage.

The clearest abuses involve the primary sector. Increasingly, countries that have already liquidated their own natural assets—or that are trying to save what is left of them—are in effect exporting their resource extraction industries. This trend is apparent in the United States, for instance, where mining and timber companies regularly look abroad for easier pickings.

"While environmental impact studies, reclamation, and other activities are an important and well established part of mining, extremist activities are causing some companies to move most or all of their operations abroad," notes the trade magazine, *Mining Voice*. In August 1996, U.S. President Bill Clinton unveiled a plan to halt a controversial gold- mining project on the borders of Yellowstone National Park. At roughly the same time, several U.S. companies were announcing plans to step up their gold mining overseas. The

Newmont Mining Corporation, based in Denver, began extracting gold in Peru in 1993, in Uzbekistan in 1995, and in Indonesia in 1996. Another Denver-based company, the Crown Resources Company, is now spending 80 percent of its gold exploration budget in Argentina and Peru.

A similar dynamic is at work in the timber industry. Luke Popovich of the American Forest and Paper Association told the *Journal of Commerce* that U.S. companies are going abroad to escape the "constant green harassment" they feel they are subjected to at home. But the forests elsewhere have grown increasingly crowded with competing firms from other countries where large-scale wood production is either impossible or increasingly difficult. Indonesia and Malaysia, for instance, have already been subjected to widespread international criticism for systematically liquidating their own forests. Now their timber companies are also aggressively hunting forests in other parts of the world. In recent years, companies from these two countries, along with firms from China, South Korea, and elsewhere have won timber concessions that could deforest large swaths of the globe. Among the countries offering the concessions are Brazil, Cambodia, Cameroon, Gabon, Guyana, Nicaragua, Nigeria, Papua New Guinea, the Solomon Islands, and Suriname. Some of the companies involved have a long history of catastrophic environmental destruction, tax evasion, and other forms of corruption—a fact that doesn't auger well for their new hosts.

As with resource extraction, the current surge of international investment in manufacturing also carries grave environmental risks. Hazardous industries—from small-scale battery recyclers to huge chemical plants—may come to be increasingly concentrated in countries ill-equipped to handle the pollution. The 1993 debate over the North American Free Trade Agreement (NAFTA) put the spotlight on an example of this activity in northern Mexico, along the border with the United States. That area is the site of nearly 2,000 mostly foreign-owned manufacturing plants known as maquiladoras. In the town of Mexicali, on the California border, more than a quarter of factory owners surveyed in the late eighties acknowledged that Mexico's lax environmental enforcement influenced their decision to locate there.

On the books, Mexico's environmental laws are roughly comparable to and in some cases actually stricter than those in the United States. But enforcement has been lax; an official of the Mexican environment ministry estimated in 1991 that only 35 percent of the U.S.-owned factories along the border comply with Mexican toxic waste laws. A 1991 survey conducted by the U.S. National Toxics Campaign found toxic discharges at three-quarters of the maquiladoras sampled. Chemicals known to cause cancer, birth defects, and brain damage were being emptied into open ditches that ran through the shanty-towns around the factories. Despite hopes that NAFTA's environmental "side agreements" would lead to stricter enforcement, a 1995 report found that a full quarter of maquiladora hazardous waste—some 44 tons daily—could not be accounted for, presumably because it continues to be dumped in the ditches.

The infrastructure boom is also fraught with environmental peril. For instance, Asea Brown Boveri, a Swiss-based engineering group, sullied its environmental reputation when it became the main contractor for Malaysia's Bakun Dam project on Borneo. If built as planned, this 2,400 megawatt hydro-electric project would require the clearing of 69,000 hectares of rainforest, the flooding of an area the size of Singapore, and the displacement of 9,500 indigenous people. In China, international companies are competing fiercely for contracts to help build the Three Gorges Dam on the Yangtze River. Three Gorges is expected to flood 60,750 hectares of land and 160 towns, and force the resettlement of over 1 million people. The Chinese government has announced that it will finance the dam through commercial bank loans, bond offerings, and stock investments. International investors are also queuing up to participate in the construction of the more than 500 power plants that China plans to construct by 2010. Many of these plants will be fueled by coal. Already the world's second largest emitter of carbon dioxide, China could well surpass the United States and top the list within the next 15 years.

TOWARD A GREENER PORTFOLIO

But the future need not be simply an extension of the present alarming trends. International investors already have a number of important points of leverage which they could use to help set the world's economies on a more sustainable course. One such point involves cutting-edge technologies, which are usually cleaner and more efficient in their use of energy and materials than older equipment. International investment often confers access to new technologies. For instance, a 1992 World Bank study compared the rates at which 60 countries were adopting a cleaner wood pulping process, and concluded that countries open to foreign investment acquired the new technology far more rapidly than did those that were closed to it.

Foreign investment is also promoting new energy technologies—in some cases to such a degree that developing countries have become major users or manufacturers. For example, efficient compact-fluorescent light bulbs, first produced in the United States, are increasingly manufactured in the developing world. In 1995, China made some 80-100 million of these bulbs—more than any other country in the world. The funding and technology came in part through joint ventures with lighting firms based in Hong Kong, Japan, the Netherlands, and Taiwan. India, meanwhile, has become the world's second largest wind-power producer, with an installed wind capacity of more than 800 megawatts. In large measure, the country owes that accomplishment to the advanced wind turbine production technology that it obtained through joint ventures and licensing agreements with Danish firms.

Efforts to preserve the Earth's dwindling biological diversity could also be served by innovations in private finance, for example, in "bioprospecting." Drug and seed companies have long used the genetic diversity of the developing world to create new products, but even when a traditional crop variety proves essential for breeding a new line of seeds, or when a wild plant yields some valuable new drug, corporations have rarely paid anything for access to that genetic resource. But the Convention on Biological Diversity, signed at the Rio "Earth Summit" in 1992, gives nations the right to charge for access to their genetic resources, and it allows them to pass national legislation setting the terms of any bioprospecting agreements. The intent of the treaty is to provide a strong conservation incentive by encouraging countries to view their genetic diversity as a source of potential profits. And the growing power of biotechnology, which allows for much more direct manipulation of genes than was previously possible, virtually guarantees that the profit potential will continue to grow in the years ahead.

A year before the Earth Summit, Merck and Company, the world's largest pharmaceuticals firm, and Costa Rica's National Institute of Biodiversity (INBio) reached a precedent-setting bioprospecting agreement of the kind envisioned by the treaty. Merck agreed to pay $1.35 million in support of INBio conservation programs in exchange for access to the country's plants, microbes, and insects. Should any Merck discovery make its way into a product, INBio will also collect royalties. Some critics of the agreement, however, argue that local peoples should have been granted the royalty rights instead.

Similar initiatives are getting underway elsewhere, some of which offer more equitable models for the sharing of benefits. A bioprospecting initiative in Suriname, for example, involves a number of different players, including indigenous healers, a Surinamese pharmaceutical company, the U.S.-based pharmaceutical company Bristol Myers Squibb, the environmental group Conservation International, and the Missouri Botanical Gardens. Royalties from any drugs developed will be channeled into a range of local institutions, including non-governmental organizations, the national pharmaceutical company, and the forest service. In addition, a "Forest Peoples Fund" has been established to fund small-scale development projects to benefit local indigenous peoples.

Eco-tourism may offer another opportunity to channel investment capital into the preservation of threatened ecosystems, if it is pursued in an ecologically sensitive way. Costa Rica is leading the way. The country's sandy beaches, dry deciduous forests, and moist cloud forests have made tourism its top foreign exchange earner. Costa Rica's some $600 million in tourist revenues surpass its traditional export mainstays, such as bananas and coffee. Since eco-tourism is not generally capital-intensive, domestic investment may often be sufficient for underwriting much of the industry. But even eco-tourism has its infrastructure: international investment may find a role in upgrading airports, and constructing the kind of carefully conceived, small-scale hotels that are compatible with the industry's aims.

Yet another opportunity is created by the growing international demand for sustainably produced timber. Precious Woods Management, Ltd., a Swiss-owned firm, plans to tap into this market. It has established a subsidiary in the Brazilian Amazon that is now harvesting timber from an operation certified by SmartWood as well managed. This is a certification program sponsored by the New York-based Rainforest Alliance and accredited by the Forest Stewardship Council, an independent body established established in 1993 through consultations with the forest industry, environmentalists, and representatives of forest peoples to set standards for sustainable forest production.

LEVERAGING CHANGE

These "green" investments are currently dwarfed by the vast sums pouring into the conventional environmentally-damaging operations that continue to push the world's economies along on an unsustainable course. But numerous policy tools exist that could scale up the green activities and begin to eliminate some of the brown.

National laws are the obvious place to start. Besides traditional environmental regulations, government subsidies and tax policies could be revamped to reflect environmental realities. A tax on carbon emissions, for instance, would increase the price of coal-generated electricity, thereby helping to stimulate the growth of renewable power sources, such as solar and wind. Similarly, wood from primary forests could be priced to reflect the loss of biological diversity suffered when it is harvested. That would boost demand for sustainably produced timber. The growth of these sustainable industries would then offer more opportunities to foreign investors— producing a kind of "snowballing" effect.

But the global nature of today's economy means that individual countries are not free agents when it comes to designing their environmental policies. Countries may well shy away from strict environmental regulations or comprehensive environmental tax reform, out of fear that foreign investors will take their money elsewhere. Action on the international front is therefore essential.

One promising approach is to encourage public development agencies to attach environmental conditions to programs that support private investments. In this way, a limited amount of aid money could serve as an environmental "screen" for a far larger pool of private capital. Indonesian and U.S. environmentalists attempted this strategy in April 1995, when they prevailed upon the U.S. Overseas Private Investment Corporation (OPIC) to cancel the $100 million political risk insurance policy it was providing to a New

Orleans-based mining company, Freeport McMoran Copper and Gold. The policy covered the company's operations at the Grasberg Mine, in the Indonesian province of Irian Jaya on the island of New Guinea. The mine is one of the world's largest; its enormous copper, gold, and silver deposits are reportedly worth more than $60 billion at today's market prices. Every day, the mine dumps 100,000 tons of tailings into nearby rivers and the local indigenous people say the operation is contaminating the fish they eat and the water they drink. The clogged rivers are also flooding large swaths of rainforest, and threatening a diverse array of forest species. Environmentalists argued that the mine would not have been allowed to operate in the United States, and should not therefore be eligible for OPIC support.

Despite the promise of this strategy, later developments in the Freeport case show how difficult it can be to make a victory stick. A year after its initial decision, OPIC reinstated Freeport's policy after the company agreed to establish a $100 million trust fund to clean up the site at the end of the mine's life. Then just a few months later, Freeport announced that it would not renew its policy with OPIC.

A similar case involves the U.S. Export-Import Bank, which provides government-subsidized loans to other countries for the purchase of U.S. goods and services. In May 1996, the bank announced that it would not provide this type of support for China's Three Gorges project—a blow to companies such as the heavy equipment manufacturer Caterpillar, which hopes to participate in the construction of the dam. But the bank said it might reconsider if China improved its plans for protecting water quality and preserving endangered species. Meanwhile, the bank's counterparts in Canada, France, Germany, Japan, and Switzerland have indicated that they may step into the breach. Clearly, the U.S. effort would have benefited from a much higher degree of international coordination. Stung by the experience, the United States is trying to persuade other countries to apply environmental conditions to export credit loans.

Among international organizations, perhaps the biggest opportunity involves the World Bank and two affiliated agencies, the International Finance Corporation (IFC) and the Multilateral Investment Guarantee Agency (MIGA). Though the World Bank has traditionally made loans to governments only, in the last few years it has begun to use some of its funds to back commercial lending to the private sector. The IFC, which lends directly to private enterprises, is much smaller than the Bank itself. (In 1996, the Bank had $21.5 billion committed to its regular programs, while the IFC was financing 264 projects with loans worth $3.2 billion.) But on average, each dollar the IFC lends is matched by five dollars of private investment—a ratio that greatly expands the IFC's influence. Given the World Bank's growing interest in private sector lending, the IFC is expected to expand rapidly in the years ahead. MIGA also promotes private investment, principally by insuring against political risks, such as expropriation, civil disturbance, and breach of contract. Since it issued its first contract in 1990, MIGA has guaranteed over 200 contracts involving more than $15 billion of FDI. And MIGA, too, is likely to play an increasingly prominent role in international finance.

Both the IFC and MIGA are involved in many large investment projects with heavy environmental impacts. Infrastructure, manufacturing, and mining are among the activities the agencies back. MIGA, for instance, was participating in Freeport's Grasberg Mine project—until the company canceled its MIGA policy as well. (Freeport took that action just before the agency was scheduled to send over a team of investigators to look into charges of environmental and human rights abuse.) The World Bank has an extensive set of environmental and social policies, which among other things require environmental impact assessments of bank projects and protection of the rights of indigenous peoples. Theoretically, all Bank agencies including the IFC and MIGA are bound by these policies, but critics have charged for years that the rules are rarely heeded at the Bank itself, let alone at the IFC and MIGA.

Since taking office in 1995, Bank President James Wolfensohn has indicated that he agrees with some of the past criticism—and that he is interested in stepping up environmental enforcement in all branches of the World Bank, including those that involve the private sector. Yet a recent case involving an IFC loan the construction of a series of dams on the scenic Bíobío River, whose banks are home to 8,000 indigenous people and to myriad rare plant and animal species, reveals some of the limits of the Bank's power. The IFC recently commissioned an independent review of the project; it concluded that the utility had violated massively the environmental and social conditions written into the loan agreement. Environmentalists were outraged when the Bank censored parts of this report before releasing it to the public. Meanwhile, the utility has prepaid large portions of its IFC loans in order to untie itself from any of the environmental strings attached to the money.

Still, a measure of environmental awareness does appear to be slowly emerging within the IFC. Over the past few years, the agency has collaborated with the Global Environment Facility (a joint undertaking of the U.N. Development Program, the U.N. Environment Programme, and the World Bank) to develop an explicitly green investment program to complement its standard offerings. A basic obstacle to this effort was the need to devise financing mechanisms for projects that are too small or unproven to attract standard IFC support or other sources of international capital; the average size of IFC loans is $15 million. The goal is to demonstrate the viability of these enterprises with a small injection of public funds so that they will grow in size and be able to attract private capital on their own.

Part of the agency's solution was to develop a program that channel funds through environmental NGOs, nonprofit venture capital firms, and other intermediaries to a range of small-scale, environmentally sound enterprises. Projects in renewable energy, energy efficiency, sustainable forestry and agriculture, and eco-tourism are the funding targets. The program was originally capitalized with $4.3 million of Global Environment Facility (GEF) funds. It has now been scaled up with an additional $16.5 million and will involve some 100 different projects when fully up and running. The IFC is also cooperating with the GEF to launch several other promising initiatives. For instance, a planned $20 to $25 million "Terra Capital Fund" for Latin America will finance sustainable forestry and agriculture programs and eco-tourism projects. Also in the pipeline is a $210 million venture capital fund to promote energy efficiency and renewable energy projects.

A SEARCH FOR STANDARDS

These green investment strategies will require a broad framework of international support if they are to flourish. One of the most important timbers in that frame should be an array of baseline international environmental standards, along the lines of the wood certification program already mentioned. For such standards to be effective, they will need to meet three basic standards of their own: they must be "floors" rather than "ceilings"—that is, they must block downward but not upward movement; they must be set high enough to have a real impact, rather than at a least-common-denominator level; and they must be developed in an open and inclusive process that will build a strong consensus for them. Some movement toward these goals is already underway.

Many industries may ultimately support the idea of common standards because they would tend to lower the cost of doing business in today's highly integrated global economy. Two-thirds of some 200 companies polled in a U.N. survey of corporate attitudes during the early 1990s thought that the United Nations should work toward standardizing national environmental regulations. Most multinational corporations already claim to adhere to roughly uniform environmental standards throughout their worldwide operations. And a number of international industry groups have now crafted voluntary codes of environmental conduct; many of these call for companies to adhere to the standards of their home countries abroad.

There are several arenas from which international environmental standards may emerge. One is the Geneva-based International Organization for Standardization (ISO), a worldwide federation of national standards-setting bodies, which over the last few years has been developing a series of voluntary environmental guidelines. The first set of the series, finalized in the fall of 1996, covers internal management and auditing procedures—how, for instance, a company should monitor its pollution. That's not the same thing as setting performance standard by specifying, for example, what levels of pollution would be acceptable, but it is nonetheless a useful step. Over the longer term, the ISO plans to take on eco-labeling and life-cycle analysis although it is not yet clear exactly how. A major weakness of the ISO process has been its relatively narrow base: industry has been an active player from the beginning of the process, but environmental groups did not participate until recently.

International trade and investment negotiations are another important forum for discussions about environmental standards in global commerce. Progress here could yield an enormous payoff, but these agreements have proven difficult for environmentalists to penetrate. Currently, for example, the Organization for Economic Cooperation and Development (OECD), a body composed mainly of the western, industrial countries, is negotiating a Multilateral Agreement on Investment intended to reduce obstacles to the flow of FDI. So far, at least, OECD negotiators have paid scant attention to the agreement's ecological implications, despite the efforts of environmental groups to put this issue on the table. Developments in the OECD are of global significance, since they often lay the groundwork for future accords at the World Trade Organization.

On NAFTA, NGO lobbying did produce some concrete results, albeit relatively weak ones. For instance, NAFTA was written with a clause that forbids the parties from lowering their environmental standards—or their enforcement of them—in order to attract investment. That constitutes a clear precedent for future trade negotiations. At least one other major trade regime appears to be following suit. The Asia Pacific Economic Cooperation forum (APEC) is a loose coalition of 18 Pacific Rim states, including the United States, China, and Japan. Its "Non-binding Investment Principles" contain an environmental provision similar to NAFTA's investment clause.

Finally, the United Nations could help put global commerce on a more sustainable course. Just as the International Labor Organization drafts standards on matters such as workplace safety and child labor, so could a U.N. environment agency be charged with developing environmental base lines. This effort could build upon the World Bank's environmental policies and guidelines, which are already a common point of reference for private investors.

When it comes to mandatory standards, of course, the industry ideal may not satisfy environmentalists, or governments anxious to conserve their natural resources. But standards, like industries themselves, need to be dynamic, and even an imperfect beginning may evolve with time.

REDEFINING DEVELOPMENT

The rapid pace at which the world is becoming more tightly knit—economically, environmentally, and culturally—is one of the most distinctive features of our time. As recently as a decade ago, industrial and developing countries almost seemed to exist on different planets. Yet today the distinction is eroding rapidly, as the two worlds are drawn together by a global economy that shows little regard for national borders. And increasingly, industrial and developing societies contain pockets of one another. The developing world has its rapidly modernizing industries and wealthy elites; the industrial world has its underclasses, locked out of its general prosperity.

But the world's growing economic integration is colliding with another defining feature of the age: an increasing awareness that the global economy is irrevocably damaging the natural capital on which it, and all of us, ultimately depend. Creating a sustainable global economy is thus one of the most urgent tasks before us—one that poses enormous challenges and uncertainties for governments, businesses, and people everywhere. The outlines, at least, of some possible solutions are beginning to come into view. We cannot know how far today's green investment strategies will ultimately take us. But it is clear that we have no hope of building a sustainable economy without them.

THE WORLD BANK AND THE FUTURE OF THE ENERGY ECONOMY

By Christopher Flavin

Soon after he took office as president of the World Bank in 1995, James Wolfensohn gathered 250 of his top managers for a meeting at the Bank's imposing headquarters in Washington, DC. In a fervent address, he told them that he was "troubled deeply." In his attempts to give the world's largest development institution a desperately needed revitalization, he said he felt he was up against a "glass wall." Instead of becoming infused with renewed enthusiasm for the challenge of alleviating poverty in the developing world, the Bank's bureaucracy had been reacting with "fear" and "cynicism," Wolfensohn asserted. He told them the time had come for far-reaching changes, and he wanted their support.

The audience of elite and well-paid economists gave the speech a cool, if polite, response. They were not accustomed to the passionate style of their new leader—a wealthy former investment banker, concert cellist, and confidante of world leaders who has been known to shed tears when discussing the plight of the world's poor. But they were even more uncomfortable with the prospect of refocusing the Bank's mission and introducing new performance incentives for the staff. In one of his first acts, Wolfensohn was requiring hundreds of senior managers to take courses on the process of corporate transformation, and then sending them to live for a week in the kind of Third World slum or village that the Bank's loans are supposed to assist.

Although most of Wolfensohn's reforms have been directed at improving its efficiency, consulting more closely with local citizens, and making the Bank "client friendly," he has also pushed for environmental reforms. During the past two decades, the World Bank has come under heavy criticism for its support of environmentally and socially damaging loans. The most controversial projects were large dams that displaced thousands of people, and road-building efforts in the Amazon that led to massive clearing of forests. For years, citizens' groups have fought to improve the Bank's environmental standards and assessment procedures. Despite the efforts of a newly created environment department, progress has been slow, and the world's largest development institution continues to be mired in environmental controversies.

By the mid-1990s, a growing number of World Bank critics were focusing on a new environmental problem—global climate change. Ever since the Framework Convention on Climate Change was signed in 1992, the role of developing countries in it has been controversial. Only the industrial countries, which contribute on average 10 times as much to global warming per person, were asked in the treaty to voluntarily hold their greenhouse gas emissions to the 1990 level or below in the year 2000. But developing countries' emissions have grown by nearly 75 percent since the beginning of the decade, as their economies have boomed, accompanied by a proliferation of motor vehicles, factories, power plants, and high rise buildings—most of them powered by fossil fuels. As a result, countries such as China, India, and Brazil are becoming increasingly important to the stability of the global climate.

During the past four decades, the World Bank has become the world's largest financier of oil wells, refineries, coal mines, power stations, road-building, and other projects that contribute heavily to the more than 6 billion tons of carbon being released to the atmosphere each year. Already, World Bank client countries (including those in central and eastern Europe) account for over half of global emissions of greenhouse gases. Consequently, the World Bank is now a major force in warming the planet—and potentially an important ally in slowing that warming.

In June 1997, Wolfensohn seemed to be trying to leapfrog critics of the Bank's support of fossil fuels when, on the occasion of the fifth anniversary of the Rio Earth Summit, he appeared at a Special Session of the United Nations General Assembly in New York. The occasion had been surrounded by a roiling debate over the shape of the global climate agreement that was to be signed in Kyoto, Japan later that year. The European delegates were calling for strong new measures to limit emissions, while the U.S. delegation—facing heavy pressure from some powerful fossil fuel-using industries—had opposed such standards.

Wolfensohn surprised the assembled reporters by appearing to side with the Europeans. He said that though as Bank president he could not take a position on the talks, as a private citizen he favored a strong agreement. He also proposed that the Bank serve as manager of a new Carbon Investment Bank to finance alternatives to fossil fuels. The funds would come from accounts set up under the climate treaty, allowing industrial nations to offset their emissions by investing in presumably low-cost means of reducing emissions in developing countries.

Wolfensohn's announcement was alternatively seen as a sign of bold leadership or as a gambit to deflect criticism. Asking the World Bank to lead the world away from fossil fuels might seem to some environmental skeptics like asking the National Rifle Association to lead a campaign against guns. Still, Wolfensohn and his fellow reformers in the Bank's environment department seem determined to confound the critics. With the Cold War over and the private sector now providing much of the world's development financing, the

World Bank, with its staff of 10,000 and roughly $20 billion in annual lending, is desperately seeking new missions. At a time when the U.S. Congress seems bent on slashing all support for developing countries that does not directly benefit the United States, helping to solve the world's greatest environmental problem might be a big enough job to help justify the Bank's continuation.

SINGRAULI

The scale of the challenge facing Wolfensohn and his fellow reformers can be seen half a world away from the World Bank's Washington offices. When India gained independence in 1947, the Singrauli region in the northern state of Bihar was one of the nation's most ecologically and culturally diverse areas. Located 140 kilometers south of the holy city of Varanasi, Singrauli was once home to a tropical forest that contained sizable populations of deer, wild boar, bears, and tigers, as well as to hundreds of thousands of indigenous subsistence farmers and villagers.

Today, Singrauli is one of the great monuments to the century's Faustian bargain with fossil fuels. The region contains 12 open pit coal mines and 11 coal-fired power plants that send electricity to distant industries. Twenty-four hours a day, 365 days a year, the sky above Singrauli is obscured by dark clouds of coal dust and smoke—carrying particulates, sulfur, and deadly mercury into surrounding forests and communities. In addition, the Singrauli complex now pumps over 10 million tons of carbon into the atmosphere each year, placing it among the leading global emitters of greenhouse gases.

Most of the trees and wildlife in the Singrauli region are now gone, and the once-proud villagers live in hovels on the edges of the various mines and power plant complexes. No longer working the soil (much of it now stripped away or contaminated), they have taken jobs as day laborers, and struggle with the respiratory and other health problems stemming from the pollution that surrounds them. Bruce Rich, an attorney and development expert at the Environmental Defense Fund, visited Singrauli in 1987 and described what he found there as "the inferno." A decade later, he said, there had been little improvement.

Over the past two decades, billions of dollars have been invested in the Singrauli complex, much of it from outside India. That capital has come from a range of public and private sources, but one of the chief sources of finance—and the one that many other lenders have looked to for leadership—has been the World Bank. Starting with an $850 million loan in the late 1970s, the Bank has been a regular contributor to the financing of Singrauli.

Even after protests began in India in the 1980s, and then spread abroad, the Bank continued to pour in the capital, further expanding the area's mines and building more power plants. In 1997, Indian police forcibly evicted local protesters to make way for yet another World Bank-financed addition to the Singrauli complex, leading local citizens to level charges of human rights abuses. Following a request from local citizens groups that fall, the Bank's Board authorized an Inspection Panel to investigate charges that the latest Singrauli loan had been in violation of the Bank's own policies and procedures.

Singrauli may constitute a particularly egregious case, but it is hardly an isolated one. The World Bank is heavily involved throughout India's coal industry, from its mines to its power plants, with over $300 million of additional loans now being prepared. Many other Bank-funded fossil fuel projects can be found from Mexico to South Africa. Even in Indonesia, which has an abundance of natural gas, a much cleaner fuel, the Bank is building coal plants. It is also helping Russia develop oil fields in Siberia, assisting China as it covers its rice paddies with highways, and providing financing for barge-mounted diesel generators in island nations.

POWERING DEVELOPMENT

It is difficult to comprehend how a development institution that professes alleviation of poverty to be its main goal, and environmental protection its new calling, could have found itself so deeply committed to Singrauli and scores of similar projects. It is even harder to grasp how such disregard for those goals could have continued in the past three years, despite the passionate desire of the Bank's president to reaffirm them, and the efforts of the Bank's environmental staff to support him. What accounts for this "glass wall" that has separated Wolfensohn's zeal from the actual practices of his institution?

One answer lies in the Bank's origin as a lender of last resort, created to help in the rebuilding of Europe after World War II. What Europe most needed at the time was to replace the infrastructure of dams, water systems, roads, bridges, and energy supplies that had been devastated by the war. Private banks were often eager to finance factories and commercial buildings, but they had little interest in large, government-owned projects that had little prospect of earning a profit in the near future. The Bank's success there, as part of the Marshall Plan, tended to reinforce the idea that if the physical requirements of a nation are properly taken care of, the well-being of the people will follow quickly.

Later, as the attention of the Bank was turned to meeting the development needs of Third World nations in the post-colonial era of the 1960s, the emphasis on large infrastructure projects continued. Even in the 1970s, despite Bank president Robert McNamara's directives to invest more heavily in health and education, the Bank continued to pour money into roads, hydroelectric power plants, and other large capital projects. And since at the time, many developing country governments owned not only the road and water systems but the power plants, oil wells, and refineries as well, energy came to be viewed mainly as an infrastructure investment that the

World Bank should take the lead in developing.

By the 1980s, the World Bank was devoting roughly one-fifth of its lending to electric power and another 10 percent or so to oil and gas. Some of the funds went to expanding energy transmission lines, but the lion's share went into constructing hydroelectric and fossil fuel power plants. From the start, many of these were controversial. The Kariba Dam in Zimbabwe, for example, uprooted 56,000 people and created a reservoir that allowed populations of malaria-bearing mosquitos to explode, leading to an epidemic. On the other hand, the Bank took a stand against nuclear power, aligning itself with the views of many environmentalists. Despite repeated requests from client governments, the Bank has judged the technology too complex and expensive for developing countries—and has never issued a loan for a nuclear power plant.

The Bank has never shown a similar reticence about fossil fuels, however. Following the pattern of the richer nations, the Bank and its technical consultants have encouraged developing countries to use fossil fuels—closely following the "western" model of energy development. The large capital investment required for dams and fossil fuel power plants seemed a good match for the institution, which has always prided itself on "efficiency," and likes big projects that minimize the staff time required for each dollar lent. The Bank financed many oil refineries and power plants in the 1960s and 1970s, and then turned more of its attention to coal and natural gas after oil prices skyrocketed. Providing energy for the rural poor, by contrast, has made up less than 10 percent of the Bank's energy loan portfolio. In transportation, the Bank became a heavy supporter of road building, helping its client governments to pursue an automobile- and truck-based transport model that is closer to that found in North America than to the more diversified transport systems of Europe or Japan. By comparison, bicycle paths and public transportation systems were neglected by the Bank's lenders—despite the fact that they are far more practical for the majority of the people.

Most poor nations, like their richer counterparts in Europe and North America, promoted even heavier reliance on fossil fuels by subsidizing their production and use. Some of these subsidies—in India, Indonesia, and Brazil, for example—covered as much as 25 to 50 percent of the cost. In Egypt, these subsidies used up more than 3 percent of the nation's total economic output in 1990. Imported kerosene, for example, is heavily subsidized in many countries in order to provide poor consumers with affordable cooking fuel. But the bulk of the subsidies have gone to electricity, most of which is consumed by industries and the small middle class. The Bank preached the gospel of subsidy reduction for decades, but with little effect.

Bank officials say that its support of fossil fuels has spurred economic growth and created numerous jobs in poor countries over the past three decades. But they also acknowledge that it has done so at a heavy price: it is the cities of the developing world, not Los Angeles or London, that now have the world's most poisonous air. One of the dirtiest is Mexico City, where only when it rains does the air meet U.S. federal standards—standards that the U.S. EPA now plans to tighten because they are not sufficient to protect public health. By the World Bank's own estimates, air pollution causes at least 4 million new cases of chronic bronchitis and contributes to a half million premature deaths each year. In many developing countries, air pollution costs run to as much as 2.5 percent of the annual GDP, and in China they are estimated to be 5 percent. In Shanghai alone, the health costs have reached an estimated $3.5 billion per year.

THE PUSH FOR REFORM

By the late 1980s, the World Bank's heavy involvement in the energy sector was stirring up concern among environmentalists and other reformers, though most of it was focused on large hydro projects. (Some of the most severe criticism came from an internal critic—Robert Goodland of the Bank's own environment department.) Outside energy experts, such as Howard Geller of the American Council for an Energy Efficient Economy, used insights gained in trying to reform their own countries' energy policies to show how developing nations could reduce the number of power plants they need by investing in more efficient appliances and industrial equipment.

At first, the economists who occupy many of the Bank's senior positions caustically dismissed these claims; in the world of economic theory where many of them were trained, any means of saving energy at less than the cost of producing it would have been exploited long ago. As long as energy prices were raised to the market level—which the Bank was urging developing countries to do—no investment in efficiency could be justified. Developing countries were growing, and energy use would grow with it, no matter what the Bank did, they argued—overlooking the fact that greater efficiency would allow a given level of energy investment to produce a greater amount of service. The arrogance with which Bank staff often made such arguments did not help their popularity in the environmental community.

As the 1992 Earth Summit approached, and concern about pollution in developing countries rose, pressure for reforms built. The Bank's industry and energy department prepared two new papers, and after much controversy they were approved in late 1992. According to these papers, new power loans were to be based on comprehensive energy strategies that included cost-effective opportunities to increase energy efficiency. The Bank also agreed to help developing countries improve their institutional capability to pursue energy efficiency, and to push them harder to reform energy prices and strengthen energy efficiency regulations.

The release of these papers was widely viewed by environmental organizations at the time as an important victory, with the potential to get developing country energy trends headed in a more positive direction. Few expected overnight success, but it did seem possible that some of the least efficient practices and most damaging projects would be stopped, and that developing countries could begin to catch up with the rapid gains in energy efficiency being made in industrial countries. Their hopes were soon dashed.

Among the modest successes that emerged from the Bank's 1992 reforms are policy changes recommended in its Energy Sector Management Assistance Program, which has pushed for more effective regulation of energy companies, performance-based contracts, and cuts in subsidies. In China, for example, the Bank's influence has helped to reduce fossil fuel supports from $24 billion annually in the 1980s to $10 billion in 1995. Between 1991 and 1996, India cut its fossil fuel subsidies from $4.2 billion to $2.6 billion, while Brazil virtually eliminated subsidies.

The Bank also stepped up its support of natural gas, a less polluting fossil fuel that has been under-developed in most poor countries. And it has successfully encouraged many of its client countries to make their power plants, transmission lines, and refineries more efficient. It is in the uses of energy, however, that the greatest potential for improved efficiency lies, and there the advances have been slower. One exception is a loan to Thailand, in which some of the funds are being used by the national power authority to improve the efficiency of lighting and appliances. Similar loans have been made to Colombia, Russia, and other countries.

But even with such loans, the Bank has not become a real leader on energy efficiency. Brazil, for example, has developed a strong network of energy service companies and is a leading manufacturer of energy-efficient equipment—but with very little Bank support. A 1994 review by two U.S.-based NGOs, the Environmental Defense Fund and the Natural Resources Defense Council, found that of 46 power loans worth $7 billion then under preparation, only two complied with the Bank's new policy. A later assessment by the Worldwide Fund for Nature in early 1996 found that only three of 56 loans complied with the 1992 policy papers. Overall, end-use energy efficiency still represents less than 5 percent of the Bank's total energy lending. According to Jim Barnes, a counselor with Friends of the Earth International, "the World Bank's spending on energy efficiency is still far below the levels that are justified on economic grounds alone."

SOLAR INITIATIVES

Although the World Bank has generously financed large hydroelectric projects since its earliest days, its technological conservatism and preoccupation with large-scale projects has made it slow to support the plethora of more decentralized renewable energy technologies. But as the cost of some of these new energy sources fell dramatically in the 1990s, pressure built on the Bank to fund them. As carbon-free energy sources, solar, wind, geothermal, and biomass energy are essential to helping the world slow global warming—and they would allow many developing countries to reduce their dependence on imported fuels.

In the early 1990s, Dennis Anderson, an economist on temporary assignment to the World Bank, wrote a path-breaking paper suggesting that the renewable energy potential of developing countries was huge, and that it could help them reduce their financially burdensome oil imports. He went on to argue that if funds were provided to scale up manufacturing of the needed devices, their costs would fall and markets would soar. Anderson and his colleagues were particularly enamored of the more centralized renewable energy technologies—such as large solar thermal power plants—that fit the big-project thinking to which the Bank's engineers are accustomed. Anderson recommended that the Bank consider taking on the role of a venture capitalist—providing seed capital to get the new renewable energy technologies off the ground.

After extensive internal debates and several false starts, a somewhat fragmented Solar Initiative was launched in 1994.

In its initial phase, it is intended to assist developing countries in the "preparation and finance of commercial and near-commercial applications" of renewable energy, "facilitation of international research, development, and demonstration," and removal of market barriers. In practice, it has served as an umbrella that links various modest programs. As such, it has begun to educate Bank staff, and led to a number of "experimental" renewable energy projects in developing countries, including geothermal power plants in the Philippines, wind farms in India and a credit program for off-the-grid solar home systems in Indonesia.

On a larger scale, the private sector lending arm of the World Bank, the International Finance Corporation (IFC), in 1996 approved a $100 to $200 million fund for small, commercial renewable energy projects in developing countries. This could turn out to be a real breakthrough, with the potential to jumpstart renewables in developing countries. The IFC is also working on a Photovoltaic Market Transformation Initiative that is to provide $30 million in low-interest financing to manufacturers and dealers of small solar systems in developing countries, allowing them to get new businesses going.

Dennis Anderson has since left the Bank, and skepticism about the potential of these new small-scale technologies—and a resistance to financing them—remains strong, both in the Bank's energy department and in the country departments where loans are prepared. A draft of a new Bank energy strategy produced in 1997 sounded particularly out of touch when it concluded: "By the end of the 30-year technological change horizon, renewable energy is expected to be cost competitive." The authors showed little awareness that in Europe, renewable energy markets were already booming at double digit growth rates as a result of recent policy changes, and attracting multi-billion dollar corporate investments.

FOSSIL FUELING

The Bank's glossy publications now point in glowing terms to the institution's "environmental leadership" and its support of "clean energy technologies"—a seeming vindication for those who have pushed for reforms. Unless one scans the fine-print appendices in the backs of those reports, one would never know that the Bank funds any fossil fuel projects at all. In reality, however, those projects continue to dominate the energy loan portfolio. In the power sector, for example, the Bank is still heavily committed to coal-fired power plants—from central Europe to Indonesia. China and India, in particular, are in the midst of Bank-supported oil and coal bonanzas as they seek to provide power to booming economies.

In fact, fossil fuel projects may be flowing through the Bank's loan pipeline faster than ever. In 1997, over $1 billion was on the way to China, India, and Russia for "restructuring" their state-owned coal industries. The goal was to shut down inefficient mines and improve the better ones, thereby preserving jobs. However, the practical result may be to preserve industries that would better be allowed to die gradually, replaced by less polluting energy sources. In an indication of the kind of "black hole" these projects have become, *Business Week* reported in 1997 that $100 million out of a $500 million World Bank loan for the Russian coal industry had "disappeared," apparently into the pockets of government officials and industrialists.

A June 1997 study by the Washington, DC-based Institute for Policy Studies found that the fossil fuel projects the Bank has financed since the Rio Earth Summit will put nearly 10 billion tons of carbon into the atmosphere over the next few decades—compared to current global annual emissions of 6 billion tons. It also found that the Bank was spending 100 times as much money on fossil fuel projects as it was on ones that reduce emissions. Bank officials believe that the IPS figures are overstated, and that the fossil fuel projects outweigh the greener ones by only six-to-one.

Even by that estimate, the Bank's energy loan portfolio is in no present danger of being labeled environmentally friendly. Critics argue that the power plant emission standards that it proudly describes in its public reports are still far too low. And in a 1996 internal report that was leaked to the press, the Bank admitted that its environmental assessments were being conducted too late in the loan process, allowing some environmentally damaging projects to be approved. To add insult to pollution, records show that the environmental assessments for recent fossil fuel loans do not even follow the Bank's recent, simple mandate to include estimates of the greenhouse gas emissions that will flow from them.

Bank officials do not deny many of the specific charges, but they place much of the responsibility on developing countries, which, they say, request the loans. Seemingly oblivious to the mountain of policy papers they put out, Bank officials say that they are in the end just bankers, and cannot finance projects they are never presented with. This argument contains more than a touch of disingenuousness. The World Bank's board has never been reluctant to force developing countries to accept conditions that it felt important—including politically difficult reforms of fiscal and social policy, such as reducing subsidized food prices. Moreover, money is often shoveled hastily out the door when political expediency demands it. Nancy Alexander of Bread for the World notes that some of the worst loans have been approved because the U.S. Treasury called the Bank and ordered loans to be processed "before the sun rises," demanding, "if they [the recipient countries] can't find projects, you find them."

A second line of defense sometimes used by Bank officials is to point out that with the massive flows of private capital now going to the developing world, the Bank only accounts for about 3 percent of the global total, and so has little leverage. Bank official Hiroaki Suzuki claimed earlier this year, "If the Bank didn't finance these coal-fired power projects, someone else would, but with lower environmental standards than ours." However, this claim sidesteps the fact that many projects involve packages of public and private loans, and that if such co-financing is included, the Bank's share of total energy lending is higher. Moreover, commercial banks often look to the World Bank to anchor such loans, and thereby minimize their own risk. As Wolfensohn told *The New York Times* in 1997, "It stands to reason that if our money is limited and there is great potential for the private sector, we must think in terms not just of what we do but how we can leverage what we do with the private sector." Moreover, the World Bank now provides loan guarantees for commercial loans in developing countries, and its sister institution, the Multilateral

One Step Forward . . .

Carbon emissions *reduced* by World Bank projects measure in the tens of thousands of tons per year ...

SELECTED GLOBAL ENVIRONMENT FACILITY ENERGY PROJECTS, SOME CO-FINANCED BY THE WORLD BANK

Location	Project Description	Estimated Cost	Annual Carbon Emissions Avoided (tons)
Leyte-Luzon, **Philippines**	440 MW geothermal power plant	$1.3 billion total ($30 mil. GEF) ($240 mil. World Bank)	**872,000**
Country-wide, **Indonesia**	Installation of 200,000 solar PV systems	$118 million ($24 mil. GEF) ($20 mil. World Bank)	**120,000**
Nine cities, **China**	Energy-efficiency upgrade of industrial boilers	$101 million total ($33 mil. GEF) (linked to $170 mil. World Bank project)	**41,000–68,000**
Guadalajara and Monterey, **Mexico**	Dissemination of high-efficiency lighting (1.7 mil. fluorescent lamps)	$23 million total ($10 mil. GEF) (no World Bank funds)	**32,000**

Investment Guarantee Agency, provides political risk insurance for many commercial loans. Without these supports, many fossil fuel projects would not be able to get any international financing at all.

Environmental organizations have been pushing the Bank's lenders to enforce the same environmental standards for commercial loans they support as those they require for public projects, but with limited success. More surprisingly, a close review of the Bank's recent energy loans suggests that they may be weighted toward technologies and fuels that are actually less efficient and dirtier than the average project funded by the private sector. Whereas private lenders are devoting 23 percent of their loans to coal plants and 40 per-

And a Hundred Steps Back?

... but emissions *generated* by Bank-funded projects measure in the *millions* of tons.

SELECTED FOSSIL FUEL POWER PLANTS FINANCED IN PART BY THE WORLD BANK IN THE 1990S

Location	Type of Plant	Estimated Cost	Annual Carbon Emissions (tons)
Tuoketuo, Inner Mongolia, **China**	3600 MW coal-fired power plant	$4.0 billion	**7,190,000**
Dolna Odra, **Poland**	1600 MW coal-fired power plant rehab	$300 million	**3,196,000**
Paiton, East Java, **Indonesia**	1230 MW coal-fired power plant	$1.8 billion	**2,457,000**
Pangasaman, **Philippines**	1200 MW coal-fired power plant	$1.4 billion	**2,397,000**
Hub River, **Pakistan**	1469 MW oil-fired power plant	$2.4 billion	**2,345,000**

cent to gas, the proportions appear to be reversed at the World Bank.

There may be a simple explanation for this discrepancy. Although commercial banks do not have environmental standards per se, they are by nature risk-averse, and do not want to fund projects that may run aground. As a result, they usually commission detailed analyses of the risks of loans they are considering—a process lenders call "due diligence." A Singrauli-style project might well fail such a test—partly because of the danger that it would be stopped by local protests prior to completion, and partly because of the risk of an accident that could kill or injure a large number of people and result in expensive lawsuits.

REFORMING THE REFORMS

For environmentalists, frustration with the Bank's reform efforts turned to anger in 1996 when, amid mounting criticism of the Bank's apparent failure to make the reforms outlined in its 1992 policy papers, its legal department issued an opinion that those papers were not formal Bank policies, but simply "good practices" guidelines. As such, the papers are not binding on Bank staff and cannot be appealed to its inspection panel. The situation was not improved when, in response to strong letters from environmental organizations, a senior vice president asserted that this new ruling was simply a reaffirmation of longstanding Bank policy.

The controversy over the 1992 Papers gets to the heart of the exasperation reformers experience in their attempts to change the World Bank's energy strategies. Papers such as these are written by Washington-based policy analysts. However, the core of the Bank's operations lies with its task managers and country directors, who process loans and work directly with officials in developing country governments. These managers and their clients view new directives from the policy staff as impediments to their main task—processing loans. (When Robert McNamara was president of the World Bank in the 1970s, he used to say that he had to repeat his policy speeches at least a dozen times just to get the attention of his own loan officers.) And indeed, operations staff and client governments have strongly resisted the new energy policy papers. Moreover, some reformers now fear that this resistance may be stiffened by the efforts launched by Wolfensohn, to simultaneously streamline operations and cut red tape. These efforts, which include plans to eliminate up to 700 of the 10,000 staff positions, could work to the detriment of innovative and small-scale projects. The Bank's own figures show that on average, small renewable energy and energy efficiency projects take more staff time, and cost 65 percent more to process. Wolfensohn was also pushing his managers to make the Bank more "client-friendly," but many of those clients are not friends of his energy reforms.

Meanwhile, the Bank's Board—to which everyone, including the president, formally reports—appears reluctant to push too hard for energy reforms. Although the Board is dominated by representatives of the industrial country governments that provide the bulk of the Bank's capital, it also includes officials from developing country governments who wish to follow the energy model of rich western countries—including heavy use of fossil fuels. They are skittish about being asked to make reforms that many industrial countries have not yet adopted. And even industrial country governments have mixed motivations. Some of their largest companies are eager to land contracts to build the fossil fuel projects the Bank is financing.

The Bank's strong rhetorical support for private industry involvement in the energy sector is also open to question. Though it lauds the move to "privatization" of energy industries in developing countries, the Bank's operations staff appears to have cozy relationships with many of the state-owned mining, petroleum, and power companies that are most resisting those reforms. Many of these government monopolies are now bankrupt in all but name, and World Bank loans appear to be delaying their conversion into more efficient private companies. This failure has clear environmental costs: many of the most polluting energy projects underway today are being carried out by these poorly regulated—often corrupt—state-owned companies.

At the same time, the Bank's support for energy efficiency has continued to be half-hearted. A generous $100 million World Bank/GEF loan package for Brazil's National Electricity Conservation Program was crawling through the Bank's operations bureaucracy in 1997, apparently delayed by internal resistance to the "market-interference" that it represents.

Although the Bank continues to defend its energy record publicly, the awkwardness of its position is becoming apparent. At an international environmental meeting in Rio de Janeiro in 1997, Wolfensohn was questioned about the Bank's continuing support for fossil fuel projects. He replied that most of the projects were products of an earlier era that had not yet cleared the pipeline, but then he went on to argue that developing countries could not be expected to do entirely without fossil fuels. In fact, no one had suggested going to that extreme.

A psychiatrist might conclude that the World Bank has developed a severe case of schizophrenia. While its policy staff is motivated to churn out an endless series of new policy papers and initiatives, its operations staff argues strenuously against any additional red tape that would slow down their ability to process loans for "desperately needed" fossil fuel plants. Rhetorically, the president and at least a portion of the Board are allied with the policy staff, but on the ground their priorities are less clear.

CONFRONTING THE GREENHOUSE

During the past few years, the global climate problem has dramatically raised the stakes for energy reformers at the

World Bank. Climate change presents a real threat to the development prospects of the Bank's client countries. Recent scientific studies suggest that rising seas could displace hundreds of millions of people, while shifting weather patterns begin to cut food production and spread infectious diseases.

As the single largest financier of fossil fuel projects in developing countries, the World Bank has been struggling with its appropriate role under the climate treaty. The Bank is prohibited from making loans in violation of any legally binding international agreement, but its fossil fuel lenders get around this by arguing that most client countries are not yet obligated to reduce their emissions. Meanwhile, their colleagues in other lending institutions are seeking new ways to edge developing countries toward limiting their greenhouse gas emissions.

One such funding vehicle is the Global Environment Facility (GEF), which was set up by the international community in 1991 as a new funding mechanism to provide developing countries with assistance in addressing "global" environmental problems such as the destruction of wildlife and climate change. The intent was to provide grants (not loans) for projects that might not be financially viable based on local economic considerations, but that could be justified in global environmental terms. The GEF is an independent fund, with its own governance structure, and has been designated as the interim funding arm of the Framework Convention on Climate Change. Still, the World Bank heavily influences the GEF, in part because the Bank, along with the U.N. Development Programme and the U.N. Environment Programme, is an implementing agency for the GEF. Many GEF projects are attached to larger World Bank loans, and the GEF is located just a block from the World Bank, where it has recruited some of its key staff.

Since it was founded, the GEF has provided roughly $700 million for addressing climate change—funding a number of innovative carbon-free energy projects. Some of the money has gone to improved energy efficiency, including a project to install 1.7 million high-efficiency light bulbs in the Mexican cities of Monterrey and Guadalajara. Additional funds have gone for renewable energy. India, for example, has received grants for solar and wind energy projects, supporting the booming renewables industry there. Another innovative project funded by the GEF is an effort to adapt jet engine technology to sugar cane waste in Brazil. Unlike a natural gas-fired generator, this one would add no additional carbon dioxide to the atmosphere. So far, $8 million has been spent on a system that gasifies the cane residues, which then fuel a small gas turbine to produce electricity. Studies suggest that countries with large sugar industries could provide much of their power this way—at a cost that is comparable to that of fossil fuel plants.

The scale of these projects pales in comparison to the Bank's own energy lending, but rebels inside and outside the Bank see the the GEF as a Trojan horse that might gradually infiltrate the Bank and then transform its energy loan portfolio. In practice, GEF projects have often been tacked onto much larger energy loans (in part to avoid the need to prepare entirely new projects along with their accompanying paper work), that may actually be adding to carbon emissions. In describing their energy loan portfolio, Bank officials sometimes airbrush the picture by blurring the line between Bank and GEF funds—leading some critics to fear that the GEF is becoming an excuse for not using more Bank funds for the innovative technologies. Bank environmental officials respond to these arguments by noting that combining Bank and GEF funds can sometimes provide additional "leverage" for the GEF. Moreover, they say, the presence of the GEF has encouraged the Bank's operations staff to work with the new energy technologies. Whether the Trojan horse effect will ultimately be realized remains to be seen.

In addition to working with the GEF, the World Bank's environmental staff is looking for other ways to address climate change. One initiative is the "global overlays" program, an analytical effort to build global environmental factors into the project development and energy planning efforts of developing countries. For example, a recent carbon "back-casting" study conducted by consultants to the Bank found that if even a modest "price tag" of $20 per ton of carbon emissions—reflecting the many potential costs of climate change—were placed on World Bank energy projects at the time the cost-benefit ratios are calculated, some 41 percent of them would no longer be deemed financially viable. If such criteria were used to evaluate the Bank's prospective energy loans, many of the fossil fuel projects now in the pipeline would have to be canceled. But Bank officials have not yet agreed to implement this reform.

Taking a new tack in 1997, the Bank's environment department began to explore the possibility of its managing a dedicated fund to reduce greenhouse gas emissions. Seizing on the growing interest of countries such as Norway, Costa Rica, and the United States in the possibility of including emissions trading in the global climate treaty, Bank environmental officials suggested that the Bank's lending expertise makes it an appropriate home for a new Carbon Investment Bank. This proposal caught Wolfensohn's attention, leading to his announcement at the U.N. in June. By early 1998, governments and companies had informally committed an initial $100 million to this new fund, and a dozen staff members were working on it.

The Carbon Investment Bank proposal reflects the continuing search of the Bank's policy departments for new projects and services that respond to Wolfensohn's pleas for innovation, and reflect their own openness to change. But many observers, including some in the Bank's own environment department, doubt whether this fund is an appropriate role for the World Bank. Others wonder whether, like the GEF, the new fund could become an excuse for not altering the Bank's core lending priorities. Already, the fund is absorbing policy staff time, while the operations staff keeps the fossil-fuel lending in high gear.

KYOTO AND BEYOND

The stakes of this struggle were raised in 1997 when powerful U.S. industrial interests decided that they would base their opposition to a strengthening of the climate treaty in Kyoto on the fact that developing countries are not included in the proposed limits. Reflecting this concern, the U.S. Senate adopted a nearly unanimous resolution five months before the conference, suggesting that it would not ratify a climate protocol limiting U.S. emissions unless it "mandates new specific scheduled commitments to limit or reduce greenhouse gas emissions for developing country parties."

Developing country officials expressed outrage at this resolution, believing that it unfairly placed too much of the burden of dealing with climate change on countries with per capita emissions levels that are less than one-tenth those found in industrial countries. Reflecting their concern, the Kyoto agreement does not include any binding new requirements for developing countries, but the U.S. government remains committed to adding such requirements in the future. The challenge now is to come up with a formula that would work for everyone—economically empowering climate policies in industrial and developing countries alike, with the industrial countries helping to fund new energy technologies for the poorer nations. Wolfensohn indicated that he wanted the World Bank to play a key role in that effort.

In 1997, the Bank began to develop a new "energy and environment strategy," involving extensive consultation with non-governmental organizations. For the first time, the issue of climate change was being seriously considered in the new plan—which was due to be approved by the Bank's Board in time for presentation at the climate negotiations in Kyoto. Lending weight to the effort was a mid-year decision by

Wolfensohn to replace the head of the Bank's environment department with one of the world's top climate scientists, Robert Watson. Described by *The New Scientist* as "a shaggy, outspoken English chemist who looks more like a biblical than a scientific prophet," Watson was an odd fit for the Bank's blue-suited culture. Even more distinctive was his background: he had been credited with single-handedly marshalling the scientific consensus that helped forge the historic Montreal Protocol on ozone depletion in the 1980s.

By 1997, Watson was leading not only the Bank's environment department but the International Panel on Climate Change (IPCC), the scientific body that was responsible for advising international climate negotiators. Indeed, Watson knows many of those negotiators on a first-name basis. In an indication of the kind of conflicts that were by then raging along the Bank's carpeted halls, Watson told the news daily *Greenwire* a few months before the negotiations that "we should analyze the climate consequences of all of our projects, and then we should look to see if there is a more climate-friendly alternative."

Given his views, Watson must have been discouraged by the early draft of the Bank's 1997 energy strategy paper, which appeared that August. It was academic in tone, lacked a substantive analysis of the Bank's energy lending record, and contained only a few weak policy proposals. If this was a "blueprint for reform," it seemed questionable whether the edifice would ever be completed. The forces at work in the draft could be seen in a press release that had appeared on the Bank's website earlier that summer. Apparently written by the Bank's office in India, it was an unapologetic defense of the Bank's heavy support for India's government-owned coal company—proclaiming coal as "the backbone of India's energy economy" and the "least-cost option for the bulk of India's energy needs for the foreseeable future." The paper went on to dismiss renewables and natural gas as energy options that are viable only in the long run.

Such papers lead one to despair about whether the World Bank can ever be reformed. Some might argue that at this juncture it should get out of energy entirely—and concentrate on health, education, and other social priorities. Perhaps so, but James Wolfensohn, for one, seems ready to give it one more try. As a result, the World Bank bureaucrats who are most resisting change seem to be on a collision course with the new head of the Bank's environmental department—and perhaps with its President.

The essential elements of a new climate-sensitive energy strategy for the World Bank are fairly easy to identify. The first step is for the Bank's Board to announce that from now on in the energy sector, the staff's record will be judged by the emissions reduced—not the amount of paper produced or dollars of loans processed. And what might the details of that strategy look like? Models can be found at the European Bank for Reconstruction and Development and the Asian Development Bank, each of which has already implemented important reforms. The Asian Bank has substantially increased its support of energy efficiency in the past two years, and now requires that potential climate impacts be included in all energy loan proposals. Meanwhile, the European Bank has established a special energy efficiency unit with expertise in locating and shepherding productive energy efficiency investments.

For the World Bank, an effective energy reform strategy would also include a requirement that client governments develop independently audited energy strategies that identify the least-cost mix of technologies, accounting fully for local and national environmental costs. The Bank would then work in tandem with private lenders to finance that mix—while carrying a special responsibility for financing the newer alternatives. The Bank might also insist that these energy plans contain specific policy changes—including commitments to phase out subsidies for fossil fuels, provide incentives for new technologies, and implement efficiency standards for all new automobiles, appliances, commercial buildings, and industrial equipment.

The Bank also needs broader goals to aim for in its energy lending, including a gradual re-balancing of its fossil fuel loans—reducing support for coal, and increasing that for natural gas. Another promising proposal can be found in a "background paper" issued by the Bank's environment department when Wolfensohn addressed the U.N. in New York. It proposed that the Bank commit $600 million per year over five years (20 percent of its total energy lending) for renewable energy, with the GEF providing another $150 million. This would be a large enough capital infusion to get renewable energy markets off the ground in several developing countries, but for this hope to become reality, the Bank will still have to find ways to effectively target the funds to smaller scale projects.

It is also important, in the current period of massive private capital flows, that the Bank devise new means of using its own loans for leveraging private investments. Important steps in this direction could include expanded IFC support for private energy efficiency and renewable energy projects, as well as Bank-sponsored performance guarantees for innovative, commercially-financed energy projects.

Describing these reforms is easy; navigating the political currents within the World Bank's bureaucracy and Board is far more difficult, as Wolfensohn himself soon discovered. But helping developing countries join an energy revolution, and stabilizing the world's climate, are essential goals that are well matched to the World Bank's historic legacy, as well as to the forward-looking concerns of its present chief. If these goals are not met, the Bank's central mission—reducing poverty—will eventually be undermined as well.

INDEX